THE LYRIC POTENTIAL
Arrangements and Techniques in Poetry

THE FOUNTAINHEAD SERIES

TO BE
Identity in Literature

REALITY IN CONFLICT
Literature of Values in Opposition

THE HUMAN CONDITION
Literature Written in the English Language

OF TIME AND PLACE
Comparative World Literature in Translation

THE LYRIC POTENTIAL
Arrangements and Techniques in Poetry

COMMENT
An Anthology in Prose

TRAITS & TOPICS
An Anthology of Short Stories

UPSTAGE/DOWNSTAGE
A Theater Festival

SCIENCE FACT/FICTION
FANTASY
Shapes of Things Unknown

I/YOU—WE/THEY
Literature By and About Ethnic Groups

MYTH, MIND, AND MOMENT

AMERICAN MODELS
A Collection of Modern Stories

BRITISH MOTIFS
A Collection of Modern Stories

MARQUEE
Ten Plays by American and British Playwrights

PERSON, PLACE, AND POINT OF VIEW
Factual Prose for Interpretation and Extension

LITERATURE FROM GREEK AND ROMAN ANTIQUITY

RUSSIAN AND EASTERN EUROPEAN LITERATURE

TRANSLATIONS FROM THE FRENCH

ITALIAN LITERATURE IN TRANSLATION

BLACK AFRICAN VOICES

LITERATURE OF THE EASTERN WORLD

FROM SPAIN AND THE AMERICAS
Literature in Translation

TEUTONIC LITERATURE
In English Translation

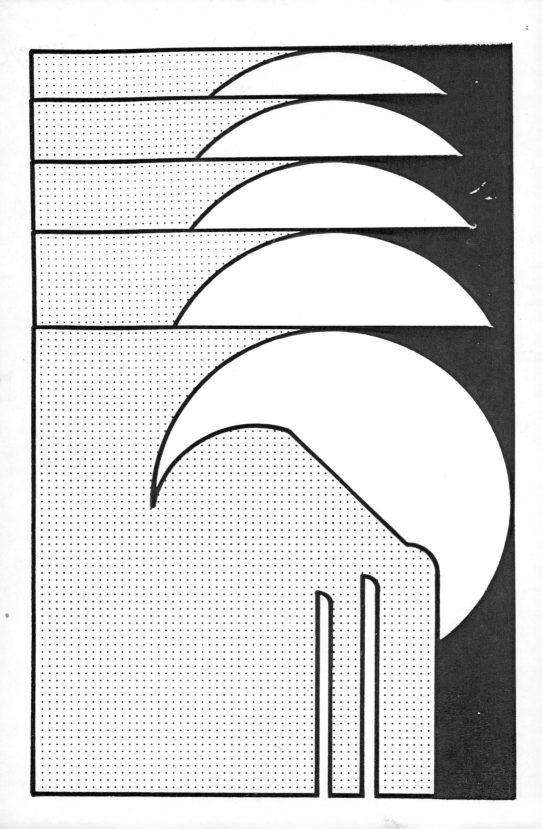

THE LYRIC POTENTIAL

Arrangements and Techniques in Poetry

JAMES E. MILLER, JR.

Professor of English, University of Chicago. Fulbright Lecturer in Naples and Rome, 1958–59, and in Kyoto, Japan, 1968. President of the National Council of Teachers of English, 1970. Awarded a Guggenheim Fellowship, 1969–1970. Author of *Quests Surd and Absurd: Essays in American Literature; Theory of Fiction: Henry James;* and *Word, Self, Reality: The Rhetoric of Imagination.*

ROBERT HAYDEN

Professor of English, University of Michigan. Formerly Bingham Professor of English, University of Louisville, Visiting Poet, University of Washington, and Professor of English, Fisk University. Recipient of the Hopwood Award, the Grand Prix de la Poesie of the First World Festival of Negro Arts, Dakar, and the Russell Loines Award. Author of *A Ballad of Remembrance, Selected Poems, Words in the Mourning Time,* and *The Night-Blooming Cereus.*

ROBERT O'NEAL

Former Professor and Chairman, English, Journalism, and Humanities, at San Antonio College, and at Berry College, Georgia. Lecturer, Georgia Institute of Higher Education. Author of *Teachers' Guide to World Literature for the High School,* (N.C.T.E.), and co-author and photographer of *English for You.*

SCOTT, FORESMAN AND COMPANY

To ascertain the tastes, the abilities, and the preferences of those for whom this book is intended, the following individuals read the many poems submitted to them, judged their appropriateness and interest, and solicited the reactions of young people. The authors and editors of *The Lyric Potential* wish to express their appreciation for this valuable assistance.

MARY ANNE BOWEN
Jackson, Mississippi

VENITA BRIDGER
Springfield, Missouri

MICHAEL G. CALLAHAN
San Mateo, California

SISTER EUGENE FOX, S.C.
Bay City, Michigan

BARBARA GOLDSMITH
Oak Park, Michigan

WILLIAM A. McCLEERY
Berea, Ohio

ROBERT P. ROMANO
Wilmington, Massachusetts

ISBN: 0-673-03417-8

Regional Offices of Scott, Foresman and Company
are located in Dallas, Texas; Glenview, Illinois;
Oakland, New Jersey; Palo Alto, California;
Tucker, Georgia; and Brighton, England.

Contents

An asterisk is used to indicate poems with accompanying commentary by the poet or a critic. No such indication has been made for commentary that is generally brief or unsigned.

Complete Poems in Handbook

Handbook of Terms and Techniques

Entries and Cross References

Acknowledgments

Cover: Needlepoint by Don Abramson. Adapted from a design by M. C. Escher.
Quotations on the opening page of each group of poems:
Page 14: Copyright 1942 by Stephen Spender. Reprinted from SELECTED POEMS, by Stephen Spender, by permission of Random House, Inc. and Harold Matson Co., Inc. Page 24: From BLUE JUNIATA: COLLECTED POEMS by Malcolm Cowley. Copyright © 1968 by Malcolm Cowley. Originally appeared in *Poetry*. Reprinted by permission of The Viking Press, Inc. Page 36: Copyright © 1964 by Karl Shapiro. Reprinted from SELECTED POEMS, by Karl Shapiro, by permission of Random House, Inc. Page 52: From REQUIEM FOR THE LIVING by C. Day Lewis. Copyright by C. Day Lewis. Reprinted by permission of Harold Matson Company, Inc. Page 66: Reprinted by permission of the publishers and the Trustees of Amherst College from Thomas H. Johnson, Editor, THE POEMS OF EMILY DICKINSON, Cambridge, Massachusetts: The Belknap Press of Harvard University Press, Copyright, 1951, 1955, by The President and Fellows of Harvard College. Page 76: From A SHROPSHIRE LAD—Authorised Edition—from THE COLLECTED POEMS OF A. E. HOUSMAN. Copyright 1939, 1940, © 1965 by Holt, Rinehart and Winston, Inc. Copyright © 1967, 1968 by Robert E. Symons. Reprinted by permission of Holt, Rinehart and Winston, Inc., The Society of Authors as the literary representative of the Estate of A. E. Housman, and Jonathan Cape Ltd., publishers of A. E. Housman's COLLECTED POEMS. Page 104: From CANE by Jean Toomer. Permission of Liveright, Publishers, New York. Copyright renewed 1951 by Jean Toomer. Page 114: Reprinted with permission of Macmillan Publishing Co., Inc., The Macmillan Company of Canada Limited, Mrs. I. Wise and Macmillan, London and Basingstoke from COLLECTED POEMS by James Stephens. Copyright 1909 by The Macmillan Company. Page 122: Reprinted with permission of Macmillan Publishing Co., Inc., Mrs. I. Wise, The Macmillan Company of Canada Limited, and Macmillan, London and Basingstoke from COLLECTED POEMS (British Title: SONGS OF CLAY) by James Stephens. Copyright 1915 by The Macmillan Company, renewed 1943 by James Stephens. Page 134: From THE EYE-BEATERS, BLOOD, VICTORY, MADNESS BUCKHEAD AND MERCY by James Dickey. Copyright © 1968, 1969, 1970 by James Dickey. Reprinted by permission of Doubleday & Company, Inc. and Theron Raines, Authors' Representative. Page 150: From THE POEMS OF DYLAN THOMAS. Copyright 1943, 1946 by New Directions Publishing Corporation. Reprinted by permission of New Directions Publishing Corporation, J. M. Dent & Sons Ltd., Publishers and the Trustees for the Copyrights of the late Dylan Thomas. Page 166: From THE COLLECTED POEMS OF LOUIS MAC-NEICE, edited by E. R. Dodds, Copyright © The Estate of Louis MacNeice 1966. Reprinted by permission of Oxford University Press and Faber and Faber Ltd. Page 176: From THE POEMS OF DYLAN THOMAS. Copyright 1943, 1946 by New Directions Publishing Corporation. Reprinted by permission of New Directions Publishing Corporation, J. M. Dent & Sons Ltd., Publishers and the Trustees for the Copyrights of the late Dylan Thomas. Page 188: From COLLECTED POEMS 1930-1965 by A. D. Hope. Copyright 1963, 1966 in all countries of the International Copyright Union by A. D. Hope. All rights reserved. Reprinted by permission of The Viking Press, Inc. and Angus & Robertson (Publishers) Pty. Ltd. Page 212: Reprinted by permission of the publishers and the Trustees of Amherst College from Thomas H. Johnson, Editor, THE POEMS OF EMILY DICKINSON, Cambridge, Massachusetts: The Belknap Press of Harvard University Press, Copyright, 1951, 1955, by The President and Fellows of Harvard College. Page 226: From THE WORLD OF GWENDOLYN BROOKS by Gwendolyn Brooks. Copyright 1949 by Gwendolyn Brooks Blakely. By permission of Harper & Row, Publishers, Inc. Page 238: From THE POETRY OF ROBERT FROST edited by Edward Connery Lathem. Copyright 1930, 1939, © 1969 by Holt, Rinehart and Winston, Inc. Copyright 1936, 1942, © 1958 by Robert Frost. Copyright © 1964, 1967, 1970 by Lesley Frost Ballantine. Reprinted by permission of Holt, Rinehart and Winston, Inc., the Estate of Robert Frost and Jonathan Cape Ltd. Page 250: From THE COLLECTED POEMS OF LOUIS MACNEICE, edited by E. R. Dodds, Copyright © the Estate of Louis MacNeice 1966. Reprinted by permission of Oxford University Press and Faber and Faber Ltd. Page 276: From THE POETRY OF ROBERT FROST, edited by Edward Connery Lathem. Copyright 1923, 1928, © 1969 by Holt, Rinehart and Winston, Inc. Copyright 1951, © 1956 by Robert Frost. Reprinted by permission of Holt, Rinehart and Winston, Inc., the Estate of Robert Frost, and Jonathan Cape Ltd. Page 288: Reprinted with permission of Macmillan Publishing Co., Inc. and Faber and Faber Ltd. from COLLECTED POEMS by Marianne Moore. Copyright 1935, renewed 1963 by Marianne Moore and T. S. Eliot. Page 308: From COLLECTED POEMS OF ARCHIBALD MACLEISH 1917-1952. Copyright © 1962 by Archibald MacLeish. Reprinted by permission of Houghton Mifflin Company.

1

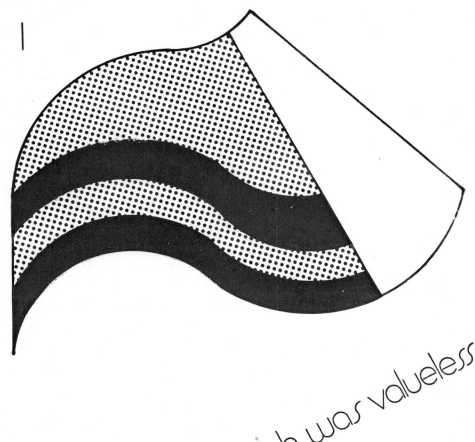

Consider his life which was valueless
In terms of employment,
hotel ledgers, news files.

STEPHEN SPENDER

THREES

CARL SANDBURG

I was a boy when I heard three red words
a thousand Frenchmen died in the streets
for: Liberty, Equality, Fraternity—I asked
why men die for words.

5 I was older; men with mustaches, sideburns,
lilacs, told me the high golden words are:
Mother, Home, and Heaven—other older men with
face decorations said: God, Duty, Immortality
—they sang these threes slow from deep lungs.

10 Years ticked off their say-so on the great clocks
of doom and damnation, soup and nuts: meteors flashed
their say-so: and out of great Russia came three
dusky syllables workmen took guns and went out to die
for: Bread, Peace, Land.

15 And I met a marine of the U.S.A., a leatherneck[1] with
a girl on his knee for a memory in ports circling the
earth and he said: Tell me how to say three things
and I always get by—gimme a plate of ham and eggs—
how much?—and, do you love me, kid?

Interpretation

1. Since each stanza alludes to a particular period or event in human history, who do you think the "I" in the poem is?
2. Why do you think Sandburg describes the three words in stanza 1 as *red*, in stanza 2 as *golden*, and the syllables in stanza 3 as *dusky*?
3. The leatherneck's "threes" are humorous, but Sandburg is making a serious point. What do you think it is?
4. Comment on Sandburg's diction. (See DICTION in *Handbook of Terms and Techniques*.)

From SMOKE AND STEEL by Carl Sandburg, copyright, 1920, by Harcourt Brace Jovanovich, Inc.; renewed, 1948, by Carl Sandburg. Reprinted by permission of the publishers.

1. *leatherneck,* a United States marine. [*Slang*]

THE CONSCIENTIOUS OBJECTOR

KARL SHAPIRO

The gates clanged and they walked you into jail
More tense than felons but relieved to find
The hostile world shut out, the flags that dripped
From every mother's windowpane, obscene
5 The bloodlust sweating from the public heart,
The dog authority slavering at your throat.
A sense of quiet, of pulling down the blind
Possessed you. Punishment you felt was clean.

The decks, the catwalks, and the narrow light
10 Composed a ship. This was a mutinous crew
Troubling the captains for plain decencies,
A Mayflower brim with pilgrims headed out
To establish new theocracies[1] to west,
A Noah's ark[2] coasting the topmost seas
15 Ten miles above the sodomites and fish.
These inmates loved the only living doves.

1. *Mayflower . . . theocracies.* The Pilgrims who sailed on the *Mayflower* and the Puritans who followed
them wished to establish a theocracy, a government ruled by religious authorities. 2. *Noah's ark.*
According to the Bible, the patriarch Noah built an ark in which he, his family, and animals of every
species survived the deluge sent by God to punish people for their sins. A dove that Noah had sent
out returned with an olive branch as a sign that the flood was subsiding. The ark came to rest on Ararat,
a mountain in eastern Turkey. (Genesis 6-8)

Like all men hunted from the world you made
A good community, voyaging the storm
To no safe Plymouth or green Ararat;
20 Trouble or calm, the men with Bibles prayed,
The gaunt politicals construed our hate.
The opposite of all armies, you were best
Opposing uniformity and yourselves;
Prison and personality were your fate.

25 You suffered not so physically but knew
Maltreatment, hunger, ennui of the mind.
Well might the soldier kissing the hot beach
Erupting in his face damn all your kind.
Yet you who saved neither yourselves nor us
30 Are equally with those who shed the blood
The heroes of our cause. Your conscience is
What we come back to in the armistice.

interpretation

1. To what is prison compared in stanzas 2–3? Explain the significance
of the allusions to the *Mayflower,* Noah's ark, Plymouth, and Ararat
in developing this idea.
2. What is Shapiro's attitude toward conscientious objectors? Which
lines in the poem make it clear?
3. What is the basic metrical pattern? (See RHYTHM in *Handbook of
Terms and Techniques.*)

ULTIMA RATIO REGUM[1]

STEPHEN SPENDER

The guns spell money's ultimate reason
In letters of lead on the Spring hillside.
But the boy lying dead under the olive trees
Was too young and too silly
5 To have been notable to their important eye.
He was a better target for a kiss.

When he lived, tall factory hooters never summoned him.
Nor did restaurant plate-glass doors revolve to wave him in.
His name never appeared in the papers.
10 The world maintained its traditional wall
Round the dead with their gold sunk deep as a well,
Whilst his life, intangible as a Stock Exchange rumour, drifted outside.

O too lightly he threw down his cap
One day when the breeze threw petals from the trees.
15 The unflowering wall sprouted with guns,
Machine-gun anger quickly scythed the grasses;
Flags and leaves fell from hands and branches;
The tweed cap rotted in the nettles.

Consider his life which was valueless
20 In terms of employment, hotel ledgers, news files.
Consider. One bullet in ten thousand kills a man.
Ask. Was so much expenditure justified
On the death of one so young, and so silly
Lying under the olive trees, O world, O death?

Interpretation

1. Spender is making an ironic statement about war—"the ultimate argument of kings." How does the death of the boy point up the irony? (See IRONY in *Handbook of Terms and Techniques*.)
2. The old or archaic meaning of *silly* is "helpless, frail"; its modern denotation is "foolish." Which meaning do you think Spender intends? Which would contribute more to the irony?

1. *Ultima Ratio Regum*, a Latin expression meaning "the ultimate argument of kings."

DOES IT MATTER?

SIEGFRIED SASSOON

Does it matter?—losing your legs? . . .
For people will always be kind,
And you need not show that you mind
When the others come in after hunting
5 To gobble their muffins and eggs.

Does it matter?—losing your sight? . . .
There's such splendid work for the blind;
And people will always be kind,
As you sit on the terrace remembering
10 And turning your face to the light.

Do they matter?—those dreams from the pit? . . .
You can drink and forget and be glad,
And people won't say that you're mad;
For they'll know that you've fought for your country,
15 And no one will worry a bit.

interpretation

1. How would you describe the tone of the poem? (See TONE in *Handbook of Terms and Techniques*.) Characterize the meter. What is its effect on the tone?
2. Why do you think a poem with a serious theme was written in this manner?

From COLLECTED POEMS by Siegfried Sassoon. Copyright 1918 by E. P. Dutton Co., renewed 1946 by Siegfried Sassoon. Reprinted by permission of The Viking Press, Inc., and G. T. Sassoon.

THE SOLDIER

RUPERT BROOKE

If I should die, think only this of me:
That there's some corner of a foreign field
That is forever England. There shall be
In that rich earth a richer dust concealed;

5 A dust whom England bore, shaped, made aware,
Gave, once, her flowers to love, her ways to roam,
A body of England's breathing English air,
Washed by the rivers, blest by suns of home.

And think, this heart, all evil shed away,
10 A pulse in the eternal mind, no less,
Gives somewhere back the thoughts by England given:
Her sights and sound; dreams happy as her day;
And laughter, learnt of friends; and gentleness,
In hearts at peace, under an English heaven.

interpretation

1. What is the speaker's attitude toward dying in combat? Contrast the tone of this poem with that of "Does It Matter?" and "Ultima Ratio Regum."

2. "The Soldier" is a sonnet. (Check the characteristics of a sonnet in *Handbook of Terms and Techniques.*) Explain ways in which the form may affect the tone of the poem.

Reprinted by permission of Dodd, Mead & Company, Inc. from THE COLLECTED POEMS OF RUPERT BROOKE. Copyright 1915 by Dodd, Mead & Company, Inc. Copyright renewed 1943 by Edward Marsh.

AN IRISH AIRMAN FORESEES HIS DEATH

WILLIAM BUTLER YEATS

I know that I shall meet my fate
Somewhere among the clouds above;
Those that I fight I do not hate,
Those that I guard I do not love;
5 My country is Kiltartan Cross,
My countrymen Kiltartan's poor,
No likely end could bring them loss
Or leave them happier than before.
Nor law, nor duty bade me fight,
10 Nor public men, nor cheering crowds,
A lonely impulse of delight
Drove to this tumult in the clouds;
I balanced all, brought all to mind,
The years to come seemed waste of breath,
15 A waste of breath the years behind
In balance with this life, this death.

commentary

Another definition of him [the dead hero] is offered in "An Irish Airman Foresees His Death." Stressing again the "balance" of his perfect man, Yeats—like Homer before him in the *Iliad*—lets his young man choose a hero's death in a war otherwise meaningless. . . . Yeats brings his hero to a moment of perception, an instance of insight that balances "all" and that makes significant (because equivalent to each other) "this life, this death."[1]

John Unterecker

1. From A READER'S GUIDE TO WILLIAM BUTLER YEATS by John Unterecker. Copyright © 1956 by John Unterecker. Published by Farrar, Straus & Giroux (The Noonday Press).

DEATH OF A WHALE

JOHN BLIGHT

When the mouse died, there was a sort of pity;
The tiny, delicate creature made for grief.
Yesterday, instead, the dead whale on the reef
Drew an excited multitude to the jetty.
5 How must a whale die to wring a tear?
Lugubrious death of a whale; the big
Feast for the gulls and sharks; the tug
Of the tide simulating life still there,
Until the air, polluted, swings this way
10 Like a door ajar from a slaughterhouse.
Pooh! pooh! spare us, give us the death of a mouse
By its tiny hole; not this in our lovely bay.
—Sorry, we are, too, when a child dies:
But at the immolation of a race, who cries?

Interpretation

1. The poet draws certain conclusions from comparing the deaths of a mouse and a whale. Do you accept his conclusions?

2. Discuss the meter and the rhyme scheme of this sonnet. Although it is neither Petrarchan nor Shakespearean, which of these types is it closer to? In what lines does slant rhyme occur? (See RHYME in *Handbook of Terms and Techniques*.) What is the effect of this rhyme on the sonnet form?

From A BEACHCOMBER'S DIARY by John Blight. Reprinted by permission of Angus & Robertson (Publishers) Pty. Ltd.

"NEXT TO OF COURSE GOD AMERICA I

E. E. CUMMINGS

"next to of course god america i
love you land of the pilgrims' and so forth oh
say can you see by the dawn's early my
country 'tis of centuries come and go
5   and are no more what of it we should worry
in every language even deafanddumb
thy sons acclaim your glorious name by gorry
by jingo by gee by gosh by gum
why talk of beauty what could be more beaut-
10 iful than these heroic happy dead
who rushed like lions to the roaring slaughter
they did not stop to think they died instead
then shall the voice of liberty be mute?"

He spoke.   And drank rapidly a glass of water

Interpretation

1. Identify the speaker.
2. Consider the use of patriotic clichés and *non sequiturs*. What is Cummings suggesting about the speaker and his ideas?
3. Why are the sentences run together without break or pause in the first thirteen lines?
4. What is the form of this poem?

2

...the boy whispers to the empty land
that folds him in, half-animal,
half-grown...

MALCOLM COWLEY

MY PARENTS KEPT ME
FROM CHILDREN WHO WERE ROUGH

STEPHEN SPENDER

My parents kept me from children who were rough
And who threw words like stones and who wore torn clothes.
Their thighs showed through rags. They ran in the street
And climbed cliffs and stripped by the country streams.

5 I feared more than tigers their muscles like iron
And their jerking hands and their knees tight on my arms.
I feared the salt coarse pointing of those boys
Who copied my lisp behind me on the road.

They were lithe, they sprang out behind hedges
10 Like dogs to bark at our world. They threw mud
And I looked another way, pretending to smile.
I longed to forgive them, yet they never smiled.

interpretation

1. How does the speaker indicate that his feelings toward the rough boys were not entirely negative? Consider some of the adjectives he uses to describe the boys and their activities.
2. What does the phrase "our world" (line 10) suggest as the reason for the boys' harsh treatment of the speaker?
3. Spender has used several striking similes in his poem. Point them out and discuss ways in which they amplify mood and meaning.

THERE WAS A NAUGHTY BOY

JOHN KEATS

There was a naughty Boy,
  And a naughty Boy was he,
He ran away to Scotland
  The people for to see—

5   Then he found
        That the ground
        Was as hard,
        That a yard
        Was as long,
10   That a song
        Was as merry,
        That a cherry
        Was as red—
        That lead
15   Was as weighty,
        That fourscore
        Was as eighty,
        That a door
        Was as wooden
20   As in England—

So he stood in his shoes
  And he wondered,
  He wondered,
He stood in his shoes
25   And he wondered.

THE DIRTY WORD

KARL SHAPIRO

The dirty word hops in the cage of the mind like the Pondicherry vulture,[1] stomping with its heavy left claw on the sweet meat of the brain and tearing it with its vicious beak, ripping and chopping the flesh. Terrified, the small boy bears the big bird of the dirty word into
5 the house, and grunting, puffing, carries it up the stairs to his own room in the skull. Bits of black feather cling to his clothes and his hair as he locks the staring creature in the dark closet.

All day the small boy returns to the closet to examine and feed the bird, to caress and kick the bird, that now snaps and flaps its wings
10 savagely whenever the door is opened. How the boy trembles and delights at the sight of the white excrement of the bird! How the bird leaps and rushes against the walls of the skull, trying to escape from the zoo of the vocabulary! How wildly snaps the sweet meat of the brain in its rage.

15 And the bird outlives the man, being freed at the man's death-funeral by a word from the rabbi.

But I one morning went upstairs and opened the door and entered the closet and found in the cage of my mind the great bird dead. Softly I wept it and softly removed it and softly buried the body of the bird in
20 the hollyhock garden of the house I lived in twenty years before. And out of the worn black feathers of the wing have I made pens to write these elegies, for I have outlived the bird, and I have murdered it in my early manhood.

Interpretation

1. Explain the metaphor of the huge bird. (See FIGURATIVE LANGUAGE in *Handbook of Terms and Techniques*.) To what extent does the metaphor seem appropriate and effective?
2. Why does the boy both "caress and kick" the bird?
3. What is the significance of the shift to "I" in the final paragraph?
4. "The Dirty Word" is a prose poem. (See PROSE POEM in *Handbook of Terms and Techniques*.) Do you think this form is effective for this particular poem? Explain your answer.

---

1. *Pondicherry vulture,* a large black vulture found in India.

BLACK JACKETS

THOM GUNN

In the silence that prolongs the span
Rawly of music when the record ends,
  The red-haired boy who drove a van
In weekday overalls but, like his friends,

5   Wore cycle boots and jacket here
To suit the Sunday hangout he was in,
  Heard, as he stretched back from his beer,
Leather creak softly round his neck and chin.

  Before him, on a coal-black sleeve
10   Remote exertion had lined, scratched, and burned
  Insignia that could not revive
The heroic fall or climb where they were earned.

  On the other drinkers bent together,
Concocting selves for their impervious kit,
15   He saw it as no more than leather
Which, taut across the shoulders grown to it,

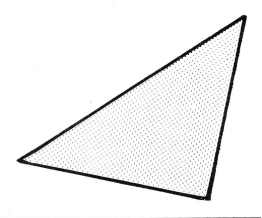

Sent through the dimness of a bar
As sudden and anonymous hints of light
As those that shipping give, that are
20   Now flickers on the Bay, now lost in night.

He stretched out like a cat, and rolled
The bitterish taste of beer upon his tongue,
And listened to a joke being told:
The present was the things he stayed among.

25   If it was only loss he wore,
He wore it to assert, with fierce devotion,
Complicity and nothing more.
He recollected his initiation,

And one especially of the rites.
30   For on his shoulders they had put tattoos:
The group's name on the left, The Knights,
And on the right the slogan Born To Lose.

1. Where does the action of the poem take place? Describe the setting
and the atmosphere.
2. We see everything from the point of view of "the red-haired boy."
How would you characterize him?
3. Why are he and his friends wearing black leather jackets? What
significance have the jackets for them?
4. What does the poem tell us about the young man's relationship to
the other "black jackets"?
5. What is your reaction to this poem?

ARMS AND THE BOY

WILFRED OWEN

Let the boy try along this bayonet-blade
How cold steel is, and keen with hunger of blood;
Blue with all malice, like a madman's flash;
And thinly drawn with famishing for flesh.

5 Lend him to stroke these blind, blunt bullet-heads
Which long to nuzzle in the hearts of lads,
Or give him cartridges of fine zinc teeth,
Sharp with the sharpness of grief and death.

For his teeth seem for laughing round an apple.
10 There lurk no claws behind his fingers supple;
And God will grow no talons at his heels,
Nor antlers through the thickness of his curls.

interpretation

1. It has often been said that man is by nature a warring animal. How does Owen seem to refute this assertion?
2. Owen personifies the instruments of war. Point out examples of such personification. What do they add to the idea the poem develops?
3. Analyze the meter and the rhyme scheme. What type of rhyme is used throughout? (See the entries for RHYTHM and RHYME in *Handbook of Terms and Techniques*.)

THE WAY IT WAS

LUCILLE CLIFTON

mornings
I got up early
greased my legs
straightened my hair and
5   walked quietly out
not touching

in the same place
the tree   the lot
the poolroom   Deacon Moore
10   everything was stayed

nothing changed
(nothing remained the same)
I walked out quietly
mornings
15   in the '40s
a nice girl
not touching
trying to be white

Reprinted from *The Massachusetts Review*, © 1971, The Massachusetts Review, Inc. Reprinted by permission.

TO DAVID, ABOUT HIS EDUCATION

HOWARD NEMEROV

The world is full of mostly invisible things,
And there is no way but putting the mind's eye,
Or its nose, in a book, to find them out,
Things like the square root of Everest
5   Or how many times Byron goes into Texas,
Or whether the law of the excluded middle[1]
Applies west of the Rockies. For these
And the like reasons, you have to go to school
And study books and listen to what you are told,
10   And sometimes try to remember. Though I don't know
What you will do with the mean annual rainfall
On Plato's Republic,[2] or the calorie content
Of the Diet of Worms,[3] such things are said to be
Good for you, and you will have to learn them
15   In order to become one of the grown-ups
Who sees invisible things neither steadily nor whole,
But keeps gravely the grand confusion of the world
Under his hat, which is where it belongs,
And teaches small children to do this in their turn.

interpretation

1. Comment on the tone of the poem. Is the voice that advises David ironic, sarcastic, disillusioned, playful, or what?
2. Why do you think the speaker employs such Alice-in-Wonderland concepts as "the square root of Everest"; "how many times Byron goes into Texas"; and the "annual rainfall / On Plato's Republic"? Mention other examples of such word play.
3. What serious comment is the poet making?

From THE NEXT ROOM OF THE DREAM, published by the University of Chicago, copyright by Howard Nemerov, 1962. Reprinted by permission of the Margot Johnson Agency.

1. *law of the excluded middle*, in formal logic, a principle for analyzing the validity of propositions. 2. *Plato's Republic*, a book by the Greek philosopher outlining an ideal society. 3. *Diet of Worms*, a deliberative assembly (diet) that met in the German city of Worms in 1521 and, among other decisions, condemned Martin Luther for heresy.

THE BALL POEM

JOHN BERRYMAN

What is the boy now, who has lost his ball,
What, what is he to do? I saw it go
Merrily bouncing, down the street, and then
Merrily over—there it is in the water!
5 No use to say "O there are other balls":
An ultimate shaking grief fixes the boy
As he stands rigid, trembling, staring down
All his young days into the harbour where
His ball went. I would not intrude on him,
10 A dime, another ball, is worthless. Now
He senses first responsibility
In a world of possessions. People will take balls,
Balls will be lost always, little boy,
And no one buys a ball back. Money is external.
15 He is learning, well behind his desperate eyes,
The epistemology[1] of loss, how to stand up
Knowing what every man must one day know
And most know many days, how to stand up.
And gradually light returns to the street,
20 A whistle blows, the ball is out of sight,
Soon part of me will explore the deep and dark
Floor of the harbour . . . I am everywhere,
I suffer and move, my mind and my heart move
With all that move me, under the water
25 Or whistling, I am not a little boy.

interpretation

1. What does the speaker mean when he declares that "no one buys a ball back" (line 14)?
2. What does the lost ball symbolize? (See SYMBOLISM in *Handbook of Terms and Techniques.*)
3. What is your understanding of the last five lines of the poem?

Reprinted with the permission of Farrar, Straus & Giroux, Inc. and Faber and Faber Ltd. From SHORT POEMS, (British title: HOMAGE TO MISTRESS BRADSTREET) by John Berryman, copyright 1948 by John Berryman.

1. *epistemology*, the science of human knowledge.

BOY IN SUNLIGHT   MALCOLM COWLEY

The boy having fished alone
down Empfield Run from where it started on stony ground,
in oak and chestnut timber,
then crossed the Nicktown Road into a stand
5   of bare-trunked beeches ghostly white in the noon twilight—

having reached a place of sunlight
that used to be hemlock woods on the slope of a broad valley,
the woods cut twenty years ago for tanbark
and then burned over, so the great charred trunks
10   lay crisscross, wreathed in briars, gray in the sunlight,
black in the shadow of saplings hardly grown
to fishing-pole size: black birch and yellow birch,
black cherry and fire cherry—

having caught four little trout that float, white bellies up,
15   in a lard bucket half-full of lukewarm water—
having unwrapped a sweat-damp cloth from a slab of pone
to eat with dewberries picked from the heavy vines—
now sprawls above the brook on a high stone,
his bare scratched knees in the sun, his fishing pole beside him,
20   not sleeping but dozing awake like a snake on the stone.

Waterskaters dance on the pool beneath the stone.
A bullfrog goes silently back to his post among the weeds.
A dragonfly hovers and darts above the water.
The boy does not look down at them
25   or up at the hawk now standing still in the pale-blue mountain sky,
and yet he feels them, insect, hawk, and sky,
much as he feels warm sandstone under his back,
or smells the punk-dry hemlock wood,
or hears the secret voice of water trickling under stone.

30   The land absorbs him into itself,
as he absorbs the land, the ravaged woods, the pale sky;
not to be seen, but as a way of seeing;
not to be judged, but as a law of judgment;
not even to remember, but stamped in the bone.
35   "Mine," screams the hawk, "Mine," hums the dragonfly,
and "Mine," the boy whispers to the empty land
that folds him in, half-animal, half-grown,
still as the sunlight, still as a hawk in the sky,
still and relaxed and watchful as a trout under the stone.

From BLUE JUNIATA: COLLECTED POEMS by Malcolm Cowley. Copyright © 1968 by Malcolm Cowley. Originally appeared in *Poetry*. Reprinted by permission of The Viking Press, Inc.

TERAN[1]

LUIS OMAR SALINAS

The children of Teran
are hungry,

they speak with ice in their
mouths.

5 They conquer
strange lands

with muddy eyes
and when harvest

time comes
10 they sit in pairs,

handsome thirteen year old
distant minstrels

of MEXICO.

Interpretation

1. The young fisherman of "Boy in Sunlight" is at home with himself and his land. Select details that show this sense of belonging. Contrast the boy's situation with that of the thirteen-year-olds of Teran.
2. Where does the first sentence of "Boy in Sunlight" end? What is the function of this sentence? How does the poem change after this sentence?

1. *Teran,* a town in southern Mexico.

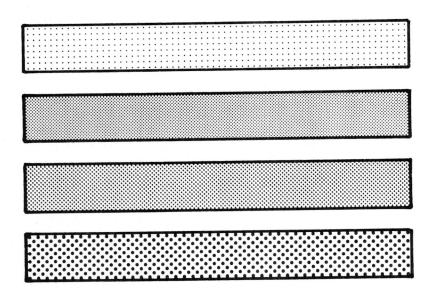

When their children begin to read poetry the parents watch them from the corner of their eye.

KARL SHAPIRO

AS YOU SAY (NOT WITHOUT SADNESS), POETS DON'T SEE, THEY FEEL

KARL SHAPIRO

As you say (not without sadness), poets don't see, they feel.
And that's why people who have turned to feelers seem
like poets. Why children seem poetic. Why when the
sap rises in the adolescent heart the young write poetry.
5 Why great catastrophes are stated in verse. Why lunatics
are named for the moon.[1] Yet poetry isn't feeling with
the hands. A poem is not a kiss. Poems are what ideas
feel like. Ideas on Sunday, thoughts on vacation.

Poets don't see, they feel. They are conductors of the senses
10 of men, as teachers and preachers are the insulators.
The poets go up and feel the insulators. Now and again
they feel the wrong thing and are thrown through a wall
by a million-volt shock. All insulation makes the poet
anxious: clothes, strait jackets, iambic five. He pulls at
15 the seams like a boy whose trousers are cutting him in
half. Poets think along the electric currents. The words
are constantly not making sense when he reads. He
flunks economics, logic, history. Then he describes what
it feels like to flunk economics, logic, history. After
20 that he feels better.

People say: it is sad to see a grown man feeling his way, sad
to see a man so naked, desireless of any defenses. The
people walk back into their boxes and triple-lock the
doors. When their children begin to read poetry the
25 parents watch them from the corner of their eye. It's
only a phase, they aver. Parents like the word "aver"
though they don't use it.

interpretation

1. By stating what poets do do, and what they don't do, Karl Shapiro
presents a definition or concept of the poet. Describe this poet in your
own words. Does this definition appear to fit the poets you have read?
2. What do "clothes, strait jackets, iambic five" have in common? (For
an explanation of *iambic five* see RHYTHM in the *Handbook of Terms and
Techniques.*) Relate this phrase to the idea expressed in the poem.
3. This is a prose poem. In what ways does it differ from conventional
poetry? (For information see the *Handbook of Terms and Techniques.*)

1. *lunatics . . . moon.* The word *lunatic* is formed from *luna,* the Latin word for moon.

IN MY CRAFT OR SULLEN ART

DYLAN THOMAS

In my craft or sullen art
Exercised in the still night
When only the moon rages
And the lovers lie abed
5 With all their griefs in their arms,
I labour by singing light
Not for ambition or bread
Or the strut and trade of charms
On the ivory stages
10 But for the common wages
Of their most secret heart.

Not for the proud man apart
From the raging moon I write
On these spindrift pages
15 Nor for the towering dead
With their nightingales and psalms
But for the lovers, their arms
Round the griefs of the ages,
Who pay no praise or wages
20 Nor heed my craft or art.

Interpretation

1. Dylan Thomas' words constantly surprise the reader because they turn up in surprising company. For example: Why is his art "sullen"? How do you interpret "singing light" (line 6)? Why does he call his pages "spindrift" (sea spray)?

2. Normally we would find lovers with their arms around each other, but in this poem their arms are around the "griefs of the ages." Is this because they are unhappy? Or is it because in their very bliss lies the seed of their future grief (and the secret of the "griefs of the ages")— that is, the passing of their happiness, the coming of age, the loss of youth and beauty, and the disappearance of romantic love? What are your ideas?

3. Much of this poem is couched in negative terms, ruling out certain motivations and certain audiences for the poet; for example, he says he does not write "for ambition or bread." What image of the poet emerges from the poem? How does Thomas' poem differ from Shapiro's?

ILLUSTRIOUS ANCESTORS

DENISE LEVERTOV

The Rav[1]
of Northern White Russia declined,
in his youth, to learn the
language of birds, because
5   the extraneous did not interest him; nevertheless
when he grew old it was found
he understood them anyway, having
listened well, and as it is said, "prayed
     with the bench and the floor." He used
10 what was at hand—as did
Angel Jones of Mold, whose meditations
were sewn into coats and britches.
     Well, I would like to make,
thinking some line still taut between me and them,
15 poems direct as what the birds said,
hard as a floor, sound as a bench,
mysterious as the silence when the tailor
would pause with his needle in the air.

---

commentary

Reading of this poem must begin with the title, as it refers directly to two of the poet's "illustrious ancestors" described in the poem. The first mentioned is the Rav of White Russia; the second is Angel Jones who came from Mold, a coal-mining center in Wales. The Russian was an intuitive and pious man of learning; the Welshman was a tailor. The poet believes that there is "some line still taut between" her and her ancestors: Her poems, she likes to think, are filled with a natural intuitive knowledge ("poems direct as what the birds said" to her Russian ancestor). She hopes they contain also the natural mystery of everyday or common experience ("mysterious as the silence" when the Welsh tailor paused between stitches). She tries to make her poems as "hard as a floor, sound as a bench." Here she is again referring to the Russian ancestor who "prayed with the bench and the floor," that is, without the ornaments and comforts found in richly appointed churches.

How does the conception of poetry which emerges here differ from the conceptions of poetry in the poems by Karl Shapiro and Dylan Thomas?

---

1. *Rav*, a variant of *rab*, or *rabbi*, the title given to a Jewish religious leader.

George Gordon, Lord Byron, the early nineteenth-century English Romantic poet, and Ogden Nash, the twentieth-century American humorous poet, have very little in common except for the poem by Byron on this page and Nash's reaction to it on the page following.

Byron's poem is based on an incident related in the Bible (II Kings 19:35). In the eighth century B.C., *King Sennacherib of Assyria led his mighty army against Jerusalem. The night before the attack the army was destroyed by a plague, which the Bible credits to direct intervention by the God of Israel, who is said to have sent an angel to assist the Jews.*

THE DESTRUCTION OF SENNACHERIB

GEORGE GORDON, LORD BYRON

The Assyrian came down like the wolf on the fold,
And his cohorts were gleaming in purple and gold;
And the sheen of their spears was like stars on the sea,
When the blue wave rolls nightly on deep Galilee.

5   Like the leaves of the forest when Summer is green,
That host with their banners at sunset were seen:
Like the leaves of the forest when Autumn hath blown,
That host on the morrow lay withered and strown.

For the Angel of Death spread his wings on the blast,
10   And breathed in the face of the foe as he passed;
And the eyes of the sleepers waxed deadly and chill,
And their hearts but once heaved, and for ever grew still!

And there lay the steed with his nostril all wide,
But through it there rolled not the breath of his pride;
15   And the foam of his gasping lay white on the turf,
And cold as the spray of the rock-beating surf.

And there lay the rider distorted and pale,
With the dew on his brow, and the rust on his mail:
And the tents were all silent, the banners alone,
20   The lances unlifted, the trumpet unblown.

And the widows of Ashur[1] are loud in their wail,
And the idols are broke in the temple of Baal[2];
And the might of the Gentile, unsmote by the sword,
Hath melted like snow in the glance of the Lord!

---

1. *Ashur,* Assyria. 2. *Baal,* the supreme divinity of the Assyrians, or Gentiles.

VERY LIKE A WHALE

OGDEN NASH

One thing that literature would be greatly the better for
Would be a more restricted employment by authors of simile and
     metaphor.
Authors of all races, be they Greeks, Romans, Teutons or Celts,
Can't seem just to say that anything is the thing it is but have to go
     out of their way to say that it is like something else.
5 What does it mean when we are told
That the Assyrian came down like a wolf on the fold?
In the first place, George Gordon Byron had had enough experience
To know that it probably wasn't just one Assyrian, it was a *lot* of
     Assyrians.
However, as too many arguments are apt to induce apoplexy and
     thus hinder longevity,
10 We'll let it pass as one Assyrian for the sake of brevity.
Now then, this particular Assyrian, the one whose cohorts were
     gleaming in purple and gold,
Just what does the poet mean when he says he came down like a
     wolf on the fold?
In heaven and earth more than is dreamed of in our philosophy there
     are a great many things,
But I don't imagine that among them there is a wolf with purple and
     gold cohorts or purple and gold anythings.
15 No, no, Lord Byron, before I'll believe that this Assyrian was actually
     like a wolf I must have some kind of proof;
Did he run on all fours and did he have a hairy tail and a big red
     mouth and big white teeth and did he say Woof woof woof?
Frankly I think it very unlikely, and all you were entitled to say, at
     the very most,
Was that the Assyrian cohorts came down like a lot of Assyrian cohorts
     about to destroy the Hebrew host.
But that wasn't fancy enough for Lord Byron, oh dear me, no, he had
     to invent a lot of figures of speech and then interpolate them,
20 With the result that whenever you mention Old Testament soldiers
     to people they say Oh yes, they're the ones that a lot of wolves
     dressed up in gold and purple ate them.
That's the kind of thing that's being done all the time by poets, from
     Homer to Tennyson;

continued

They're always comparing ladies to lilies and veal to venison,
And they always say things like that the snow is a white blanket after
      a winter storm.
Oh it is, is it, all right then, you sleep under a six-inch blanket of
      snow and I'll sleep under a half-inch blanket of unpoetical
      blanket material and we'll see which one keeps warm,
25 And after that maybe you'll begin to comprehend dimly
What I mean by too much metaphor and simile.

interpretation

1. Discuss the validity of Nash's objections to Byron's metaphors and similes. (See entries in *Handbook of Terms and Techniques*.)
2. Explore the nature of Nash's odd rhymes. How do the funny rhymes affect the way we react to what the poet says?

TO A POET, WHO WOULD HAVE ME PRAISE CERTAIN BAD POETS, IMITATORS OF HIS AND MINE

WILLIAM BUTLER YEATS

You say, as I have often given tongue
In praise of what another's said or sung,
'Twere politic to do the like by these;
But was there ever dog that praised his fleas?

In the following lines from An Essay on Criticism, *Pope is mocking both those who admire and those who write bad poetry.*

from AN ESSAY ON CRITICISM

ALEXANDER POPE

But most by numbers[1] judge a poet's song;
And smooth or rough, with them, is right or wrong:
In the bright Muse[2] though thousand charms conspire,
Her voice is all these tuneful fools admire;
5 Who haunt Parnassus[3] but to please their ear,
Not mend their minds; as some to church repair,
Not for the doctrine, but the music there.
These[4] equal syllables alone require,
Though oft the ear the open vowels tire;
10 While expletives[5] their feeble aid do join[6];
And ten low words oft creep in one dull line:
While they ring round the same unvaried chimes,
With sure returns of still expected rimes;
Where'er you find "the cooling western breeze,"
15 In the next line, it "whispers through the trees";
If crystal streams "with pleasing murmurs creep,"
The reader's threatened (not in vain) with "sleep":
Then, at the last and only couplet fraught
With some unmeaning thing they call a thought,
20 A needless Alexandrine[7] ends the song,
That like a wounded snake, drags its slow length along. . . .
True ease in writing comes from art, not chance,
As those move easiest who have learned to dance.
'Tis not enough no harshness gives offense,
25 The sound must seem an echo to the sense:
Soft is the strain when Zephyr gently blows,
And the smooth stream in smoother numbers flows;
But when loud surges lash the sounding shore,
The hoarse, rough verse should like the torrent roar.

interpretation

1. In this passage does Pope's "sound" seem "an echo to the sense"? Give examples to justify your answer.
2. Reread the first seven lines. Why does Pope censure those who judge poetry by "numbers"?

---

1. *numbers,* verses. **2.** *bright Muse,* poetry. **3.** *Parnassus,* a mountain in Greece which was sacred to Apollo, god of prophecy, music, and poetry, and to the Muses. It symbolizes poetic inspiration. **4.** *These,* these individuals. **5.** *expletives,* words added to fill out a line of poetry. **6.** *join.* In the eighteenth century the pronunciation of *join* rhymed with *line.* **7.** *Alexandrine,* a line containing twelve syllables, iambic hexameter. The next line is an illustration.

I KNOW I'M NOT SUFFICIENTLY OBSCURE

RAY DUREM

I know I'm not sufficiently obscure
to please the critics—nor devious enough.
Imagery escapes me.
I cannot find those mild and gracious words
5 to clothe the carnage.
Blood is blood and murder's murder.
What's a lavender word for lynch?
Come, you pale poets, wan, refined and dreamy:
here is a black woman working out her guts
10 in a white man's kitchen
for little money and no glory.
How should I tell that story?
There is a black boy, blacker still from death,
face down in the cold Korean mud.
15 Come on with your effervescent jive
explain to him why he ain't alive.
Reword our specific discontent
into some plaintive melody,
a little whine, a little whimper,
20 not too much—and no rebellion!
God, no! Rebellion's much too corny.
You deal with finer feelings,
very subtle—an autumn leaf
hanging from a tree—I see a body!

interpretation

1. Is the speaker in this poem really interested in being "sufficiently obscure / to please the critics"? Explain why you think he is, or is not.
2. How does Durem's conception of the poet's function differ from Shapiro's? from Thomas'? from Levertov's?

From TAKE NO PRISONERS by Ray Durem. Copyright © 1962, 1971 by Dorothy Durem. Reprinted by permission of the publishers, Paul Breman Limited.

PRIMITIVES

DUDLEY RANDALL

Paintings with stiff
homuncules,[1] flat in iron
draperies, with distorted
bodies against spaceless
5 landscapes.

Poems of old
poets in stiff
metres whose harsh
syllables
10 drag like
dogs with
crushed
backs.

We go back to
15 them, spurn difficult
grace and
symmetry,
paint tri-faced
monsters,
20 write lines that
do not sing, or
even croak, but that
bump,
jolt, and are hacked
25 off in the mid-
dle, as if by these dis-
tortions, this
magic, we can
exorcise
30 horror, which we
have seen and fear to
see again:

hate deified,
fears and
35 guilt conquering,
turning cities to
gas, powder and a
little rubble.

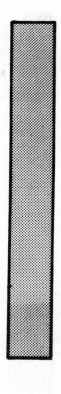

interpretation

1. What do the works of the modern poets of protest have in common with the work of primitive painters and primitive poets?

2. What is the horror these modern poets are trying to "exorcise"?

3. What resemblances can you find in "Primitives" to the idea developed in "I Know I'm Not Sufficiently Obscure"?

From CITIES BURNING, © 1968 by Dudley Randall. Reprinted by permission of Broadside Press.
1. *homuncules* (hō mung′kyə ləs), little men, dwarfs. See Pronunciation Key on page 401.

LAST ANSWERS

CARL SANDBURG

I wrote a poem on the mist
And a woman asked me what I meant by it.
I had thought till then only of the beauty of the mist, how pearl and
      gray of it mix and reel,
And change the drab shanties with lighted lamps at evening into
      points of mystery quivering with color.

  I answered:
The whole world was mist once long ago and some day it will all go
      back to mist,
Our skulls and lungs are more water than bone and tissue
And all poets love dust and mist because all the last answers
Go running back to dust and mist.

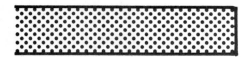

ONE MODERN POET

CARL SANDBURG

          Having heard the instruction:
             "Be thou no swine,"
          He belabored himself and wrote:
             "Beware of the semblance
5   of lard at thy flanks."

THE SNOWFLAKE WHICH IS NOW AND HENCE FOREVER

ARCHIBALD MACLEISH

Will it last? he says.
Is it a masterpiece?
Will generation after generation
Turn with reverence to the page?

5 Birdseye scholar of the frozen fish,
What would he make of the sole, clean, clear
Leap of the salmon that has disappeared?

To *be*, yes!—whether they like it or not!
But not to last when leap and water are forgotten,
10 A plank of standard pinkness in the dish.

They also live
Who swerve and vanish in the river.

interpretation

1. The speaker of the first stanza is a conventional or traditional scholar asking the trite question as to whether a particular poem will really last; he is a "birdseye scholar of the frozen fish." Why *birdseye?* Why *frozen* fish? What other words express the same idea?
2. What does the snowflake of the title have to do with the meaning of the poem?

From COLLECTED POEMS OF ARCHIBALD MACLEISH 1917-1952. Copyright © 1962 by Archibald MacLeish. Reprinted by permission of Houghton Mifflin Company.

ELEGY FOR A NATURE POET

HOWARD NEMEROV

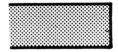

It was in October, a favorite season,
He went for his last walk. The covered bridge,
Most natural of all the works of reason,
Received him, let him go. Along the hedge

5 He rattled his stick; observed the blackening bushes
In his familiar field; thought he espied
Late meadow larks; considered picking rushes
For a dry arrangement; returned home, and died

Of a catarrh caught in the autumn rains
10 And let go on uncared for. He was too rapt
In contemplation to recall that brains
Like his should not be kept too long uncapped

In the wet and cold weather. While we mourned,
We thought of his imprudence, and how Nature,
15 Whom he'd done so much for, had finally turned
Against her creature.

His gift was daily his delight, he peeled
The landscape back to show it was a story;
Any old bird or burning bush revealed
20 At his hands just another allegory.

Nothing too great, nothing too trivial
For him; from mountain range or humble vermin
He could extract the hidden parable—
If need be, crack the stone to get the sermon.

25 And now, poor man, he's gone. Without his name
The field reverts to wilderness again,
The rocks are silent, woods don't seem the same;
Demoralized small birds will fly insane.

Rude Nature, whom he loved to idealize
30 And would have wed, pretends she never heard
His voice at all, as, taken by surprise
At last, he goes to her without a word.

HOWARD NEMEROV WRITES ABOUT "ELEGY FOR A NATURE POET":
The poem was written at Bennington, Vermont, and the covered bridge
is one of three that cross the Walloomsack River below the College on
the way south to town. The poet in question is in the first place, I
suppose, myself, under his own ruefully humorous regard.

interpretation

1. What added insights about the poem does the poet's own comment
give you?
2. In what sense, do you suppose, does the field revert to "wilderness"
in the absence of the poet?
3. Why is this poem called an elegy? (See *Handbook of Terms and
Techniques.*) How does it differ in tone from the traditional elegy?
4. Discuss the irony of the last line . . . the poet goes to Nature "without
a word." (See IRONY in the *Handbook of Terms and Techniques.*)

TO THE STONE-CUTTERS

ROBINSON JEFFERS

Stone-cutters fighting time with marble, you foredefeated
Challengers of oblivion
Eat cynical earnings, knowing rock splits, records fall down,
The square-limbed Roman letters
5 Scale in the thaws, wear in the rain. The poet as well
Builds his monument mockingly;
For man will be blotted out, the blithe earth die, the brave sun
Die blind and blacken to the heart:
Yet stones have stood for a thousand years, and pained thoughts found
10 The honey of peace in old poems.

NOT MARBLE, NOR THE GILDED MONUMENTS *(Sonnet 55)*

WILLIAM SHAKESPEARE

Not marble, nor the gilded monuments
Of princes, shall outlive this pow'rful rhyme;
But you shall shine more bright in these contents
Than unswept stone besmeared with sluttish time.
5 When wasteful war shall statues overturn,
And broils root out the work of masonry,
Nor Mars his sword nor war's quick fire shall burn
The living record of your memory.
'Gainst death and all-oblivious enmity
10 Shall you pace forth; your praise shall still find room
Even in the eyes of all posterity
That wear this world out to the ending doom.
　So, till the judgement that yourself arise,
　You live in this, and dwell in lovers' eyes.

Interpretation

Both of these poems take solace in the fact that poetry outlasts human
life, and indeed bestows as much immortality as humans can know
firsthand. But Shakespeare appears to be more affirmative, Jeffers
more bitter. Explain.

AS FOR POETS

GARY SNYDER

As for Poets,
The Earth Poets,
Who write small poems,
Need help from no man.

5 The Air Poets
Play on the swiftest gales
And sometimes loll in the eddies.
Poem after poem
Curling back on the same thrust.

10 At fifty below
Fuel oil won't flow
And propane stays in the tank.
Fire poets
Burn at absolute zero
15 Fossil love pumped back up.

The first
Water poet
Stayed down six years.
He was covered with seaweed.
20 The life in his poem
Left millions of tiny
Different tracks
Criss-crossing through the mud.

With the Sun and Moon
In his belly,   25
The Space Poet,
Sleeps.
No end to the sky—
But his poems,
Like wild geese,   30
Fly off the edge.

A Mind Poet
Stays in the house.
The house is empty
And it has no walls.   35
The poem
Is seen from all sides,
Everywhere,
At once.

Interpretation

To the traditional four basic elements of Earth, Air, Fire, and Water, Gary Snyder has added Space and Mind. In a playful mood he suggests that every poet fits into one of these categories. When asked to name poets who fill the qualifications for a particular group, he replied: "As for explanation—it's tempting—but may be more fun for teachers and students to play with it themselves."

Suggest poets that in your opinion might fit each of the six categories. Where, for example, would you place Dylan Thomas? Carl Sandburg? Ogden Nash?

From *The New American Review*, #15. Copyright © 1972 by Gary Snyder. Reprinted by permission.

Squirrel, go climb a tree.
You are too like me.
C. DAY LEWIS

THE BEAR

GALWAY KINNELL

1

In late winter
I sometimes glimpse bits of steam
coming up from
some fault in the old snow
5 and bend close and see it is lung-colored
and put down my nose
and know
the chilly, enduring odor of bear.

2

I take a wolf's rib and whittle
10 it sharp at both ends
and coil it up
and freeze it in blubber and place it out
on the fairway of the bears.

And when it has vanished
15 I move out on the bear tracks,
roaming in circles
until I come to the first, tentative, dark
splash on the earth.

And I set out
20 running, following the splashes
of blood wandering over the world.
At the cut, gashed resting places
I stop and rest,
at the crawl-marks
25 where he lay out on his belly
to overpass some stretch of bauchy[1] ice
I lie out
dragging myself forward with bear-knives in my fists.

3

On the third day I begin to starve,
30 at nightfall I bend down as I knew I would
at a turd sopped in blood,
and hesitate, and pick it up,
and thrust it in my mouth, and gnash it down,
and rise
35 and go on running.

---

1. *bauchy*, weak.

On the seventh day,
living by now on bear blood alone,
I can see his upturned carcass far out ahead, a scraggled,
steamy hulk,
40   the heavy fur riffling in the wind.

I come up to him
and stare at the narrow-spaced, petty eyes,
the dismayed
face laid back on the shoulder, the nostrils
45   flared, catching
perhaps the first taint of me as he
died.

I hack
a ravine in his thigh, and eat and drink,
50   and tear him down his whole length
and open him and climb in
and close him up after me, against the wind,
and sleep.

5

And dream
55   of lumbering flatfooted
over the tundra,[2]
stabbed twice from within,
splattering a trail behind me,
splattering it out no matter which way I lurch,
60   no matter which parabola of bear-transcendence,
which dance of solitude I attempt,
which gravity-clutched leap,
which trudge, which groan.

6

Until one day I totter and fall—
65   fall on this
stomach that has tried so hard to keep up,
to digest the blood as it leaked in,
to break up
and digest the bone itself: and now the breeze
70   blows over me, blows off
the hideous belches of ill-digested bear blood
and rotted stomach
and the ordinary, wretched odor of bear,

---

2. *tundra,* a treeless terrain, with a permanently frozen subsoil, characteristic of the arctic and sub-arctic regions.

blows across
75 my sore, lolled tongue a song
or screech, until I think I must rise up
and dance. And I lie still.

7

I awaken I think. Marshlights
reappear, geese
80 come trailing again up the flyway.
In her ravine under old snow the dam-bear[3]
lies, licking
lumps of smeared fur
and drizzly eyes into shapes
85 with her tongue. And one
hairy-soled trudge stuck out before me,
the next groaned out,
the next,
the next,
90 the rest of my days I spend
wandering: wondering
what, anyway,
was that sticky infusion, that rank flavor of blood, that poetry, by
        which I lived?

GALWAY KINNELL WRITES ABOUT "THE BEAR":
As for "The Bear"—I can't explain exactly, even to myself—what it
means, and yet when I read it I understand it very well. Also I'm
probably not in a good position to comment on the poem, because I
still remember those intentions and forethoughts that became irrelevant
as the poem gathered a life of its own.

Interpretation

1. On perhaps the simplest level, this poem is an account by the hunter-
speaker of how he brought about the death of a bear, and how he afterwards crawled inside the carcass and fell asleep, dreaming he himself
had become the bear. What stanzas cover the physical action of the
poem? By what means does the hunter kill the bear? Why does he crawl
inside the bear's body?
2. Comment on the hunter's dream. Discuss the various ways in which
the pursuit and killing of the bear might suggest the quest of the poet,
the artist.

---

3. *dam-bear,* mother bear.

THE BEAR ON THE DELHI[1] ROAD

EARLE BIRNEY

Unreal   tall as a myth
by the road the Himalayan bear
is beating the brilliant air
with his crooked arms
5   About him two men   bare
spindly as locusts   leap

One pulls on a ring
in the great soft nose   His mate
flicks   flicks with a stick
10   up at the rolling eyes

They have not led him here
down from the fabulous hills
to this bald alien plain
and the clamorous world   to kill
15   but simply to teach him to dance

They are peaceful both   these spare
men of Kashmir[2]   and the bear
alive is their living   too
If   far on the Delhi way
20   around him galvanic they dance
it is merely to wear   wear
from his shaggy body the tranced
wish forever to stay
only an ambling bear
25   four-footed in berries

It is no more joyous for them
in this hot dust to prance
out of reach of the praying claws
sharpened to paw for ants
30   in the shadows of deodars[3]
It is not easy to free
myth from reality
or rear this fellow up
to lurch   lurch with them
35   in the tranced dancing of men

From SELECTED POEMS by Earle Birney. Reprinted by permission of The Canadian Publishers, McClelland and Stewart Limited, Toronto.

1. *Delhi* (del'ē), a city in northern India. 2. *Kashmir*, a mountainous area north of India, claimed by both India and Pakistan. 3. *deodars* (dē'ə därz), cedar trees of the Himalayas.

...I think I am grateful to this poem for lessening a feeling of guilt within me. The summer before, I had spent five weeks in India. I'd never been in Asia before, then, suddenly—five weeks in the heart of it. I'm still only a grown-up Alberta ranch boy, and I was drowned in strangeness, objects unthought of, people unimagined: the hollow tombs and the seething streets, the empty peace of a houseboat in the Vale of Kashmir, a child left to die of cholera on the banks of the Jumna, cocktails at an embassy, the sun battering on Ghandi's tomb. And always the presence of the poor, the millions upon millions of incredibly poor, sick or half well, infants or old-men-of-thirty. And the need to say something to encompass them, and the sense of shame in not finding a way to say anything.

Of course I've not shaken off my guilt here, for that is lodged in something deeper even than my conscience as a writer, in that uneasy *imago* of myself as an over-privileged Western man. But I have, in this poem, worked from a sudden vision of a reality otherwise inexpressible for me into an expression of some small part of that compassion and fear and love and despair that overwhelmed me when I was in India. Perhaps I managed also to evoke something about the oddness of Myth, but if so it was accidental. I'm grateful enough to have appeased one of my thronging ghosts.

Earle Birney

1. Compare this poem with Galway Kinnell's "The Bear." What are the essential differences between the two in regard to the human/animal relationships described?
2. Kinnell's poem moves from the realistic into the mythical and symbolic. How would you describe the movement of this poem?

Published in POET'S CHOICE, edited by Paul Engle. © 1962 by Earle Birney. Reprinted by permission of McClelland and Stewart Limited.

GREY SQUIRREL: GREENWICH PARK[1]

C. DAY LEWIS

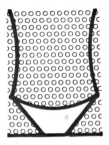

You with the panache[2] tail,
The dowdy old ash-bin fur—
What are you *for*, zigzagging so sprucely
And so obtusely
5 Over the autumn leaves, stopping so dead
The eye shoots ahead of you? What main chance
Are you after, my prancing dear?
You cover the autumn grass with a row
Of lolloping shorthand signs and no
10 Hesitation or apparent destination;
Then pose upright, paws on chest
Like a politician clasping his top-hat on
A solemn occasion, or a hospital matron
Attending some lord of the wards.
15 They say you are vermin, but I cannot determine
What no good you're up to. Possibly the odium
Attaches to you for ganging[3] so thoroughly
Your own mad, felicitous gait, not doing
A hand's turn for State, Church, Union, or Borough.[4]

20 Squirrel, go climb a tree.
You are too like me.

interpretation

1. Why do you think the speaker asks "What are you *for*, . . ." (line 3)?
2. Why does the speaker conclude by saying to the squirrel, "You are too like me"?
3. Find examples of unexpected images. (See IMAGERY in *Handbook of Terms and Techniques*.) Note the way in which rhyme is used. What effect do the uses of imagery and rhyme have on the tone of the poem?

From REQUIEM FOR THE LIVING by C. Day Lewis. Copyright by C. Day Lewis. Reprinted by permission of Harold Matson Company, Inc.

1. *Greenwich Park* (gren′ich), a park in London. **2.** *panache* (pə nash′), a plume or tuft of feathers used for decoration. The word suggests flamboyance or dash. **3.** *ganging,* going. [*Scottish*] **4.** *Borough,* in England, a town or other urban community that has been incorporated for self-government.

ESTHER'S TOMCAT

TED HUGHES

Daylong this tomcat lies stretched flat
As an old rough mat, no mouth and no eyes.
Continual wars and wives are what
Have tattered his ears and battered his head.

5 Like a bundle of old rope and iron
Sleeps till blue dusk. Then reappear
His eyes, green as ringstones: he yawns wide red,
Fangs fine as a lady's needle and bright.

A tomcat sprang at a mounted knight,
10 Locked round his neck like a trap of hooks
While the knight rode fighting its clawing and bite.
After hundreds of years the stain's there

On the stone where he fell, dead of the tom:
That was at Barnborough. The tomcat still
15 Grallochs¹ odd dogs on the quiet,
Will take the head clean off your simple pullet,

Is unkillable. From the dog's fury,
From gunshot fired point-blank he brings
His skin whole, and whole
20 From owlish moons of bekittenings

Among ashcans. He leaps and lightly
Walks upon sleep, his mind on the moon
Nightly over the round world of men
Over the roofs go his eyes and outcry.

1. *gralloch* (gra'lək), disembowel.

PROPINQUITY

ALASTAIR REID

is the province of cats. Living by accident,
lapping the food at hand, or sleeking down
in an adjacent lap when sleep occurs to them,
never aspiring to consistency
5   in homes or partners, unaware of property,
cats take their chances, love by need and nearness
as long as the need lasts, as long as the nearness
is near enough. The code of cats is simply
to take what comes. And those poor souls who claim
10   to own a cat, who long to recognize
in bland and narrowing eyes a look like love,
are bound to suffer should they expect
cats to come purring punctually home.
Home is only where the food and the fire are,
15   but might be anywhere. Cats fall on their feet,
nurse their own wounds, attend to their own laundry,
and purr at appropriate times. O folly, folly
to love a cat, and yet
we dress with love the distance that they keep,
20   the hair-raising way they have, and easily blame
all the abandoned litters and torn ears
on some marauding tiger. Well, no matter;
cats do not care.

       Yet part of us is cat. Confess—
25 love turns on accident, and needs
    nearness; and the various selves we have
    all come from our cat-wanderings, our chance
    crossings. Imagination prowls at night,
    cat-like among odd possibilities.
30 Only our dog-sense brings us faithfully homeward,
    makes meaning out of accident, keeps faith,
    and, cat-and-dog, the arguments go at it.
    But every night, outside, cat-voices call
    us out to take a chance, to leave
35 the safety of our baskets, and to let
    what happens, happen. "Live, live!" they catcall.
    "Each moment is your next! Propinquity,
    propinquity is all!"

interpretation

1. The title, "Propinquity," which in this context means "nearness in place," is also the first word of the poem. Explain why the first statement may be considered the theme of the poem.

2. From your own experience with cats, are you inclined to agree or disagree with the statements in the first part of the poem?

3. Comment on the accuracy or inaccuracy of the second part of the poem, which develops the idea that "part of us is cat."

4. How would you interpret the "cat-voices" that call to human beings?

THE LIZARD   THEODORE ROETHKE

He too has eaten well—
I can see that by the distended pulsing middle;
And his world and mine are the same,
The Mediterranean sun shining on us, equally,
5 His head, stiff as a scarab, turned to one side,
His right eye staring straight at me,
One leaf-like foot hung laxly
Over the worn curb of the terrace,
The tail straight as an awl,
10 Then suddenly flung up and over,
Ending curled around and over again,
A thread-like firmness.

(Would a cigarette disturb him?)

At the first scratch of the match
15 He turns his head slightly,
Retiring to nudge his neck half-way under
A dried strawberry leaf,
His tail gray with the ground now,
One round eye still toward me.
20 A white cabbage-butterfly drifts in,
Bumbling up and around the bamboo windbreak;
But the eye of the tiny lizard stays with me.
One greenish lid lifts a bit higher,
Then slides down over the eye's surface,
25 Rising again, slowly,
Opening, closing.

To whom does this terrace belong?—
With its limestone crumbling into fine grayish dust,
Its bevy of bees, and its wind-beaten rickety sun-chairs.
30 Not to me, but this lizard,
Older than I, or the cockroach.

Interpretation

1. What seems to be the speaker's attitude toward the tiny Mediterranean lizard with whom he shares a few moments of his life? Why does he decide that the terrace and the landscape belong not to him but the lizard?
2. What details indicate Roethke has carefully observed the lizard?

THE GULL   MICHAEL THWAITES

Riding the wind, in planetary sweep
The gull wheels on the radius of a wing;
Ocean and air, concourse of height and deep,
Acclaim the exultant orbit of their king.

5   Precise he lands, defter than any dancer,
Red legs, red eye, white body whiter than foam;
No loveliest yacht so light to lean and answer,
No soul so white in its celestial home.

O Attic[1] joy, O grace made visible,
10   Beauty and power embodied into bird!
Malice, or truth—which is it pricks your spell
With sarcasm of the loathsome and absurd?

Those lacquered feathers, sleek to wind and wave,
Or downy to the softly-fingering breeze,
15   Are an infested jungle, a living grave,
The haunt of lice, mites, parasites, and fleas.

Filth feeds that savage beauty; when head, beak, eyes
Plunge in the putrid whale, or, harsh as sin,
Are stretched agape, with cannibalistic cries,
20   To tear the wounded body of his kin.

O beauty born of death, to death returning,
You are our Middle Earth,[2] nor Heaven nor Hell;
You are ourselves, our turning globe still turning,
The fractured light in which we have to dwell.

25   Here truth is ever tangent. Therefore, gull,
Gorged with the stinking offal that you eat,
Rise in the light, infested, beautiful,
In fragmentary loveliness complete.

Interpretation

1. How does the speaker view the gull in the first ten lines of the poem?
How does he see it in the fourth and fifth stanzas?
2. What do the last two stanzas seem to suggest about appearance and
reality—or the ideal and the real?

Reprinted by permission of G. P. Putnam's Sons from THE JERVIS BAY AND OTHER POEMS
by Michael Thwaites. Copyright 1942 by Michael R. Thwaites.

1. *Attic,* classical, elegant. 2. *Middle Earth,* our Earth, when conceived of as lying midway between
the upper regions (Paradise) and the lower regions (Hell).

THE QUAGGA[1]

D. J. ENRIGHT

By mid-century there were two quaggas left,
And one of the two was male.
The cares of office weighed heavily on him.
When you are the only male of a species,
5   It is not easy to lead a normal sort of life.

The goats nibbled and belched in casual content;
They charged and skidded up and down their concrete mountain.
One might cut his throat on broken glass,
Another stray too near the tigers.
10   But they were zealous husbands; and the enclosure was always full,
Its rank air throbbing with ingenuous voices.

The quagga, however, was a man of destiny.
His wife, whom he had met rather late in her life,
Preferred to sleep, or complain of the food and the weather.
15   For their little garden was less than paradisiac,
With its artificial sun that either scorched or left you cold,
And savants with cameras eternally hanging around,
To perpetuate the only male quagga in the world.

Perhaps that was why he failed to do it himself.
20   It is all very well for goats and monkeys—
But the last male of a species is subject to peculiar pressures.
If ancient Satan had come slithering in, perhaps . . .
But instead the savants, with cameras and notebooks,
Writing sad stories of the decadence of quaggas.

From SELECTED POEMS. © D. J. Enright. Reprinted by permission of Open Court Publishing
Company and Chatto & Windus, Ltd.

1. *Quagga*, an African mammal, related to the horse and the zebra, which was hunted for its skin and
exterminated in the nineteenth century.

25 And then one sultry afternoon he started raising Cain.
This angry young quagga kicked the bars and broke a camera;
He even tried to bite his astonished keeper.
He protested loud and clear against this and that,
Till the other animals became quite embarrassed
30 For he seemed to be calling them names.

Then he noticed his wife, awake with the noise,
And a curious feeling quivered round his belly.
He was Adam: there was Eve.
Galloping over to her, his head flung back,
35 He stumbled, and broke a leg, and had to be shot.

interpretation

1. What is the setting of the poem? Describe the situation in which the male quagga finds himself.
2. The poet has given the quagga human attributes. Name some of these. How does this treatment of the quagga affect your attitude toward him?
3. Find allusions in the poem to the story of Adam and Eve in the Garden of Eden. Why are these allusions pertinent?
4. Why did the male quagga start "raising Cain" one afternoon? Comment on the effectiveness of "Cain" as a pun.
5. Comment on the irony in the last two lines.

5

Ourself behind ourself, concealed—
EMILY DICKINSON

THE SECRET SHARER

THOM GUNN

Over the ankles in snow and numb past pain
I stared up at my window three stories high:
From a white street unconcerned as a dead eye,
I patiently called my name again and again.

5 The curtains were lit, through glass were lit by doubt
And there was I, within the room alone.
In the empty wind I stood and shouted on:
But O, what if the strange head should peer out?

Suspended taut between two equal fears
10 I was like to be torn apart by their strong pull:
What, I asked, if I never hear my call?
And what if it reaches my insensitive ears?

Fixed in my socket of thought I saw them move
Aside, I saw that some uncertain hand
15 Had touched the curtains. Mine, I wondered? And,
At this instant, the wind turned in its groove.

The wind turns in its groove and I am here
Lying in bed, the snow and street outside;
Fire-glow still reassuring; dark defied.
20 The wind turns in its groove: I am still there.

interpretation

1. Where do you think the speaker actually is, inside or outside his
room? The first three lines of the last stanza seem to say that he is in
the room; but then the last line asserts that he is still outside. How do
you interpret these lines?
2. Note the repetition of the expression "... the wind turned (turns)
in its groove" (lines 16, 17, 20). What does it mean? Explain its function
in the poem.

From FIGHTING TERMS. Reprinted by permission of Faber and Faber Ltd.

A GAME OF GLASS

ALASTAIR REID

I do not believe this room
with its cat and its chandelier,
its chessboard-tiled floor,
and its shutters that open out
5 on an angel playing a fountain,
and the striped light slivering in
to a room that looks the same
in the mirror over my shoulder,
with a second glass-eyed cat.

10 My book does not look real.
The room and the mirror seem
to be playing a waiting game.
The cat has made its move,
the fountain has one to play,
15 and the thousand eyes of the angel
in the chandelier above
gleam beadily, and say
the next move is up to me.

How can I trust my luck?
20 Whatever way I look,
I cannot tell which is the door,
and I do not know who is who—
the thin man in the mirror,
or the watery one in the fountain.
25 The cat is eyeing my book.
What am I meant to do?
Which side is the mirror on?

commentary

"A Game of Glass" is the one poem of mine which *occurred* to me, as an actual happening—the only thing I had to do was to catch it and hold it in words as clearly as possible.

I was sitting in my workroom in Spain, one morning very early, writing. The room was exactly as reconstituted in the poem—a large mirror on the wall behind me, shutters in front of me opening to the fountained garden, a huge chandelier, a black and white tiled floor, and my writing table in the middle. All at once, I looked up, and caught the eyes of the cat gazing at me intently—and I felt, for an endless moment, a realisation of utter mystery, in which I existed in no familiar sense, but was simply one element in a vast, inexplicable game, which the cat understood more completely than I. There was something of Through the Looking Glass about it; the feeling was awesome. The coinciding reflections, the chessboard, the un-recognition, all sustained the moment; the poem followed almost at once. I cannot be sure that my profound astonishment is properly contained in it; but I do know that whenever I happen to read it over, I reenter the moment most vividly, as more than a memory.

Except in the manner of its happening, the poem is not out of key with the rest of my work, since to explore the amazement of finding myself alive has been my preoccupation. But this poem reassures me; through it, I can feel beyond words to the happening itself, and realise always that the mystery *does* exist, prior to them.

Alastair Reid

GLASS

W. S. MERWIN

One day you look at the mirror and it's open
and inside the place where the eyes were
is a long road gray as water
and on it someone is running away
5   a little figure in a long pale coat
and you can't move you can't call
it's too late
who was it

then
10 there are many of them
with their backs to you and their arms in the air
and no shadows
running away on the road gray as ice
with the leaves flying after them
15 and the birds in great flocks the dust
the stones the trees
all your terrors running away from you
too late
into a cloud

20 and you fall on your knees and try to call to them
far in the empty face

---

interpretation

1. Something of the Through-the-Looking-Glass feeling that Alastair Reid writes about (page 69) pervades this poem. A mirror opens and in a gray landscape pale figures and trees and birds and dust fade into the distance—"all your terrors running away from you." Speculate as to why the "terrors" are described as such unterrible things.

2. Why do you think the speaker tries to call the phantoms back? Has it anything to do with the fact that he now has an "empty face" (line 21)?

From WRITINGS TO AN UNFINISHED ACCOMPANIMENT by W. S. Merwin. Copyright © 1972 by W. S. Merwin. Reprinted by permission of Atheneum Publishers and Harold Ober Associates Incorporated. Appeared originally in *The New Yorker*.

SCHIZOPHRENIC   P. K. PAGE

Nobody knew when it would start again —
the extraordinary beast go violent in her blood;
nobody knew the virtue of her need
to shape her face to the giant in her brain.

5 Certainly friends were sympathetic, kind,
gave her small handkerchiefs and showed her tricks,
built her life to a sort of "pick-up sticks"
simplification — as if she were a child.

Malleable she wore her lustre nails
10 daily like a debutante and smoked,
watching the fur her breath made as they joked,
caught like a wind in the freedom of their sails.

While always behind her face, the giant's face
struggled to break the matte mask of her skin —
15 and, turned about at last, be looking in —
tranquilly *in* to that imprisoned place.

Strong for the dive he dived one day at tea —
the cakes like flowers, the cups dreamy with cream —
he saw the window a lake and with a scream
20 nobody heard, shot by immediacy

he forced the contours of her features out.
Her tea-time friends were statues as she passed,
pushed, but seemingly drawn towards the glass;

her tea-time friends were blind, they did not see
25 the violence of his struggle to get free,
and deaf, and deaf, they did not hear his shout.

The waters of his lake were sharp and cold —
splashed and broke, triangular on the floor
after the dive from his imagined shore
30 in a land where all the inhabitants are old.

interpretation

Examine the concluding stanzas of the poem closely, distinguishing
event from metaphor, reality from fantasy, window glass from lake
waters. What is the effect of the poet's mingling and entangling the two?

From A CANADIAN ANTHOLOGY. Published by McClelland and Stewart Limited. Reprinted by
permission.

THE TWINS

MONA VAN DUYN

My sweet-faced, tattle-tale brother was born blind,
but the colors drip in his head. He paints with his fingers.
All day with his pots and paper he follows me around
wherever I set up my easel, till I pinch his bat ears,

5 then before he goes he swears he didn't feel anything.
But he knows my feelings, sneaks them out of my skin.
The things he knows! Leaving me squeezed and sulking,
he pretends he felt them himself and tells everyone.

Nobody ever blames him. He's terribly talented.
10 The world, glimpsing itself through him, will grow
sick with self-love, it seems, and under his eyelid
lie down, in burning shame, with its own shadow,

whereas, on my canvas, it wears its gray and brown
like a fat beaver, and even as I sweat on my brush,
15 all forms, at its simple-minded toothy grin,
branches, limbs, trunks, topple in a watery backwash.

When he goes to sleep, he says, the world stays in his head
like a big spiderweb strung between ear and ear,
buzzing like telephone wires, and what he has heard
20 all night, next morning has happened, is true, is there.

Though it always comes back for me, thick, bathed, grateful,
everything has to be re-imagined each sunrise
when I crawl from my black comfort. But I can't make a phone call.
I have to talk to something in front of my eyes.

25   You'd never know we were close. When we meet strangers
they poke my round stomach and pat his long bare legs,
I gush, and he, or that's what it looks like, glares,
then he stomps on my oils and we fight like cats and dogs.

But when it rains sometimes, and he feels it and I hear it,
30   and he closes my eyes with his fingers to stop my raining,
and one tear falls before everything is quiet,
and his tear is the color of cinnamon on my tongue,

oh then we leave together and nobody can find us.
Not even our mother, if she came, could tell us apart.
35   Only the stars can see, who cluster around us,
my painted person crouched in his painted heart.

commentary

I would prefer this poem, out of all my poems, to appear without au-
thorial interpretation. I have intended it to be "open" and I would not
wish to "close" it with a commentary. It is my hope that the poem will
go out to meet the experiences and emotions of the reader in not one
but many contexts, some of which I may not even have foreseen. Those
who are familiar with the concerns of my poetry will know that "The
Twins," like many of my other poems, operates in the subject realms
of both love and art.

Mona Van Duyn

ONE NEED NOT BE A CHAMBER—TO BE HAUNTED—

EMILY DICKINSON

One need not be a Chamber—to be Haunted—
One need not be a House—
The Brain has Corridors—surpassing
Material Place—

5   Far safer, of a Midnight Meeting
External Ghost
Than its interior Confronting—
That Cooler Host.

Far safer, through an Abbey gallop,
10   The Stones a'chase—
Than Unarmed, one's a'self encounter—
In lonesome Place—

Ourself behind ourself, concealed—
Should startle most—
15   Assassin hid in our Apartment
Be Horror's least.

The Body—borrows a Revolver—
He bolts the Door—
O'erlooking a superior spectre—
20   Or More—

Interpretation

Although Emily Dickinson's cryptic style is sometimes puzzling, her poetic genius is nearly always startling in its brilliance. In this poem, she develops a simple comparison between the fears that lurk outside and the horrors that lurk inside the individual. Each stanza devotes, first, two lines to the external threat, and then two lines to the internal, an order shifted only once, in the next-to-last stanza.

1. What are some of the possible reasons for speaking of the internal threat as the "Cooler Host"?

2. How does the poet make her point that the greatest threat lies within?

Reprinted by permission of the publishers and the Trustees of Amherst College from Thomas H. Johnson, Editor, THE POEMS OF EMILY DICKINSON, Cambridge, Mass.: The Belknap Press of Harvard University Press. Copyright, 1951, 1955, by The President and Fellows of Harvard College.

MARSHALL

GEORGE MACBETH

It occurred to Marshall
that if he were a vegetable, he'd
be a bean. Not
one of your thin, stringy
5 green beans, or your

dry, marbly
Burlotti beans. No, he'd be
a broad bean,
a rich, nutritious,
10 meaningful bean,

alert for advantages,
inquisitive with potatoes,
mixing with every kind
and condition of vegetable,
15 and a good friend

to meat and lager. Yes, he'd
leap from his huge
rough pod with a loud
popping sound
20 into the pot: always

in hot water
and out of it with a soft
heart inside
his horny carapace. He'd
carry the whole   25

world's hunger on
his broad shoulders, green
with best butter
or brown with gravy. And if
some starving Indian saw his   30

flesh bleeding
when the gas was turned on
or the knife went in
he'd accept the homage and
    prayers,
and become a god, and die like   35
    a man,

which, as things were, wasn't
    so easy.

commentary

It's a funny poem that turns serious, and the first of a number of rather surrealist vegetable pieces I've done—a recent sequence of twenty-four includes, for example, "The Great Crested Cucumber" and "The Vampire Marrow" (i.e. vegetables as macabre animals you wouldn't like to meet in a dark restaurant). The Aztecs, of course, thought beans were alive because they seemed to bleed to death in hot water.

George MacBeth

From THE NEW POETRY. Published by Scorpion Press. Reprinted by permission.

6

Ah, spring was sent for lass and lad...

A. E. HOUSMAN

CHERRYLOG ROAD

JAMES DICKEY

Off Highway 106
At Cherrylog Road I entered
The '34 Ford without wheels,
Smothered in kudzu,
5 With a seat pulled out to run
Corn whiskey down from the
      hills,

And then from the other side
Crept into an Essex
With a rumble seat of red
      leather
10 And then out again, aboard
A blue Chevrolet, releasing
The rust from its other color,

Reared up on three building
      blocks.
None had the same body heat;
15 I changed with them inward,
      toward
The weedy heart of the junkyard,
For I knew that Doris Holbrook
Would escape from her father at
      noon

And would come from the farm
20 To seek parts owned by the sun
Among the abandoned chassis,
Sitting in each in turn
As I did, leaning forward
As in a wild stock-car race

25 In the parking lot of the dead.
Time after time, I climbed in
And out the other side, like
An envoy or movie star
Met at the station by crickets.
30 A radiator cap raised its head,

Become a real toad or a
      kingsnake
As I neared the hub of the yard,
Passing through many states,
Many lives, to reach
Some grandmother's long
      Pierce-Arrow   35
Sending platters of blindness
      forth

From its nickel hubcaps
And spilling its tender
      upholstery
On sleepy roaches,
The glass panel in between   40
Lady and colored driver
Not all the way broken out,

The back-seat phone
Still on its hook.
I got in as though to exclaim,   45
"Let us go to the orphan asylum,
John; I have some old toys
For children who say their
      prayers."

I popped with sweat as I thought
I heard Doris Holbrook scrape   50
Like a mouse in the
      southern-state sun
That was eating the paint in
      blisters
From a hundred car tops and
      hoods.
She was tapping like code,

Loosening the screws,   55
Carrying off headlights,
Sparkplugs, bumpers,

Cracked mirrors and gear-knobs,
Getting ready, already,
60 To go back with something to
    show
[STANZA BREAK]
Other than her lips' new
    trembling
I would hold to me soon, soon,
Where I sat in the ripped back
    seat
Talking over the interphone,
65 Praying for Doris Holbrook
To come from her father's farm

[Stanza break]
And to get back there   *notelltale signs*
With no trace of me on her face
To be seen by her red-haired
    father
70 Who would change, in the
        squalling barn,
Her back's pale skin with a
        strop,
Then lay for me

In a bootlegger's roasting car
With a string-triggered 12-gauge
        shotgun
75 To blast the breath from the air.
Not cut by the jagged
        windshields,
Through the acres of wrecks she
        came
With a wrench in her hand.

Through dust where the
        blacksnake dies   *dull dead petting*
80 Of boredom, and the beetle
        knows
The compost has no more life.
Someone outside would have
        seen

The oldest car's door
        inexplicably   *wins her.*
Close from within:

I held her and held her and   85
        held her,   *in contrast*
Convoyed at terrific speed
By the stalled, dreaming traffic
        around us,
So the blacksnake, stiff
With inaction, curved back
Into life, and hunted the mouse   90
        "like a mouse"
With deadly overexcitement,
The beetles reclaimed their
        field
As we clung, glued together,
With the hooks of the seat
        springs
Working through to catch us   95
        red-handed
Amidst the gray, breathless
        batting
That burst from the seat at our
        backs.
We left by separate doors
Into the changed, other bodies
Of cars, she down Cherrylog   100
        Road
And I to my motorcycle
Parked like the soul of the
        junkyard   *he restores it*

Restored, a bicycle fleshed
With power, and tore off
Up Highway 106, continually   105
Drunk on the wind in my
        mouth,
Wringing the handlebar for
        speed,
Wild to be wreckage forever.

"Cherrylog Road" is a much-anthologized piece. I think it's sort of funny and innocent. It seems to me to have a Huckleberry Finn quality about it, even though it deals with motorcycles and junk yards. What I attempted to show by means of a boy and girl having a . . . rendezvous in an old junk yard full of bootleggers' cars and wrecked stock cars was that magical moment when you realize that this year you can do a lot of things you couldn't do last year. You know, last year you were riding around on a bicycle, and this year you've got a big, powerful motorcycle.

Junk yards are oddly surrealistic. Growth is heavy in the South. If junked automobiles are left in a lot, it's going to look like a jungle in a few months, especially in summertime. Kudzu vines will be growing through the cars; and snakes, turtles, roaches, mice, toads—everything you can think of—will be living there. It is a strange place for human love; where man's castoff goods and nature meet. And I suppose the factual experience is changed somewhat simply by virtue of writing about it in one way rather than another. I don't think Cherrylog Road was the name of the road. It's a place name I picked up on a fishing trip I took one time, but it seemed like a good name. I realize it doesn't matter whether the incidents in a poem are true, but people might be interested to know that in this case they really are.

James Dickey

THE GOOD MORROW

JOHN DONNE

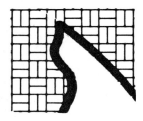

> I wonder, by my troth, what thou and I
> Did till we loved? were we not weaned till then,
> But sucked on country pleasures, childishly?
> Or snorted we in the Seven Sleepers' den?[1]
> 5   'Twas so; but this, all pleasures fancies be.
> If ever any beauty I did see
> Which I desired, and got, 'twas but a dream of thee.
>
> And now good morrow to our waking souls,
> Which watch not one another out of fear;
> 10   For love all love of other sights controls,
> And makes one little room an everywhere.
> Let sea-discoverers to new worlds have gone;
> Let maps to other, worlds on worlds have shown;
> Let us possess one world; each hath one, and is one.
>
> 15   My face in thine eye, thine in mine appears,
> And true, plain hearts do in the faces rest;
> Where can we find two better hemispheres
> Without sharp north, without declining west?
> Whatever dies, was not mixed equally;
> 20   If our two loves be one, or thou and I
> Love so alike that none do slacken, none can die.

---

1. *Seven Sleepers' den.* According to an ancient legend, seven young men fled from religious persecution to a cavern, where they slept for over two hundred years.

The first stanza of this poem is devoted to speculation on what pleasures could possibly have existed before the lovers discovered their love for each other. They must have been like unweaned babies in that they must have experienced ("sucked") only childish pleasures, or "snorted" in the "Seven Sleepers' den." But in comparison with this new-found love, all their pleasures must have been only "fancies." If the lover ever before saw beauty, it was but a pale copy (dream) of the present love.

Stanza 2 moves from past to present with a salutation (good morrow) to the souls of the lovers newly awakened by love. Genuine love is so commanding that it controls the lesser love of "other sights." By looking at each other, the lovers discover (and create) one world, an "every-where," and need no other—not the new worlds explorers have discovered, nor the worlds shown on maps. Each of the lovers has a world in the other, and is one in his (or her) own being.

The geographical imagery continues in Stanza 3, as the lovers see their faces reflected in each others' eyes, and as their hearts are reflected in their faces. Thus, in each other they possess two "hemispheres," which are better than actual hemispheres because they do not have rigidly fixed or patterned directions (as in reality or on a map). Since their love is perfectly shared ("mixed equally"), it cannot die: only what is unequally mixed can die, and their two loves are one, or they are so equal ("so alike"), that neither can "slacken." Thus the speaker convinces himself and perhaps the reader, that his love is a world unto itself and eternal.

James E. Miller, Jr.

This poem has the structure of an argument. If you were to debate with this lover, what weaknesses would you point out in his argument? Do these weaknesses make any difference in the lover's basic purpose or intent in the poem?

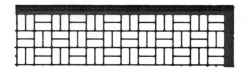

BEHOLD, thou art fair, my love; behold, thou art fair; thou hast
doves' eyes within thy locks: thy hair is as a flock of goats,
that appear from mount Gilead.

2 Thy teeth are like a flock of sheep that are even shorn, which
came up from the washing; whereof every one bear twins, and none is
barren among them.

3 Thy lips are like a thread of scarlet, and thy speech is comely:
thy temples are like a piece of a pomegranate within thy locks.

4 Thy neck is like the tower of David builded for an armory,
whereon there hang a thousand bucklers, all shields of mighty men.

5 Thy two breasts are like two young roes that are twins, which
feed among the lilies.

6 Until the day break, and the shadows flee away, I will get me
to the mountain of myrrh, and to the hill of frankincense.

7 Thou art all fair, my love; there is no spot in thee.

8 Come with me from Lebanon, my spouse, with me from Lebanon:
look from the top of Amana, from the top of Shenir and Hermon, from
the lions' dens, from the mountains of the leopards.

9 Thou hast ravished my heart, my sister, my spouse; thou hast
ravished my heart with one of thine eyes, with one chain of thy neck.

10 How fair is thy love, my sister, my spouse! how much better
is thy love than wine! and the smell of thine ointments than all
spices!

11 Thy lips, O my spouse, drop as the honeycomb: honey and milk
are under thy tongue; and the smell of thy garments is like the
smell of Lebanon.

12 A garden inclosed is my sister, my spouse; a spring shut up,
a fountain sealed.

13 Thy plants are an orchard of pomegranates, with pleasant
fruits; camphire, with spikenard,

14 Spikenard and saffron; calamus and cinnamon, with all trees
of frankincense; myrrh and aloes, with all the chief spices:

15 A fountain of gardens, a well of living waters, and streams
from Lebanon.

16 Awake, O north wind; and come, thou south; blow upon my
garden, that the spices thereof may flow out. Let my beloved come
into his garden, and eat his pleasant fruits.

This poem appears to be the address, used in Eastern marriage ceremonies, of a bridegroom to his bride. Although sometimes considered a religious allegory, the poem with its elaborate, sensuous imagery functions most successfully as a human love poem. The pastoral imagery relies heavily on hyperbole. In Verse 1, the statement, "Thy hair is as a flock of goats," is based on the speaker's visualization of a herd of goats winding down the mountainside. His bride's teeth, even and gleaming, are likened to "a flock of sheep that are even shorn" (Verse 2). Her neck is firm and graceful as a tower; such a tower would have been worthy of David, the shepherd boy that became king of Israel. Around her neck are rows of necklaces that suggest the shields of mighty men (Verse 4). The lover portrays his bride's fragrance, desirability, and worth, as well as his ultimate union with her, in terms of the conquest of "the mountain of myrrh" and "the hill of frankincense" (Verse 6). Repetition of the invitation, "Come with me from Lebanon, my spouse, with me from Lebanon," serves rhetorically to emphasize the lover's passion, while the geographical details suggest the bride's inaccessibility, distance, superiority, faithfulness, and vulnerability (Verse 8). "Sister," a common term in love poetry of the time and place, indicates the fraternal closeness and tenderness of the lovers (Verses 9 and 10). The bride's speech is sweet as honey; the scent of her garments as fragrant as the cedars of Lebanon. Lebanon can be translated literally as "the white," calling to mind the maiden's chastity (Verse 11). Images of containment and untouchability, the enclosed garden and sealed fountain suggest the exclusivity and purity of their relationship (Verse 12). A catalogue of plants in Verses 13 and 14 indicates the fragrance and salutary powers of the beloved. The bridegroom's rhapsody culminates in Verse 15 with a series of images suggesting cool, running water—the sources and sustaining power of life. Finally, in Verse 16, the bride responds to her lover with an invitation to be united with her and reap the pleasures of love.

This passionate lyric is based on images which may seem foreign to a modern reader. Yet, the place names and references to plants, foods, and animals were familiar to an inhabitant of ancient Syria. It is the skillful use of allusions, their appropriateness, and their sensuous detail that make this excerpt from *The Song of Solomon* an example of great love poetry. The ardent bridegroom expresses himself not only through images he chooses, but through the tone he adopts and the rhythms of his speech. Through his eyes, we see the bride—chaste, beautiful, and silent until the end. In the final verse, however, she emerges from the highly idealized portrait to speak. It is with her invitation that she shifts from an object of worship to a partner in love.

DANCE FIGURE   *For the Marriage in Cana of Galilee*[1]

EZRA POUND

Dark eyed,
O woman of my dreams,
Ivory sandaled,
There is none like thee among the dancers,
5 None with swift feet.

I have not found thee in the tents,
In the broken darkness.
I have not found thee at the well-head
Among the women with pitchers.

10 Thine arms are as a young sapling under the bark;
Thy face as a river with lights.

White as an almond are thy shoulders;
As new almonds stripped from the husk.
They guard thee not with eunuchs;
15 Not with bars of copper.

Gilt turquoise and silver are in the place of thy rest.
A brown robe, with threads of gold woven in patterns, hast thou
       gathered about thee.
O Nathat-Ikanaie, "Tree-at-the-river."

As a rillet among the sedge are thy hands upon me;
20 Thy fingers a frosted stream.

Thy maidens are white like pebbles;
Their music about thee!

There is none like thee among the dancers;
None with swift feet.

interpretation

1. There are many ways to praise a woman's beauty. In what way does each of the following contribute to Pound's homage: use of negatives? syntax (arrangement of words within a sentence), especially in stanza 1? choice of images?
2. Compare the imagery here with that of the excerpt from *The Song of Solomon.*

From PERSONAE, (British title: COLLECTED SHORTER POEMS). Copyright 1926 by Ezra Pound. Reprinted by permission of New Directions Publishing Corporation and Faber and Faber Ltd.

1. *For the Marriage . . . Galilee.* The dedication refers to the Biblical account of a wedding feast in Cana, a village of Galilee, at which Jesus changed water to wine (John 2:1-10). There is probably little connection between the dedication and Pound's poem, other than a general Biblical motif.

THE SILKEN TENT

ROBERT FROST

She is as in a field a silken tent
At midday when a sunny summer breeze
Has dried the dew and all its ropes relent,
So that in guys[1] it gently sways at ease,
5 And its supporting central cedar pole,
That is its pinnacle to heavenward
And signifies the sureness of the soul,
Seems to owe naught to any single cord,
But strictly held by none, is loosely bound
10 By countless silken ties of love and thought
To everything on earth the compass round,
And only by one's going slightly taut
In the capriciousness of summer air
Is of the slightest bondage made aware.

interpretation

In order to understand the extended metaphor which is the basis of
this poem, a reader should try to visualize the silken tent. It is very
likely the elaborate, colorful sort of stately pavilion used in the Middle
Ages for tournaments. At any rate, it is a structure, made of silk, an-
chored by a central pole and several supporting ropes, whose move-
ments are affected by the wind.
1. In what way do the following characteristics of the tent offer a parallel
to those of the beloved: the supporting central pole? the pole's "pinnacle
to heavenward"? the "going slightly taut"?
2. This sonnet consists of one long sentence. Can you justify the critic's
observation that this one-sentence technique strengthens the poem
by unifying it and providing a cumulative effect? Why or why not?

From THE POETRY OF ROBERT FROST edited by Edward Connery Lathem. Copyright 1930,
1939, © 1969 by Holt, Rinehart and Winston, Inc. Copyright 1936, 1942, © 1958 by Robert Frost.
Copyright © 1964, 1967, 1970 by Lesley Frost Ballantine. Reprinted by permission of Holt, Rinehart
and Winston, Inc., the Estate of Robert Frost and Jonathan Cape Ltd.

1. *guys*, poles or ropes used to anchor or steady anything.

I THOUGHT I SAW STARS

R. P. LISTER

I thought I saw stars, when first I saw your eyes,
So luminous they were, and such an enormous size;
I fell on the floor and foamed at the mouth, with inconsequential cries.

Now, when I look in your eyes, I do not flinch;
5 Heaven forgive me, I am not even tempted to lynch
The men who, standing beside you, display an inclination to pinch.

For this insensitivity may I be pardoned.
I looked in your eyes too often, and in the end became hardened;
There came a day when Adam turned his back upon Eve, and gardened.

THE LONELINESS OF THE LONG DISTANCE RUNNER

ALDEN NOWLAN

My wife bursts into the room
where I'm writing well
of my love for her

and because now
5 the poem is lost

I silently curse her.

Interpretation

1. Both of these poems include a change of attitude. Find the reason
for the change in each case.
2. Is the change of attitude described in "I Thought I Saw Stars" usual
or unusual?
3. Is "The Loneliness of the Long Distance Runner" a love poem or
a hate poem? Explain.

COMPLAINT

JAMES WRIGHT

She's gone. She was my love, my moon or more.
She chased the chickens out and swept the floor,
Emptied the bones and nut-shells after feasts,
And smacked the kids for leaping up like beasts.
5   Now morbid boys have grown past awkwardness;
The girls let stitches out, dress after dress,
To free some swinging body's riding space
And form the new child's unimagined face.
Yet, while vague nephews, spitting on their curls,
10   Amble to pester winds and blowsy girls,
What arm will sweep the room, what hand will hold
New snow against the milk to keep it cold?
And who will dump the garbage, feed the hogs,
And pitch the chickens' heads to hungry dogs?
15   Now my lost hag who dumbly bore such pain:
Childbirth and midnight sassafras and rain.
New snow against her face and hands she bore,
And now lies down, who was my moon or more.

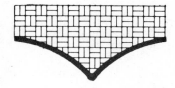

Interpretation

1. What clues do you find that the wife of the speaker has died?
2. On the evidence of the poem, what was the nature of the relationship between the speaker and his wife?
3. The speaker calls his wife "my love, my moon," but he also refers to her as "my lost hag." This appears contradictory. Explain.

SHE WAS A PHANTOM OF DELIGHT

WILLIAM WORDSWORTH

She was a Phantom of delight
When first she gleamed upon my sight;
A lovely Apparition, sent
To be a moment's ornament;
5 Her eyes as stars of Twilight fair;
Like Twilight's, too, her dusky hair;
But all things else about her drawn
From May-time and the cheerful Dawn;
A dancing Shape, an Image gay,
10 To haunt, to startle, and waylay.

I saw her upon nearer view,
A Spirit, yet a Woman too!
Her household motions light and free,
And steps of virgin-liberty;
15 A countenance in which did meet
Sweet records, promises as sweet;
A Creature not too bright or good
For human nature's daily food;
For transient sorrows, simple wiles,
20 Praise, blame, love, kisses, tears, and smiles.

And now I see with eye serene
The very pulse of the machine;
A Being breathing thoughtful breath,
A Traveller between life and death;
25 The reason firm, the temperate will,
Endurance, foresight, strength, and skill;
A perfect Woman, nobly planned,
To warn, to comfort, and command;
And yet a Spirit still, and bright
30 With something of angelic light.

JUKE BOX LOVE SONG

LANGSTON HUGHES

I could take the Harlem night
and wrap around you,
Take the neon lights and make a crown,
Take the Lenox Avenue buses,
5 Taxis, subways,
And for your love song tone their rumble down.
Take Harlem's heartbeat,
Make a drumbeat,
Put it on a record, let it whirl,
10 And while we listen to it play,
Dance with you till day—
Dance with you, my sweet brown Harlem girl.

interpretation

1. There are three views of the woman in "She Was a Phantom of Delight." How do they differ? Which is the reality? none? one? all?
2. Both the first stanza of "She Was a Phantom of Delight" and "Juke Box Love Song" make use of exaggerated images. Point out some of the images in each. (See IMAGERY in *Handbook of Terms and Techniques*.) Comment on the effect achieved by the combination of images.
3. Both of these poems are love songs. Study the rhythm and rhyme in each. Then try to explain how the differences in rhythm and rhyme affect the tone.

SONG

WILLIAM BLAKE

How sweet I roamed from field to field,
  And tasted all the summer's pride,
'Till I the prince of love beheld,
  Who in the sunny beams did glide!

5 He showed me lilies for my hair,
   And blushing roses for my brow;
He led me through his gardens fair,
  Where all his golden pleasures grow.

With sweet May dews my wings were wet,
10   And Phoebus fired my vocal rage[1];
He caught me in his silken net,
  And shut me in his golden cage.

He loves to sit and hear me sing,
  Then, laughing, sports and plays with me;
15 Then stretches out my golden wing,
  And mocks my loss of liberty.

interpretation

1. What statement about love is Blake making in this poem?
2. What metaphor does the poet use to make his point? Do you find it effective?

---

1. *Phoebus . . . vocal rage.* The lover credits the passionate song to Phoebus (Apollo), god of inspiration.

OH SEE HOW THICK THE GOLDCUP FLOWERS

A. E. HOUSMAN

Oh see how thick the goldcup flowers
    Are lying in field and lane,
With dandelions to tell the hours
    That never are told again.
5 Oh may I squire you round the meads
    And pick you posies gay?
—'T will do no harm to take my arm.
    "You may, young man, you may."

Ah, spring was sent for lass and lad,
10   'Tis now the blood runs gold,
And man and maid had best be glad
    Before the world is old.
What flowers today may flower tomorrow,
    But never as good as new.
15 —Suppose I wound my arm right round—
    "'Tis true, young man, 'tis true."

Some lads there are, 'tis shame to say,
    That only court to thieve,
And once they bear the bloom away
20   'Tis little enough they leave.
Then keep your heart for men like me
    And safe from trustless chaps.
My love is true and all for you.
    "Perhaps, young man, perhaps."

25 Oh, look in my eyes then, can you doubt?
    —Why, 'tis a mile from town.
How green the grass is all about!
    We might as well sit down.
—Ah, life, what is it but a flower?
30   Why must true lovers sigh?
Be kind, have pity, my own, my pretty,—
    "Good-bye, young man, good-bye."

From A SHROPSHIRE LAD—Authorised Edition—from THE COLLECTED POEMS OF A. E.
HOUSMAN. Copyright 1939, 1940, © 1965 by Holt, Rinehart and Winston, Inc. Copyright © 1967,
1968 by Robert E. Symons. Reprinted by permission of Holt, Rinehart and Winston, Inc., The Society
of Authors as the literary representative of the Estate of A. E. Housman, and Jonathan Cape Ltd.,
publishers of A. E. Housman's COLLECTED POEMS.

HOW SHE RESOLVED TO ACT

MERRILL MOORE

"I shall be careful to say nothing at all
About myself, or what I know of him,
Or the vaguest thought I have, no matter how dim,
Tonight, if it so happen that he call."
5   And not ten minutes later the door-bell rang,
And into the hall he stepped as he always did,
With a face and a bearing that quite poorly hid
His brain that burned, and his heart that fairly sang,
And his tongue that wanted to be rid of the truth.

10 As well as she could, for she was very loath
To signify how she felt, she kept very still.
But soon her heart cracked loud as a coffee-mill,
And her brain swung like a comet in the dark,
And her tongue raced like a squirrel in the park.

interpretation

1. What is the girl's resolve? Why is she unable to live up to it?
2. Which simile in the last three lines do you consider most effective? Why?
3. Analyze the form of this sonnet. How is it like and unlike the traditional sonnet form? (See SONNET in *Handbook of Terms and Techniques*.)

From POEMS OF AMERICAN LIFE. Reprinted by permission of Philosophical Library, Inc.

PARTING, WITHOUT A SEQUEL

JOHN CROWE RANSOM

> She has finished and sealed the letter
> At last, which he so richly has deserved,
> With characters venomous and hatefully curved,
> And nothing could be better.
>
> 5 But even as she gave it,
> Saying to the blue-capped functioner of doom,
> "Into his hands," she hoped the leering groom
> Might somewhere lose and leave it.
>
> Then all the blood
> 10 Forsook the face. She was too pale for tears.
> Observing the ruin of her younger years.
> She went and stood
>
> Under her father's vaunting oak
> Who kept his peace in wind and sun, and glistened
> 15 Stoical in the rain; to whom she listened
> If he spoke.
>
> And now the agitation of the rain
> Rasped his sere leaves, and he talked low and gentle,
> Reproaching the wan daughter by the lintel;
> 20 Ceasing and beginning again.
>
> Away went the messenger's bicycle,
> His serpent's track went up the hill forever,
> And all the time she stood there hot as fever
> And cold as any icicle.

interpretation

1. We learn nothing about the relationship of the man and woman in this poem, nor do we know why the woman has decided to end the relationship. Yet we have some insight into the emotions of the woman. What do we learn? What evidence is there that she has doubt about her own actions?

2. What is suggested by the merging of her father and the "vaunting oak"? What is the message the father-oak seems to send the woman?

3. This poem has a regular rhyme scheme, yet in some stanzas the rhyme goes almost unnoticed. Why is this so?

AGAINST STILL LIFE

MARGARET ATWOOD

Orange in the middle of a table:

It isn't enough
to walk around it
at a distance, saying
5   it's an orange:
nothing to do
with us, nothing
else: leave it alone

I want to pick it up
10 in my hand
I want to peel the
skin off; I want
more to be said to me
than just Orange:
15 want to be told
everything it has to say

And you, sitting across
the table, at a distance, with
your smile contained, and like
the orange
20 in the sun: silent:

Your silence
isn't enough for me
now, no matter with what
contentment you fold
25 your hands together; I want
anything you can say
in the sunlight:

stories of your various
childhoods, aimless journeyings,
30 your loves; your articulate
skeleton; your posturings; your
lies.

These orange silences
(sunlight and hidden smile)
make me want to
wrench you into saying: 35
now I'd crack your skull
like a walnut, split it like a
    pumpkin
to make you talk, or get
a look inside

But quietly: 40
if I take the orange
with care enough and hold it
gently

I may find
an egg   45
a sun
an orange moon
perhaps a skull; centre
of all energy
resting in my hand   50

can change it to
whatever I desire
it to be

and you, man, orange afternoon
lover, wherever   55
you sit across from me
(tables, trains, buses)

if I watch
quietly enough
and long enough   60

at last, you will say
(maybe without speaking)

From THE CIRCLE GAME. Reprinted by permission of House of Anansi Press Limited.

(there are mountains
inside your skull
65 garden and chaos, ocean

and hurricane; certain
corners of rooms, portraits
of great-grandmothers, curtains
of a particular shade;
70 your deserts; your private
dinosaurs; the first
woman)

all I need to know:
tell me
75 everything
just as it was
from the beginning.

interpretation

1. *Still life* is a term from painting, usually indicating inanimate objects arranged on a table—a bottle, a bowl, a toy, an orange. Explain the word *against* in the title. How are the orange and the man related in the poem?

2. The poem is divided into two parts, the second beginning with the line "But quietly." What is the speaker's mood in the first part? How does it change in the second part? By the end of the poem, what strategy has the speaker decided on?

3. Several pairs of parentheses are used in the poem. Explain their use. Explore the meaning of the last long parenthetical insertion (lines 63–72)—for example, how can mountains be inside a man's skull?

FAIR YOU BE SURE

(Sonnet 56)

EDMUND SPENSER

Fair you be sure, but crue and unkind,
As is a tiger that with greediness
Hunts after blood, when he by chance does find
A feeble beast, does felly[1] him oppress.
5 Fair be you sure, but proud and pitiless,
As is a storm, that all things do prostrate:
Finding a tree alone all comfortless,
Beats on it strongly it to ruinate,
Fair be you sure, but hard and obstinate,
10 As is a rock amid the raging floods:
'Gainst which a ship of succor desolate,
Does suffer wreck both of herself and goods.
That ship, that tree, and that same beast am I,
Whom you do wreck, do ruin, and destroy.

interpretation

1. The lady addressed in this poem is described as cruel, proud, and hard. Locate the simile used to describe each of these elements of her personality.

2. How are the last two lines of the sonnet related to the foregoing twelve?

1. *felly*, cruelly.

LINES: WHEN THE LAMP IS SHATTERED

PERCY BYSSHE SHELLEY

When the lamp is shattered
The light in the dust lies dead—
When the cloud is scattered
The rainbow's glory is shed.
5 When the lute is broken,
Sweet tones are remembered not;
When the lips have spoken,
Loved accents are soon forgot.

As music and splendor
10 Survive not the lamp and the lute,
The heart's echoes render
No song when the spirit is mute—
No song but sad dirges,
Like the wind through a ruined cell,
15 Or the mournful surges
That ring the dead seaman's knell.

When hearts have once mingled
Love first leaves the well-built nest;
The weak one is singled
20 To endure what it once possessed.
O Love! who bewailest
The frailty of all things here,
Why choose you the frailest
For your cradle, your home, and your bier?

25 Its passions will rock thee
As the storms rock the ravens on high;
Bright reason will mock thee,
Like the sun from a wintry sky.
From thy nest every rafter
30 Will rot, and thine eagle home
Leave thee naked to laughter,
When leaves fall and cold winds come.

interpretation

1. Note the images in the first stanza. What use is made of these images
in the second stanza?
2. Explain lines 19–20.
3. Study the imagery and figurative language of the last stanza and
discuss their appropriateness to the ideas and attitudes they embody.
4. Trace the progression of idea from stanza to stanza of the poem.

FOR ANNE GREGORY

W. B. YEATS

"Never shall a young man,
Thrown into despair
By those great honey-coloured
Ramparts at your ear,
5 Love you for yourself alone
And not your yellow hair."

"But I can get a hair-dye
And set such colour there,
Brown, or black, or carrot,
10 That young men in despair
May love me for myself alone
And not my yellow hair."

"I heard an old religious man
But yesternight declare
15 That he had found a text to prove
That only God, my dear,
Could love you for yourself alone
And not your yellow hair."

POLITICS

W. B. YEATS

*"In our time the destiny of man
presents its meaning in political
terms."*—Thomas Mann

How can I, that girl standing
    there,
My attention fix
On Roman or on Russian
Or on Spanish politics?
Yet here's a travelled man that knows   5
What he talks about,
And there's a politician
That has read and thought,
And maybe what they say is true
Of war and war's alarms,   10
But O that I were young again
And held her in my arms!

---

interpretation

1. "For Anne Gregory" seems to be a conversation, beginning perhaps in the middle, between a man and a young girl about the nature of love. What does the young girl propose to do? Is the statement in the last stanza witty, conclusive, convincing, true?

2. Read the quotation from Thomas Mann that precedes "Politics." What is the relationship between the quotation and the poem itself?

3. Is the experience described in "Politics" a common one? The last two lines are frequently quoted. Why do you think they are often remembered?

---

*The clavier is a musical instrument with a keyboard; Peter Quince is
the stage manager of the group of rustics who stage a play for the nobles in
Shakespeare's play,* A Midsummer-Night's Dream. *In Stevens'
poem the music played on the clavier is related to the story of Susanna, a
heroine of one of the apocryphal books of the Old Testament.*

*Susanna, a beautiful woman, was married to a wealthy man who had a
fine house in Babylon with a secluded garden adjoining it. One
day when Susanna was bathing in the garden, two evil elders who had
hidden there to watch her came forth and made advances. When Susanna
repelled them, they declared that she had had a tryst in the garden with a
young man. The elders summoned the people and demanded Susanna's death
for unchastity. A devout young man named David questioned the old
men separately. When he determined they were lying, they were executed.*

PETER QUINCE AT THE CLAVIER

WALLACE STEVENS

I

Just as my fingers on these keys
Make music, so the self-same sounds
On my spirit make a music, too.

Music is feeling, then, not sound;
5 And thus it is that what I feel,
Here in this room, desiring you,

Thinking of your blue-shadowed silk,
Is music. It is like the strain
Waked in the elders by Susanna.

10 Of a green evening, clear and warm,
She bathed in her still garden, while
The red-eyed elders, watching, felt

The basses of their being throb
In witching chords, and their thin blood
15 Pulse pizzicati of Hosanna.[1]

continued

1. *Pulse pizzicati of Hosanna.* The musical term *pizzicato* (pit'sə kä'tō) refers to the plucking of the
strings of a bowed instrument, like a violin. The quickened pulses of the elders were a sort of hosanna
or exclamation of praise to the beautiful Susanna.

II

In the green water, clear and warm,
Susanna lay.
She searched
The touch of springs,
20 And found
Concealed imaginings.
She sighed
For so much melody.

Upon the bank she stood
25 In the cool
Of spent emotions.
She felt, among the leaves,
The dew
Of old devotions.

30 She walked upon the grass,
Still quavering.
The winds were like her maids,
On timid feet,
Fetching her woven scarves,
35 Yet wavering.

A breath upon her hand
Muted the night.
She turned—
A cymbal crashed,
40 and roaring horns.

III

Soon, with a noise like tambourines,
Came her attendant Byzantines.[2]

They wondered why Susanna cried
Against the elders by her side;

45 And as they whispered, the refrain
Was like a willow swept by rain.

Anon their lamps' uplifted flame
Revealed Susanna and her shame.

And then, the simpering Byzantines
50 Fled, with a noise like tambourines.

---

2. *attendant Byzantines*, Susanna's ladies-in-waiting. The word *Byzantine* suggests the mystery and romance of the East.

IV

Beauty is momentary in the mind—
The fitful tracing of a portal;
But in the flesh it is immortal.
The body dies; the body's beauty lives.
55 So evenings die, in their green going,
A wave, interminably flowing.
So gardens die, their meek breath scenting
The cowl of winter, done repenting.
So maidens die, to the auroral
60 Celebration of a maiden's choral.
Susanna's music touched the bawdy strings
Of those white elders; but, escaping,
Left only Death's ironic scraping.
Now, in its immortality, it plays
65 On the clear viol of her memory,
And makes a constant sacrament of praise.

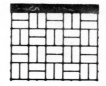

commentary

Peter Quince is the stage manager of the rustic actors in *A Midsummer-Night's Dream*. He is perhaps à propos as the speaker of the poem in that, as he day dreams at the key board, he is in a sense the stage manager of the imagination. The poem is a flight of imagination that takes place as Peter Quince plays, and one should note the high frequency of musical terms used. It is like a key board impromptu in which each of the four sections resembles a "movement" whose metrical tempo helps set its mood.

As the player strikes the keys of the clavier (I), so the sounds produced strike a music from his spirit. By logical extension, then, the music is essentially the feeling it produces; since music is feeling, the desire he feels for the woman of whom he is thinking is a kind of music. There follows a projection of this feeling into the story of Susanna, the story serving as an extended simile for the feeling. (The poem is in this respect a compliment to the woman, referred to in the second and third stanzas, desire for whom provokes the reflective revery that follows.) This projection becomes a speculation on the nature of desire and the bodily beauty that is its object. Susanna awakened a similar music, or "strain" (tune, tension: desire) in the elders. Since their lust is, in terms of the poem, a kind of music, it is appropriately described in musical terms (note especially the triple meaning of "The basses of their beings" —"bass" as musical term or instrument, as depth, and as evil).

The poem then gives a description of the music of Susanna's feelings (II). The warmth of the water, its sensuous "touch," brings forth in her "melody" of sensual day dreams or fantasies ("concealed imaginings"). The cooler air as she stands on the bank is echoed by her "spent emotions." She feels, "among the leaves," a gentle residue, or nostalgia ("dew") for her amorous attachments of the past ("old devotions"). As she walks away she still trembles ("quaver," a trill or tremolo in music) with the emotions she has just felt. Then the breath of the elders suddenly deadens ("muted") the feelings which the night had evoked in her, and their intrusion is put in terms of the brash, brassy interruption of the cymbal and horns.

The "attendant Byzantines" (III) serve as a choral expression of feeling about the elders' accusation. They are silly ("simpering"), frightened. Their "refrain" (or possibly Susanna's) is weeping, like a willow in windy rain.

The mind's response to beauty comes and goes (IV); it is spasmodic, changeable, giving only the vaguest suggestion of access to beauty as it exists in the flesh ("The fitful tracing of a portal"). But "in the flesh" beauty never dies. The apparent paradox is immediately qualified and then resolved in three metaphors. Though the body itself dies, bodily beauty lives on in new embodiments. In the same way evenings die: the "green" of their "going" is descriptively apt, but also indicates that it is a "going" that is perpetually renewed, just as a wave flowing through the sea at the same time both passes and continues. Gardens die under the "cowl of winter" (winter covering the landscape, and also, a monk's cowl, winter itself like a monk now finished with its seasonal repentance), but they die to be reborn in the spring. Maidens die in marriage, to be replaced by other maidens who will, in their turn, die a similar death. The lust that Susanna's beauty aroused in the elders' minds was momentary and left only the prospect of their mortality (the "white" elders; "Death's ironic scraping"—in the *Apocrypha*, after falsely accusing Susanna, they are put to death). But Susanna's beauty has become immortal. Her beauty, her "music," is reborn in memory of her, and serves to consecrate that memory in praise.

Ronald Sukenick

30 CENTS, TWO TRANSFERS, LOVE

RICHARD BRAUTIGAN

Thinking hard about you
I got onto the bus
and paid 30 cents car fare
and asked the driver for two transfers
5 before discovering that I was alone.

VISTA

ALFRED KREYMBORG

The snow,
ah yes, ah yes, indeed,
is white and beautiful, white and beautiful,
verily beautiful—
5 from my window.
The sea,
ah yes, ah yes, indeed,
is green and alluring, green and alluring,
verily alluring—
10 from the shore.
Love?—
ah yes, ah yes, ah yes, indeed,
verily yes, ah yes, indeed.

interpretation

1. What are the successive statements made about snow, the sea, and love in "Vista"? What, finally, does the poem imply about love?
2. What do you think of the idea of love expressed in the poem?

7

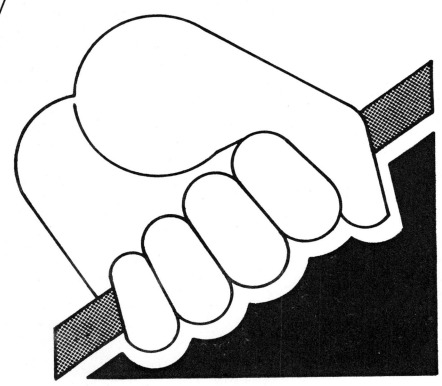

...with the sound of steel on stones...

JEAN TOOMER

FINE WORK WITH PITCH AND COPPER

WILLIAM CARLOS WILLIAMS

Now they are resting
in the fleckless light
separately in unison

like the sacks
5   of sifted stone stacked
regularly by twos

about the flat roof
ready after lunch
to be opened and strewn

10 The copper in eight
foot strips has been
beaten lengthwise

down the center at right
angles and lies ready
15 to edge the coping

One still chewing
picks up a copper strip
and runs his eye along it

interpretation

No ideas except in things, Williams wrote again and again as the key to his poetry. If this poem has any ideas, they must be in the things seen and carefully recorded. Roofers are resting and eating their lunch, their materials waiting for them to continue their work. The scene contains great power and strength, but it remains static until the last stanza.

Why do you suppose Williams chose this particular moment for his poem, rather than an earlier or later moment when the men were at work and the materials in use?

REAPERS

JEAN TOOMER

Black reapers with the sound of steel on stones
Are sharpening scythes. I see them place the hones
In their hip-pockets as a thing that's done,
And start their silent swinging, one by one.
5 Black horses drive a mower through the weeds,
And there, a field rat, startled, squealing bleeds,
His belly close to ground. I see the blade,
Blood-stained, continue cutting weeds and shade.

interpretation

Black reapers, black horses, and a bleeding field rat—a peaceful scene
marred by a minor instance of violence? What is suggested by the quiet
continuance of the bloodstained mower?

THE PERFORMERS

ROBERT HAYDEN

Easily, almost matter-of-factly they step,
two minor Wallendas,[1] with pail and squeegee along
the wintry ledge, hook their harness to the wall
and leaning back into a seven-story angle of space
5   begin washing the office windows. I
am up there too until straps break
and iron paper apple of iron I fall
through plateglass wind onto stalagmites below.

But am safely at my desk again by the time
10 the hairline walkers, high-edge
balancers end their center-ring routine
and crawl inside. A rough day, I remark,
for such a risky business. Many thanks.
Thank *you,* sir, one of the men replies.

interpretation

1. Explain the speaker's falling but not falling. What is suggested by "plateglass wind" and "stalagmites"?
2. The poem is action-packed but the ending is quite matter-of-fact. Try to explain the reason for this change.
3. Who are the "performers"?

From NIGHT-BLOOMING CEREUS. Copyright © 1972 by Robert Hayden. Reprinted by permission of October House Inc.

1. *Wallendas,* a high-wire team, originally from Germany, who became a famous circus act in America.

DIVER

ROBERT FRANCIS

> Diver go down
> Down through the green
> Inverted dawn
> To the dark unseen
> 5   To the never day
> The under night
> Starless and steep
> Deep beneath deep
> Diver fall
> 10   And falling fight
> Your weed-dense way
> Until you crawl
> Until you touch
> Weird water land
> 15   And stand.
>
> Diver come up
> Up through the green
> Into the light
> The sun   the seen
> 20   But in the clutch
> Of your dripping hand
> Diver bring
> Some uncouth thing
> That we could swear
> 25   And would have sworn
> Was never born
> Or could ever be
> Anywhere
> Blaze on our sight
> 30   Make us see.

interpretation

1. The first stanza is concerned with the diver's descent, the second with his ascent. Compare the imagery of these stanzas.

2. In addition to imagery, what devices does the poet use to suggest a descent to the bottom of the sea?

3. Why does the speaker ask the diver to bring up "Some uncouth thing"? What are the ramifications or reverberations of the last line, "Make us see"?

Reprinted by permission of Robert Francis and The University of Massachusetts Press from COME OUT INTO THE SUN: POEMS NEW AND SELECTED, 1965.

SKY DIVING

RICHMOND LATTIMORE

They step from the high plane and begin to tumble
down. Below is the painted ground, above
is bare sky. They do not fumble
with the catch, but only fall; drop sheer; begin to move

5   in the breakless void; stretch and turn, freed
from pressure; stand in weightless air
and softly walk across their own speed;
gather and group, these dropping bundles, where

the neighbor in the sky stands, reach touch
10 and clasp hands, separate and swim
back to station (did swimmer ever shear such
thin water?) falling still. Now at last pull the slim

cord. Parasols bloom in the air, slow
the swift sky fall. Collapsed tents cover
15 the ground. They rise up, plain people now.
Their little sky-time is over.

interpretation

1. Compare the sky diving in this poem with the water descent in
Francis' "Diver." Discuss the effect of these phrases: "painted ground"
(line 2); "softly walk" (line 7); "Parasols bloom" (line 13); "Collapsed
tents" (line 14).
2. Both "Diver" and "Sky Diving" make use of a great number of run-
on lines. What effect does this device have on the rhyme? How does the
device affect the movement of the poems?
3. Why, at the end of "Sky Diving," does the speaker call the divers
"plain people now"?

SKIERS

(from In the Mountains)

ROBERT PENN WARREN

> With the motion of angels, out of
> Snow-spume and swirl of gold mist, they
> Emerge to the positive sun. At
> That great height, small on that whiteness,
> 5 With the color of birds or of angels,
> They swoop, sway, descend, and descending,
> Cry their bright bird-cries, pure
> In the sweet desolation of distance.
> They slowly enlarge to our eyes. Now
>
> 10 On the flat where the whiteness is
> Trodden and mud-streaked, not birds now,
> Nor angels even, they stand. They
>
> Are awkward, not yet well adjusted
> To this world, new and strange, of Time and
> 15 Contingency, who now are only
> Human. They smile. The human
>
> Face has its own beauty.

interpretation

1. As the poem develops, the skiers are changed from angels to men. What is the meaning of the concluding statement: "—The human / Face has its own beauty"? Compare the conclusion of this poem with that of "Sky Diving."

2. This free-verse poem makes use of assonance, consonance, and alliteration. Find examples of these techniques and explain their effect.

FELIX RANDAL

GERARD MANLEY HOPKINS

Felix Randal the farrier,[1] O he is dead then? my duty all ended,
Who have watched his mold of man, big-boned and hardy-handsome
Pining, pining, till time when reason rambled in it and some
Fatal four disorders, fleshed there, all contended?

5 Sickness broke him. Impatient he cursed at first, but mended
Being anointed[2] and all; though a heavenlier heart began some
Months earlier, since I had our sweet reprieve and ransom[3]
Tendered to him. Ah well, God rest him all road[4] ever he offended!

This seeing the sick endears them to us, us too it endears.
10 My tongue had taught thee comfort, touch had quenched thy tears,
Thy tears that touched my heart, child, Felix, poor Felix Randal;

How far from then forethought of, all thy more boisterous years,
When thou at the random grim forge, powerful amidst peers,
Didst fettle[5] for the great grey drayhorse his bright and battering
        sandal!

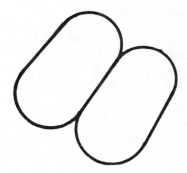

Interpretation

1. Who is the speaker? What has been his relation to Felix Randal?
2. Discuss the ways Felix' profession gives him identity and individuality. (Note particularly the last three lines.)

From POEMS OF GERARD MANLEY HOPKINS, 4th Edition. Published by Oxford University Press, London.

1. *farrier,* a smith who shoes horses. 2. *anointed,* the sacrament of Extreme Unction, usually administered by a priest to someone in danger of death. 3. *reprieve and ransom,* the sacraments of Penance (confession) and Holy Communion. 4. *all road,* in every way. 5. *fettle,* prepare.

AFTER APPLE-PICKING   ROBERT FROST

My long two-pointed ladder's sticking through a tree
Toward heaven still,
And there's a barrel that I didn't fill
Beside it, and there may be two or three
5   Apples I didn't pick upon some bough.
But I am done with apple-picking now.
Essence of winter sleep is on the night,
The scent of apples: I am drowsing off.
I cannot rub the strangeness from my sight
10   I got from looking through a pane of glass
I skimmed this morning from the drinking trough
And held against the world of hoary grass.
It melted, and I let it fall and break.
But I was well
15   Upon my way to sleep before it fell,
And I could tell
What form my dreaming was about to take.
Magnified apples appear and disappear,
Stem end and blossom end,
20   And every fleck of russet showing clear.
My instep arch not only keeps the ache,
It keeps the pressure of a ladder-round.
I feel the ladder sway as the boughs bend.
And I keep hearing from the cellar bin
25   The rumbling sound
Of load on load of apples coming in.
For I have had too much
Of apple-picking: I am overtired
Of the great harvest I myself desired.
30   There were ten thousand thousand fruit to touch,
Cherish in hand, lift down, and not let fall.
For all
That struck the earth,
No matter if not bruised or spiked with stubble,
35   Went surely to the cider-apple heap
As of no worth.
One can see what will trouble
This sleep of mine, whatever sleep it is.
Were he not gone,
40   The woodchuck could say whether it's like his
Long sleep, as I describe its coming on,
Or just some human sleep.

One of his [Frost's] best examples of management of tone occurs in "After Apple-Picking," a poem in which he extends his symbolism further, and achieves more intensity, than is usual for him. But to demonstrate this is to indicate that the poem is in reality a symbolist poem.

The concrete experience of apple-picking is communicated firmly and realistically; but the poem invites a metaphorical extension. The task of apple-picking, it is suggested, is any task; it is life.

The drowsiness which the speaker feels after the completion of the task is associated with the cycle of the seasons. Its special character is emphasized by a bit of magic, even though the magic is whimsical (lines 7–13). The speaker goes on to speculate playfully on the form that his dreaming will take. It will surely be about apples, for his instep arch still feels the pressure of the ladder rung, and his ears are still full of the rumble of apples rolling into the cellar bin. But he returns to the subject of his drowsiness, and the phrase, "whatever sleep it is," renews the suggestion that his sleepiness may not be merely ordinary human sleepiness (lines 39–42).

The end of the labor leaves the speaker with a sense of completion and fulfillment—in short, with a sense of ripeness which savors of the fruit with which he has been working and of the season in which the work has been done. The ice sheet through which he has looked signals the termination of the harvest and the summons to the winter sleep of nature. The woodchuck has already begun his hibernation. The speaker does not overemphasize his own connection with nature— the reference to the woodchuck is merely one more piece of whimsy— but the connection is felt.

The poem even suggests that the sleep is like the sleep of death. We are not to feel that the speaker is necessarily conscious of this. But perhaps we are to feel that, were the analogy to present itself to him, he would accept it. In the context defined in the poem, death might be considered as something eminently natural, as a sense of fulfillment mixed with a great deal of honest weariness and a sense of something well done—though with too much drowsiness for one to bother that every one of the apples had not been picked. The theme thus turns out to be a sort of rustic New England version of "Ripeness is all," though the theme is arrived at casually—stumbled over, almost— and with no effect of literary pretentiousness.

Cleanth Brooks

From MODERN POETRY AND THE TRADITION by Cleanth Brooks. Reprinted by permission of The University of North Carolina Press.

8

I saw God. Do you doubt it?

JAMES STEPHENS

GOD OPENS HIS MAIL   LARRY RUBIN

Dear Sir:
                 Your poem interested us
Somewhat, but we do not consider it
Entirely successful. For one thing,
5   Your floral diction blooms in the right places,
But there are bugs which seem almost deliberately
Placed. Then, again, life breathes everywhere
In your work, yet you cancel it
Later in the lines with a disdain
10   No artist with a trace of self-respect
Would dare to show (not to mention compassion
For the child of his brain, but let
That pass). Do you have a friend
Who might perhaps be willing to read your work
15   Before you send it out? Just a suggestion,
But beginners must be guided. Another thing:
Your images, though pleasant taken singly,
Fail to fuse properly. We find a sly
Intent to suggest an over-all design,
20   And yet the reader sees no real organic
Whole. Your metaphors stand isolated;
No poem can carry such disparities
As shooting stars and glory-holes, no matter
How securely yoked. Creation carries
25   Certain responsibilities, and we
Are unconvinced you have accepted these.
There are other problems, of course,
But our staff is limited, and time is short.
You have, we feel, much to learn, but your talent
30   Will help.
                 Cordially,
                          The Editors.

P.S. Since half the battle is knowing
Your market, perhaps you would care to subscribe.

interpretation

1. What is the "poem" that the "Editors" are rejecting? Note the use
of terms commonly used in criticizing poetry: *diction, images,* and
metaphors. Suggest meanings for these terms in the poem's context.
2. The "Editors" say that they find "a sly / Intent to suggest an over-
all design." What do they mean? Is it true that "the reader sees no real
organic / Whole"? What reader is meant?

From *Harper's Magazine*, (July 1961). Copyright © 1961, by Minneapolis Star and Tribune Co., Inc.
Reprinted by permission of the author. Published in THE WORLD'S OLD WAY, University of
Nebraska Press, 1963.

115

THE PULLEY

GEORGE HERBERT

When God at first made man,
Having a glass of blessings standing by,
　"Let us," said he, "pour on him all we can.
Let the world's riches, which dispersèd lie,
5　　Contract into a span."

So strength first made a way;
Then beauty flowed, then wisdom, honor, pleasure.
　When almost all was out, God made a stay,
Perceiving that, alone of all his treasure,
10　　Rest in the bottom lay.

"For if I should," said he,
"Bestow this jewel also on my creature,
　He would adore my gifts instead of me,
And rest in Nature, not the God of Nature;
15　　So both should losers be.

"Yet let him keep the rest,
But keep them with repining restlessness.
　Let him be rich and weary, that at least,
If goodness lead him not, yet weariness
20　　May toss him to my breast."

1. What gifts did God give man? What gift did he withhold? Why?
2. Explain the relationship between the effect of the gift withheld and
the title, "The Pulley."

GOD FASHIONED THE SHIP OF THE WORLD CAREFULLY

STEPHEN CRANE

God fashioned the ship of the world carefully.
With the infinite skill of an All-Master
Made He the hull and the sails,
Held He the rudder
5   Ready for adjustment.
Erect stood He, scanning His work proudly.
Then—at fateful time—a wrong called,
And God turned, heeding.
Lo, the ship, at this opportunity, slipped slyly,
10   Making cunning noiseless travel down the ways.
So that, for ever rudderless, it went upon the seas
Going ridiculous voyages,
Making quaint progress,
Turning as with serious purpose
15   Before stupid winds.
And there were many in the sky
Who laughed at this thing.

interpretation

1. Trace the ship metaphor throughout the poem.
2. How is the God of Herbert's "The Pulley" different from the God of Crane's poem? Which is closer to your idea of God?

LOOK, HOW BEAUTIFUL

ROBINSON JEFFERS

There is this infinite energy, the power of God forever working—toward
          what purpose?—toward none.
This is God's will; he works, he grows and changes, he has no object.
No more than a great sculptor who has found a ledge of fine marble,
          and lives beside it, and carves great images,
And casts them down. That is God's will: to make great things and
          destroy them, and make great things
And destroy them again. With war and plague and horror, and the
          diseases of trees and the corruptions of stone
He destroys all that stands. But look how beautiful—
Look how beautiful are all the things that He does. His signature
Is the beauty of things.

WHEN GOD DECIDED TO INVENT

E. E. CUMMINGS

when god decided to invent
everything he took one
breath bigger than a circustent
and everything began

5 when man determined to destroy
himself he picked the was
of shall and finding only why
smashed it into because

interpretation

1. Cummings frequently uses one part of speech for another, as, for example, a verb or connective for a noun. Discuss the new meanings given *was, shall, why,* and *because* by their becoming new parts of speech in the second stanza.
2. Both the Cummings poem and the Jeffers poem which precedes it are in some sense about destruction, but the poets distribute the responsibility differently. Explain.

YET DO I MARVEL

COUNTEE CULLEN

I doubt not God is good, well-meaning, kind,
And did He stoop to quibble could tell why
The little buried mole continues blind,
Why flesh that mirrors Him must some day die,
5 Make plain the reason tortured Tantalus
Is baited by the fickle fruit,[1] declare
If merely brute caprice dooms Sisyphus
To struggle up a never-ending stair.[2]
Inscrutable His ways are, and immune
10 To catechism by a mind too strewn
With petty cares to slightly understand
What awful brain compels His awful hand.
Yet do I marvel at this curious thing:
To make a poet black, and bid him sing!

Interpretation

1. The octave of this sonnet refers to Tantalus, Sisyphus, and other tortured creatures. Explain their relationship to the paradox posed in the last line of the poem.
2. Why is this paradox a paradox? (See *Handbook of Terms and Techniques.*) What is the social situation the poet expects the reader to understand?

From ON THESE I STAND by Countee Cullen. Copyright, 1925 by Harper & Row, Publishers, Inc.; renewed, 1953 by Ida M. Cullen. By permission of Harper & Row, Publishers, Inc.
1. *Tantalus...fruit.* The mythological Tantalus displeased the gods by divulging their secrets to mortals. As a punishment, he was plunged chin-deep in the river of Hades. Fruit and drink, placed within his grasp, moved beyond his reach when he tried to procure them, dooming him to a life of hunger, thirst, and unfulfillment. 2. *Sisyphus...stair.* Sisyphus was a legendary king whose task in the immortal world was to roll a huge stone up a hill; when the stone reached the top, it rolled down again, making the task of Sisyphus an eternal endeavor.

WHAT THOMAS AN BUILE[1] SAID IN A PUB

JAMES STEPHENS

I saw God. Do you doubt it?
  Do you dare to doubt it?
I saw the Almighty Man. His hand
Was resting on a mountain, and
5 He looked upon the World and all about it:
I saw Him plainer than you see me now,
  You mustn't doubt it.

He was not satisfied;
  His look was all dissatisfied.
10 His beard swung on a wind far out of sight
Behind the world's curve, and there was light
Most fearful from His forehead, and He sighed,
"That star went always wrong, and from the start
  I was dissatisfied."

15 He lifted up His hand—
  I say He heaved a dreadful hand
Over the spinning Earth. Then I said, "Stay,
You must not strike it, God; I'm in the way;
And I will never move from where I stand."
20 He said, "Dear child, I feared that you were dead,"
  And stayed His hand.

interpretation

1. "Thomas an Buile" means "Thomas the Mad." What is Thomas'
vision of God? According to Thomas, why does God not strike the earth?
2. Why do you think the poet makes the speaker a madman? Why does
he locate the speaker in a pub?

Reprinted with permission of Macmillan Publishing Co., Inc., The Macmillan Company of Canada
Limited, Mrs. I. Wise and Macmillan, London and Basingstoke from COLLECTED POEMS by James
Stephens. Copyright 1909 by The Macmillan Company.

1. *Buile* (bi′li).

PIED BEAUTY

GERARD MANLEY HOPKINS

Glory be to God for dappled things—
 For skies of couple-colour as a brinded cow;
  For rose-moles all in stipple upon trout that swim;
Fresh-firecoal chestnut-falls[1]; finches' wings;
 5   Landscape plotted and pieced[2]—fold, fallow, and plough;
  And áll trádes, their gear and tackle and trim.

All things counter,[3] original, spare, strange;
 Whatever is fickle, freckled (who knows how?)
  With swift, slow; sweet, sour; adazzle, dim;
10 He fathers-forth whose beauty is past change:
    Praise him.

---

interpretation

1. What dappled things can you think of? Can these things be described as "counter, original, spare, strange"?
2. Note the series of ANTITHESES in line 9. (See *Handbook of Terms and Techniques.*) Why do you think these antitheses are included in the poem?
3. The things of nature portrayed in this poem are varied and changing. How does the idea of God suggested in the last two lines differ from and yet embrace this concept of "pied beauty"?

From **POEMS OF GERARD MANLEY HOPKINS**, 4th Edition. Published by Oxford University Press, London.

1. *chestnut-falls,* chestnuts newly stripped of their husks. 2. *plotted and pieced,* divided into fields.
3. *counter,* contrary to what is expected.

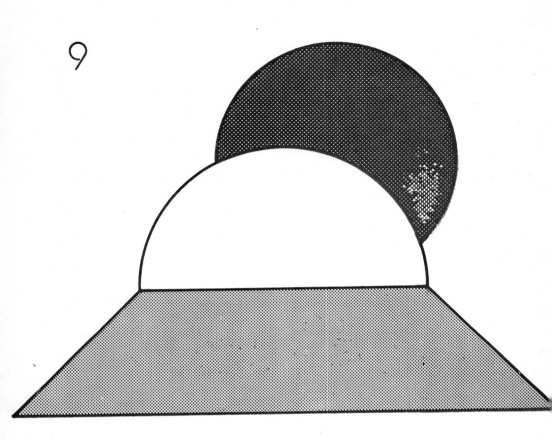

9

We dive, each man,
into his secret house...
JAMES STEPHENS

THE ROAD

JAMES STEPHENS

Because our lives are cowardly and sly,
Because we do not dare to take or give,
Because we scowl and pass each other by,
We do not live; we do not dare to live.

5   We dive, each man, into his secret house,
And bolt the door, and listen in affright,
Each timid man beside a timid spouse,
With timid children huddled out of sight.

Kissing in secret, fighting secretly!
10 We crawl and hide like vermin in a hole,
Under the bravery of sun and sky,
We flash our meannesses of face and soul.

Let us go out and walk upon the road,
And quit for evermore the brick-built den,
15 And lock and key, the hidden, shy abode
That separates us from our fellow-men.

And by contagion of the sun we may,
Catch at a spark from that primeval fire,
And learn that we are better than our clay,
20 And equal to the peaks of our desire.

Interpretation

1. Is the impulse to withdraw or stand apart as universal as this poem implies?
2. What does the poet mean by "a spark from that primeval fire" (line 18)? What would be the effect of catching at such a spark?

Reprinted with permission of Macmillan Publishing Co., Inc., Mrs. I. Wise, The Macmillan Company of Canada Limited, and Macmillan, London and Basingstoke from COLLECTED POEMS (British title: SONGS OF CLAY) by James Stephens. Copyright 1915 by The Macmillan Company, renewed 1943 by James Stephens.

THE BYSTANDER

ROSEMARY DOBSON

I am the one who looks the other way.
In any painting you may see me stand
Rapt at the sky, a bird, an angel's wing,
While others kneel, present the myrrh,[1] receive
5   The benediction from the radiant hand.

I hold the horses while the knights dismount
And draw their swords to fight the battle out,
Or else in dim perspective you may see
My distant figure on the mountain road
10   When in the plain the hosts are put to rout.

I am the silly soul who looks too late,
The dullard dreaming, second from the right.
I hang upon the crowd, but do not mark
(Cap over eyes) the slaughtered Innocents,[2]
15   Or Icarus,[3] his downward-plunging flight.

Once in a Garden[4]—back view only there;
How well the painter placed me, stroke on stroke,
Yet scarcely seen among the flowers and grass—
I heard a voice say "Eat," and would have turned—
20   I often wonder who it was that spoke.

---

interpretation

1. Each of the stanzas appears to suggest one or more paintings. Identify the subject of as many of these paintings as you can. (The footnotes provide clues.)
2. The speaker places himself in each painting. What do the descriptions "I hold the horses while the knights dismount" (line 6) or "second from the right" (line 12) indicate about the speaker?
3. What is the speaker's situation in stanza 4? What point do you think the speaker is making?

From CHILD WITH A COCKATOO. Reprinted by permission of Angus & Robertson (Publishers) Pty. Ltd.

1. *myrrh*, a fragrant gum resin used for perfume, ointment, and incense. Myrrh was one of the gifts the wise men from the East presented to the Christ child. 2. *slaughtered Innocents*. Herod, when he heard that a child who would become the future king of the Jews had been born in Bethlehem, issued an order that all children from the area, two years old and under, should be slain. 3. *Icarus* (ik′ər əs). In Greek mythology Icarus and his father Daedalus (ded′əl əs) escaped the labyrinth with the aid of wax wings. Despite his father's warnings, Icarus flew too close to the sun, which melted his wings and caused him to drown in the sea. 4. *Garden*, the Garden of Eden. According to the Bible, it was in the Garden that the serpent tempted Eve by asking her to eat the forbidden fruit.

SOLEDAD[1]
(And I, I am no longer of that world)

ROBERT HAYDEN

Naked, he lies in the blinded room
chainsmoking, cradled by drugs, by jazz
as never by any lover's cradling flesh.

Miles Davis[2] coolly blows for him:
5   *O pena negra,*[3] sensual Flamenco blues;
the red clay foxfire voice of Lady Day[4]

(lady of the pure black magnolias)
sobsings her sorrow and loss and fare you well,
dryweeps the pain his treacherous jailers

10   have released him from for awhile.
His fears and his unfinished self
await him down in the anywhere streets.

He hides on the dark side of the moon,
takes refuge in a stained-glass cell,
15   flies to a clockless country of crystal.

Only the ghost of Lady Day knows where
he is. Only the music. And he swings
oh swings: beyond complete immortal now.

interpretation

1. This might be termed "an escape poem." Discuss the poet's use of images, both literal and figurative, to suggest insulation and escape.
2. Comment on the effectiveness of poetic coinages such as "sobsings" and "dryweeps."

From WORDS IN THE MOURNING TIME. Copyright © 1970 by Robert Hayden. Reprinted by permission of October House Inc.

1. *Soledad* (sô le däd′), a Spanish word that suggests loneliness or alienation. **2.** *Miles Davis*, jazz trumpeter, composer, and combo leader. **3.** *O pena negra* (ō pe′nä ne′grä), a Spanish expression used to indicate dark pain or anguish. **4.** *Lady Day*, singer Billie Holiday, queen of the blues during the forties.

INVERT

F. R. SCOTT

Casting about for love, when his eye rested, even for a moment,
His longing poured forth a whole cathedral of worship and prayer
Over the miraculous cause of his conversion.
Up went the pillar and the arching roof
5   While lights flared in the chancel, and a boy at the altar
Offered a single candle to the Madonna.
But always he came away with his own lost soul
Wrapped round the cold stone fact he would not face
Till, lonely amid the flux, his ego turned
10 And creeping back upon its source, was left
Beside its own true love, himself, in the crypt of his heart.

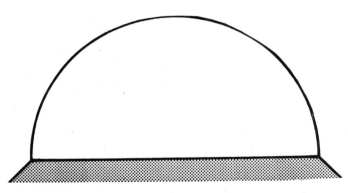

interpretation

1. An *invert* is an individual who is turned in upon himself. Cite expressions in the poem which bear out this definition.
2. In line 2 we read, "His longing poured forth a whole cathedral of worship and prayer. . . ." What does this mean? What does it tell you about where the action of the poem actually takes place?
3. Why is the cathedral an appropriate image for the invert's longing?
4. What was "the cold stone fact he would not face" (line 8)?

From A CANADIAN ANTHOLOGY. Reprinted by permission.

THE ENAMEL GIRL   GENEVIEVE TAGGARD

Fearful of beauty, I always went
Timidly indifferent:

Dainty, hesitant, taking in
Just what was tiniest and thin;

5 Careful not to care
For burning beauty in blue air;

Wanting what my hand could touch—
That not too much;

Looking not to left or right
10 On a honey-silent night;

Fond of arts and trinkets, if
Imperishable and stiff.

They never played me false, nor fell
Into fine dust. They lasted well.

15 They lasted till you came, and then
When you went, sufficed again.

But for you, they had been quite
All I needed for my sight.

You faded. I never knew
20 How to unfold as flowers do,

Or how to nourish anything
To make it grow. I wound a wing

With one caress; with one kiss
Break most fragile ecstasies . . .

25 Now terror touches me when I
Dream I am touching a butterfly.

Interpretation

1. What do you imagine happened between the speaker and the "you"
of the poem?
2. Relate the title to the meaning of the poem.

THE LADY OF SHALOTT

ALFRED, LORD TENNYSON

PART I

On either side the river lie
Long fields of barley and of rye,
That clothe the wold[1] and meet the sky;
And through the field the road runs by
5   To many-towered Camelot;
And up and down the people go,
Gazing where the lilies blow
Round an island there below,
     The island of Shalott.

10 Willows whiten, aspens quiver,
Little breezes dusk and shiver
Through the wave that runs for ever
By the island in the river
     Flowing down to Camelot.
15 Four gray walls, and four gray towers,
Overlook a space of flowers,
And the silent isle imbowers
     The Lady of Shalott.

By the margin, willow-veiled,
20 Slide the heavy barges trailed
By slow horses; and unhailed
The shallop flitteth silken-sailed
     Skimming down to Camelot:
But who hath seen her wave her hand?
25 Or at the casement seen her stand?
Or is she known in all the land,
     The Lady of Shalott?

Only reapers, reaping early
In among the bearded barley,
30 Hear a song that echoes cheerly
From the river winding clearly,
     Down to towered Camelot;
And by the moon the reaper weary,
Piling sheaves in uplands airy,
35 Listening, whispers "'Tis the fairy
     Lady of Shalott."

---

1. *wold,* open country.

PART II

There she weaves by night and day
A magic web with colors gay.
She has heard a whisper say,
40 A curse is on her if she stay[2]
     To look down to Camelot.
She knows not what the curse may be,
And so she weaveth steadily,
And little other care hath she,
45   The Lady of Shalott.

And moving through a mirror clear
That hangs before her all the year,
Shadows of the world appear.
There she sees the highway near
50   Winding down to Camelot;
There the river eddy whirls,
And there the surly village churls,[3]
And the red cloaks of market girls,
     Pass onward from Shalott.

55 Sometimes a troop of damsels glad,
An abbot on an ambling pad,[4]
Sometimes a curly shepherd lad,
Or long-haired page in crimson clad,
     Goes by to towered Camelot;
60 And sometimes through the mirror blue
The knights come riding two and two:
She hath no loyal knight and true,
     The Lady of Shalott.

But in her web she still delights
65 To weave the mirror's magic sights,
For often through the silent nights
A funeral, with plumes and lights
     And music, went to Camelot;
Or when the moon was overhead,
70 Came two young lovers lately wed:
"I am half sick of shadows," said
     The Lady of Shalott.

---

2. *stay*, stop. **3.** *churls*, peasants. **4.** *ambling pad*, easy-paced horse.

PART III

A bow-shot from her bower-eaves,
He rode between the barley sheaves,
75　The sun came dazzling through the leaves,
And flamed upon the brazen greaves⁵
　　　Of bold Sir Lancelot.
A red-cross knight for ever kneeled
To a lady in his shield,
80　That sparkled on the yellow field,
　　　Beside remote Shalott.

The gemmy bridle glittered free,
Like to some branch of stars we see
Hung in the golden Galaxy.
85　The bridle bells rang merrily
　　　As he rode down to Camelot;
And from his blazoned baldric⁶ slung
A mighty silver bugle hung,
And as he rode his armor rung,
90　　　Beside remote Shalott.

All in the blue unclouded weather
Thick-jeweled shone the saddle-leather,
The helmet and the helmet-feather
Burned like one burning flame together,
95　　　As he rode down to Camelot;
As often through the purple night,
Below the starry clusters bright,
Some bearded meteor, trailing light,
　　　Moves over still Shalott.

100　His broad clear brow in sunlight glowed;
On burnished hooves his war horse trode;
From underneath his helmet flowed
His coal-black curls as on he rode,
　　　As he rode down to Camelot.
105　From the bank and from the river
He flashed into the crystal mirror,
"Tirra lirra," by the river
　　　Sang Sir Lancelot.

---

5. *greaves*, armor for the leg below the knee. 6. *baldric*, a belt that is usually ornamented and worn over the shoulder.

She left the web, she left the loom,
110　She made three paces through the room,
She saw the water lily bloom,
She saw the helmet and the plume,
　　She looked down to Camelot.
Out flew the web and floated wide;
115　The mirror cracked from side to side;
"The curse is come upon me," cried
　　The Lady of Shalott.

PART IV

In the stormy east wind straining,
The pale yellow woods were waning,
120　The broad stream in his banks complaining,
Heavily the low sky raining
　　Over towered Camelot;
Down she came and found a boat
Beneath a willow left afloat,
125　And round about the prow she wrote
　　The Lady of Shalott.

And down the river's dim expanse
Like some bold seër in a trance,
Seeing all his own mischance—
130　With a glassy countenance
　　Did she look to Camelot.
And at the closing of the day
She loosed the chain, and down she lay;
The broad stream bore her far away,
135　　The Lady of Shalott.

Lying, robed in snowy white
That loosely flew to left and right—
The leaves upon her falling light—
Through the noises of the night
140　　She floated down to Camelot;
And as the boat-head wound along
The willowy hills and fields among,
They heard her singing her last song,
　　The Lady of Shalott.

145   Heard a carol, mournful, holy
     Chanted loudly, chanted lowly,
     Till her blood was frozen slowly,
     And her eyes were darkened wholly,
        Turned to towered Camelot.
150   For ere she reached upon the tide
     The first house by the waterside,
     Singing in her song she died,
        The Lady of Shalott.

     Under tower and balcony,
155   By garden-wall and gallery,
     A gleaming shape she floated by,
     Dead-pale between the houses high,
        Silent into Camelot.
     Out upon the wharfs they came,
160   Knight and burgher,[7] lord and dame,
     And round the prow they read her name,
        The Lady of Shalott.

     Who is this? and what is here?
     And in the lighted palace near
165   Died the sound of royal cheer;
     And they crossed themselves for fear,
        All the knights of Camelot:
     But Lancelot mused a little space;
     He said, "She has a lovely face;
170   God in his mercy lend her grace,
        The Lady of Shalott."

interpretation

1. On her island of Shalott, the lady of this poem lived one of the most isolated and insulated lives in all literature. In Part I how does the poet provide a sense of life and activity for a subject that is removed and static? In Part II the activity continues but the sense of participation is removed. What device does the poet use to create this effect?
2. At the end of Part II what clue do you find that the Lady of Shalott will, in spite of the curse placed upon her, look directly out the window? What irony do you find in the last stanza of the poem?
3. Can you relate this poem to "The Enamel Girl"?
4. Critics have praised Tennyson's creation of rich and varied melodies in "The Lady of Shalott." To discover what makes this poem unusually melodious, consider the following questions: What meter predominates? What variations in the basic rhythm do you find? What is the rhyme scheme? What effect is created by the occasional use of feminine rhyme? What use is made of the refrain? Are alliteration, assonance, and consonance used frequently? To what effect?

---

7. *burgher*, a freeman in a borough.

THE PURE SUIT OF HAPPINESS

MAY SWENSON

The pure suit of happiness,
not yet invented. How I long
to climb into its legs,

fit into its sleeves, and zip
5 it up, pull the hood
over my head. It's got

a face mask, too, and gloves
and boots attached. It's
made for me. It's blue. It's

10 not too heavy, not too
light. It's my right.
It has its own weather,

which is youth's breeze,
equilibrated by the ideal
15 thermostat of maturity,

and, built-in to begin with,
fluoroscopic goggles of
age. I'd see through

everything, yet be happy.
20 I'd be suited for life. I'd
always look good to myself.

interpretation

1. The pursuit of happiness is one of the "inalienable rights" proclaimed by the American Declaration of Independence. How does the speaker in the poem regard this right? What elements of youth, maturity, and age would the speaker hope to find in the "suit" of happiness?
2. How would the speaker regard being "suited for life"?
3. Should the reader take this poem seriously? Can one be insulated and happy?

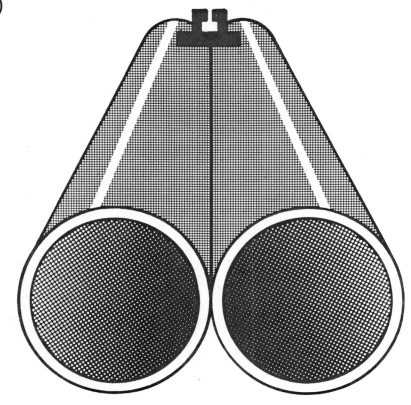

10

LEAP STAND KILL DIE STRIKE

JAMES DICKEY

THE PARABLE OF THE OLD MAN AND THE YOUNG

WILFRED OWEN

So Abram rose, and clave[1] the wood, and went,
And took the fire with him, and a knife.
And as they sojourned both of them together,
Isaac the first-born spake and said, My Father,
5 Behold the preparations, fire and iron,
But where the lamb for this burnt offering?[2]
Then Abram bound the youth with belts and straps,
And builded parapets and trenches there,
And stretchèd forth the knife to slay his son.
10 When lo! an angel called him out of heav'n,
Saying, Lay not thy hand upon the lad,
Neither do anything to him. Behold,
A ram, caught in a thicket by its horns;
Offer the Ram of Pride instead of him,
15 But the old man would not so, but slew his son,—
And half the seed of Europe, one by one . . .

Interpretation

1. The first fourteen lines of the poem tell the story of Abram and Isaac as it is recounted in the Bible (Genesis 22:1–18), but line 15 varies from the Biblical version—Abram spared his son but sacrificed the ram the Lord had provided. Why do you think Owen changed the story?
2. What is a parable? What significance do you find in the title?

From COLLECTED POEMS by Wilfred Owen. Copyright Chatto & Windus Ltd., 1946, © 1963. Reprinted by permission of New Directions Publishing Corporation, the Executors of the Estate of Harold Owen and Chatto & Windus Ltd.

1. *clave,* archaic form of *cleaved, split.* 2. *burnt offering,* a sacrifice burned upon an altar to a god.

CAIN

IRVING LAYTON

Taking the air rifle from my son's hand,
I measured back five paces, the Hebrew
In me, narcissist, father of children,
Laid to rest. From there I took aim and fired.
5 The silent ball hit the frog's back an inch
Below the head. He jumped at the surprise
Of it, suddenly tickled or startled
(He must have thought) and leaped from the wet sand
Into the surrounding brown water. But
10 The ball had done its mischief. His next spring
Was a miserable flop, the thrust all gone
Out of his legs. He tried—like Bruce[1]—again,
Throwing out his sensitive pianist's
Hands as a dwarf might or a helpless child.
15 His splash disturbed the quiet pondwater
And one old frog behind his weedy moat
Blinking, looking self-complacently on.
The lin's[2] surface at once became closing
Eyelids and bubbles like notes of music
20 Liquid, luminous, dropping from the page
White, white-bearded, a rapid crescendo
Of inaudible sounds and a crone's whispering
Backstage among the reeds and bulrushes
As for an expiring Lear or Oedipus.[3]

25 But death makes us all look ridiculous.
Consider this frog (dog, hog, what you will)
Sprawling, his absurd corpse rocked by the tides
That his last vain spring had set in movement.
Like a retired oldster, I couldn't help sneer,
30 Living off the last of his insurance:
Billows—now crumbling—the premiums paid.

From COLLECTED POEMS by Irving Layton reprinted by permission of The Canadian Publishers, McClelland and Stewart Limited, Toronto.

1. *Bruce*, Robert Bruce, liberator and King (as Robert I, 1306–29) of Scotland. **2.** *lin*, pond. [*Scottish*]
3. *Lear or Oedipus*. Both are tragic figures who die on stage. Lear is forsaken by all in Shakespeare's *King Lear*. Oedipus gouges out his eyes after discovering he has unwittingly killed his father and married his mother in the Greek drama *Oedipus Rex*.

Absurd, how absurd, I wanted to kill
At the mockery of it, kill and kill
Again—the self-infatuate frog, dog, hog,
35 Anything with the stir of life in it,
Seeing the dead leaper, Chaplin-footed,[4]
Rocked and cradled in this afternoon
Of tranquil water, reeds, and blazing sun,
The hole in his back clearly visible
40 And the torn skin a blob of shadow
Moving when the quiet poolwater moved.
O Egypt, marbled Greece, resplendent Rome,
Did you also finally perish from a small bore
In your back you could not scratch? And would
45 Your mouths open ghostily, gasping out
Among the murky reeds, the hidden frogs,
We climb with crushed spines toward the heavens?

When the next morning I came the same way
The frog was on his back, one delicate
50 Hand on his belly, and his white shirt front
Spotless. He looked as if he might have been
A comic, tapdancer apologizing
For a fall, or an Emcee, his wide grin
Coaxing a laugh from us for an aside
55 Or perhaps a joke we didn't quite hear.

commentary

Lin is a Scottish word, still in use, meaning "pond." It can also be spelled with a double _n_. I might have used either _pond_ or _pool_ but settled for _lin_ because it wore an air of mystery and remoteness, echoing the mysteriousness of the impulse that seized me to aim and fire at the innocent frog. With no other reason than the blind impulse to kill, I grabbed the air rifle from my son and shot away at the frog croaking happily among the reeds that sunny early morning. I can explain my action only by supposing that we are all descendants of the first murderer, Cain, and wear his mark on our foreheads, invisible to us only because we don't look hard enough.

Irving Layton

4. _Chaplin-footed,_ splayfooted. A trademark of Charlie Chaplin in one of his most famous comic guises was flattened, spread-out feet.

LAMKIN

ANONYMOUS

It's Lamkin was a mason good
  As ever built wi' stane;
He built lord Wearie's castle,
  But payment got he nane.

5 O pay me, lord Wearie,
  Come, pay me my fee.
I canna pay you, Lamkin,
  For I maun gang¹ o'er the sea.

O pay me now, lord Wearie,
10   Come, pay me out o' hand.
I canna pay you, Lamkin,
  Unless I sell my land.

O gin ye winna² pay me
  I here sall mak a vow,
15 Before that ye come hame again,
  Ye sall ha'e cause to rue.

Lord Wearie got a bonny ship
  To sail the saut sea faem,³
Bade his lady weel the castle
    keep
20   Ay till he should come hame.

But the nourice⁴ was a fause
    limmer⁵
  As e'er hung on a tree;
She laid a plot wi' Lamkin
  Whan her lord was o'er the
    sea.

25 She laid a plot wi' Lamkin
  When the servants were
    awa',
Loot him in at a little shot
    window⁶
  And brought him to the ha'.

O whare's a' the men o' this
    house
  That ca' me Lamkin?   30
They're at the barnwall
    thrashing,
  'Twill be lang ere they come
    in.

And whare's the women o' this
    house
  That ca' me Lamkin?
They're at the far well washing, 35
  'Twill be lang ere they come
    in.

And whare's the bairns o' this
    house
  That ca' me Lamkin?
They're at the school reading,
  'Twill be night or they come 40
    hame.

O whare's the lady o' this
    house
  That ca's me Lamkin?
She's up in her bower⁷ sewing,
  But we soon can bring her
    down.

Then Lamkin's tane a sharp 45
    knife
  That hang down by his
    gaire,⁸
And he has gi'en the bonny
    babe
  A deep wound and a sair.⁹

Then Lamkin he rocked
  And the fause nourice sang, 50

From THE OXFORD BOOK OF BALLADS, edited by James Kinsley. Copyright © 1969 by Oxford
University Press. Reprinted by permission of The Clarendon Press.

1. *maun gang*, must go. **2.** *gin ye winna*, if you will not. **3.** *saut sea faem*, salt sea foam. **4.** *nourice*,
nurse. **5.** *fause limmer*, false jade; deceitful woman. **6.** *shot window*, casement. **7.** *bower*, chamber.
8. *by his gaire*, near his knee. **9.** *sair*, sore; serious.

Till frae ilkae bore[10] o' the
    cradle
  The red blood out sprang.

Then out it spak the lady
  As she stood on the stair:
55 What ails my bairn, nourice,
  That he's greeting[11] sae sair?

O still my bairn, nourice,
  O still him wi' the pap.[12]
He winna still, lady,
60   For this, nor for that.

O still my bairn, nourice,
  O still him wi' the wand.
He winna still, lady,
  For a' his father's land.

65 O still my bairn, nourice,
  O still him wi' the bell.
He winna still, lady,
  Till ye come down yoursel.

O the firsten step she steppit,
70   She steppit on a stane;
But the neisten step she steppit,
  She met him, Lamkin.

O mercy, mercy, Lamkin,
  Ha'e mercy upon me!
75 Though you've ta'en my young
    son's life
  Ye may let mysel be.

O sall I kill her, nourice?
  Or sall I let her be?
O kill her, kill her, Lamkin,
80   For she ne'er was good to me.

O scour the bason, nourice,
  And mak it fair and clean,
For to keep this lady's heart's
    blood;
  For she's come o' noble kin.

There need nae bason, Lamkin, 85
  Lat it run through the floor;
What better is the heart's blood
  O' the rich than o' the poor?

But ere three months were at
    an end
  Lord Wearie came again; 90
But dowie, dowie[13] was his heart
  When first he came hame.

O wha's blood is this, he says,
  That lies in the châmer?
It is your lady's heart's blood, 95
  'Tis as clear as the lamer.[14]

And wha's blood is this, he says,
  That lies in my ha'?
It is your young son's heart's
    blood,
  'Tis the clearest ava.[15] 100

O sweetly sang the black-bird
  That sat upon the tree;
But sairer grat[16] Lamkin
  When he was condemn'd to
    die.

And bonny sang the mavis[17] 105
  Out o' the thorny brake;
But sairer grat the nourice
  Whe she was tied to the
    stake.

---

10. *ilkae bore*, each crevice. 11. *greeting*, crying. 12. *still him wi' the pap*, nurse him. 13. *dowie*, sad.
14. *lamer*, amber. 15. *ava*, of all. 16. *grat*, wept; lamented. 17. *mavis*, thrush.

FRANKIE AND JOHNNY

ANONYMOUS

Frankie and Johnny were lovers,
Lordy, how they could love,
Swore to be true to each other,
True as the stars above,
5   *He was her man, but he done her wrong.*

Little Frankie was a good gal,
As everybody knows,
She did all the work around the house,
And pressed her Johnny's clothes,
10   *He was her man, but he done her wrong.*

Johnny was a yeller man,
With coal black, curly hair,
Everyone up in St. Louis
Thought he was a millionaire,
15   *He was her man, but he done her wrong.*

Frankie went down to the barroom,
Called for a bottle of beer,
Says, "Looky here, Mister Bartender,
Has my lovin' Johnny been here?
20   *He is my man, and he's doin' me wrong."*

"I will not tell you no story,
I will not tell you no lie.
Johnny left here about an hour ago,
With a gal named Nelly Bly,
25   *He is your man, and he's doing you wrong."*

Little Frankie went down Broadway,
With her pistol in her hand,
Said, "Stand aside you chorus gals,
I'm lookin' for my man,
30   *He is my man, and he's doin' me wrong."*

The first time she shot him, he staggered,
The next time she shot him, he fell,
The last time she shot, O Lawdy,
There was a new man's face in hell,
35   *She shot her man, for doin' her wrong.*

"Turn me over, doctor,
Turn me over slow,
I got a bullet in my left hand side,
Great God, it's hurtin' me so.
40   *I was her man, but I done her wrong.*"

It was a rubber-tired buggy,
Decorated hack,
Took poor Johnny to the graveyard,
Brought little Frankie back,
45   *He was her man, but he done her wrong.*

It was not murder in the first degree,
It was not murder in the third,
A woman simply dropped her man
Like a hunter drops his bird,
50   *She shot her man, for doin' her wrong.*

The last time I saw Frankie,
She was sittin' in the 'lectric chair,
Waitin' to go and meet her God
With the sweat runnin' out of her hair,
55   *She shot her man, for doin' her wrong.*

Walked on down Broadway,
As far as I could see,
All I could hear was a two string bow
Playin' "Nearer my God to thee,"
60   *He was her man, and he done her wrong.*

interpretation

1. Ballads have traditionally been filled with violence. In which ballad—"Lamkin" or "Frankie and Johnny"—are you more affected by the violence? What things about the ballad cause this reaction?

2. Study the refrain of "Frankie and Johnny," noting both what changes and what remains the same. What functions does this refrain serve? (See REFRAIN in *Handbook of Terms and Techniques*.)

FAREWELL TO BARN AND STACK AND TREE

A. E. HOUSMAN

"Farewell to barn and stack and tree,
   Farewell to Severn shore.
Terence, look your last at me,
   For I come home no more.

5   "The sun burns on the half-mown hill,
   By now the blood is dried;
And Maurice amongst the hay lies still
   And my knife is in his side.

"My mother thinks us long away;
10   'Tis time the field were mown.
She had two sons at rising day,
   Tonight she'll be alone.

"And here's a bloody hand to shake,
   And oh, man, here's good-bye;
15 We'll sweat no more on scythe and rake,
   My bloody hands and I.

"I wish you strength to bring you pride,
   And a love to keep you clean,
And I wish you luck, come Lammastide,[1]
20   At racing on the green.

"Long for me the rick will wait,
   And long will wait the fold,
And long will stand the empty plate,
   And dinner will be cold."

interpretation

1. This modern literary ballad might be compared with the foregoing traditional ballads. (See *Handbook of Terms and Techniques.*) Is the violence here the center of interest? If not, what seems to be?
2. Like "Lamkin," Housman's poem uses the rhythm of the ballad stanza; but it does not follow the traditional rhyme scheme. How does the rhyme scheme differ? Discuss the important differences between this literary ballad and traditional ballads like "Lamkin."

From A SHROPSHIRE LAD—Authorised Edition—from THE COLLECTED POEMS OF A. E. HOUSMAN. Copyright 1939, 1940, © 1965 by Holt, Rinehart and Winston, Inc. Copyright © 1967, 1968 by Robert E. Symons. Reprinted by permission of Holt, Rinehart and Winston, Inc., The Society of Authors as the literary representative of the Estate of A. E. Housman, and Jonathan Cape Ltd., publishers of A. E. Housman's COLLECTED POEMS.

1. *Lammastide,* a harvest festival held on August 1.

SUICIDE

VERNON SCANNELL

Alone, he came to his decision,
The sore tears stiffening his cheeks
As headlamps flicked the ceiling with white dusters
And darkness roared downhill with nervous brakes.
5 Below, the murmuring and laughter,
The baritone, tobacco-smelling jokes;
And then his misery and anger
Suddenly became articulate:
"I wish that I was dead. Oh, they'll be sorry then!
10 I hate them and I'll kill myself tomorrow.
I want to die. I hate them, hate them. Hate."

And kill himself in fact he did,
But not next day as he'd decided.
The deed itself, for thirty years deferred,
15 Occurred one wintry night when he was loaded.
Belching with scotch and misery
He turned the gas tap on and placed his head
Gently, like a pudding, in the oven.
"I want to die. I'll hurt them yet," he said,
20 And once again: "I hate them, hate them. Hate."
The lampless darkness roared inside his skull
Then sighed into a silence in which played
The grown up voices, still up late,
Indifferent to his rage as to his fate.

Interpretation

1. The suicide is described as putting his head in the oven, "gently, like a pudding." Why is this simile effective?
2. Certain words and phrases in the first stanza are repeated exactly or with slight changes in the second stanza. Find examples of this technique. What do these repetitions suggest?

Reprinted by permission of the author.

IN THE POCKET

JAMES DICKEY

Going backward
All of me and some
Of my friends are forming a shell   my arm is looking
Everywhere and some are breaking
5   In   breaking down
And out   breaking
Across, and one is going deep   deeper
Than my arm.   Where is Number One hooking
Into the violent green alive
10   With linebackers?   I cannot find him he cannot beat
His man   I fall back more
Into the pocket   it is raging and breaking
Number Two has disappeared into the chalk
Of the sideline   Number Three is cutting with half
15   A step of grace   my friends are crumbling
Around me the wrong color
Is looming   hands are coming
Up and over between
My arm and Number Three: throw it hit him in
20   the middle
Of his enemies   hit move scramble
Before death and the ground
Come up   LEAP STAND KILL DIE STRIKE
Now.

interpretation

1. What game is being played? What words and phrases suggest the violence of the game and the desperation of the speaker?
2. Discuss the ways in which line length, arrangement of lines, and spacing between words contribute to the suggestion of a violent game in progress.

From THE EYE-BEATERS, BLOOD, VICTORY, MADNESS, BUCKHEAD AND MERCY by James Dickey. Copyright © 1968, 1969, 1970 by James Dickey. Reprinted by permission of Doubleday & Company, Inc. and Theron Raines, Authors' Representative.

THE PRIZE CAT

E. J. PRATT

Pure blood domestic, guaranteed,
Soft-mannered, musical in purr,
The ribbon had declared the breed,
Gentility was in the fur.

5   Such feline culture in the gads,[1]
No anger ever arched her back—
What distance since those velvet pads
Departed from the leopard's track!

And when I mused how Time had thinned
10   The jungle strains within the cells,
How human hands had disciplined
Those prowling optic parallels;

I saw the generations pass
Along the reflex of a spring,
15   A bird had rustled in the grass,
The tab had caught it on the wing:

Behind the leap so furtive-wild
Was such ignition in the gleam,
I thought an Abyssinian child
20   Had cried out in the whitethroat's scream.

interpretation

1. What does the title tell you about the cat?
2. What train of thought is set in motion by watching the cat?

From THE COLLECTED POEMS OF E. J. PRATT, Second Edition, © 1962 The Macmillan Company of Canada Limited. Reprinted by permission of the Macmillan Company of Canada Limited.

1. *gads,* meanderings.

THE ARMADILLO
(For Robert Lowell[1])

ELIZABETH BISHOP

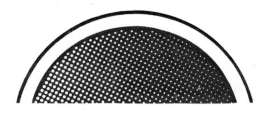

This is the time of year
when almost every night
the frail, illegal fire balloons appear.
Climbing the mountain height,

5 rising toward a saint
still honored in these parts,
the paper chambers flush and fill with light
that comes and goes, like hearts.

Once up against the sky it's hard
10 to tell them from the stars—
planets, that is—the tinted ones:
Venus going down, òr Mars,

or the pale green one. With a wind,
they flare and falter, wobble and toss;
15 but if it's still they steer between
the kite sticks of the Southern Cross,[2]

receding, dwindling, solemnly
and steadily forsaking us,
or, in the downdraft from a peak,
20 suddenly turning dangerous.

From QUESTIONS OF TRAVEL. Copyright © 1957 by Elizabeth Bishop. Reprinted by permission of Farrar, Straus & Giroux, Inc. and Chatto & Windus Ltd.

1. *Robert Lowell,* American poet. Lowell's poem, "Skunk Hour" (page 284), is dedicated to Elizabeth Bishop. **2.** *kite sticks . . . Southern Cross.* The Southern Cross is a constellation of four bright stars in the Southern Hemisphere; its four points are situated to form the extremities of a cross.

Last night another big one fell.
It splattered like an egg of fire
against the cliff behind the house.
The flame ran down. We saw the pair

25   of owls who nest there flying up
and up, their whirling black-and-white
stained bright pink underneath, until
they shrieked up out of sight.

The ancient owls' nest must have burned.
30   Hastily, all alone,
a glistening armadillo left the scene,
rose-flecked, head down, tail down,

and then a baby rabbit jumped out,
short-eared, to our surprise.
35   So soft!—a handful of intangible ash
with fixed, ignited eyes.

Too pretty, dreamlike mimicry!
O falling fire and piercing cry
and panic, and a weak mailed fist
40   *clenched ignorant against the sky!*

Interpretation

1. What is the central situation described in the poem? What clues to setting can you find? What is an armadillo?
2. Whose is the "weak mailed fist / clenched ignorant against the sky"?
3. Why do you think the poem was titled "The Armadillo" rather than "The Owl's Nest" or "The Baby Rabbit"?

THE ARRIVAL OF THE BEE BOX

SYLVIA PLATH

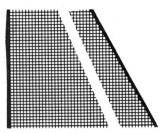

I ordered this, this clean wood box
Square as a chair and almost too heavy to lift.
I would say it was the coffin of a midget
Or a square baby
5 Were there not such a din in it.

The box is locked, it is dangerous.
I have to live with it overnight
And I can't keep away from it.
There are no windows, so I can't see what is in there.
10 There is only a little grid, no exit.

I put my eye to the grid.
It is dark, dark,
With the swarmy feeling of African hands
Minute and shrunk for export,
15 Black on black, angrily clambering.

How can I let them out?
It is the noise that appals me most of all,
The unintelligible syllables.
It is like a Roman mob,
20 Small, taken one by one, but my god, together!

I lay my ear to furious Latin.
I am not a Caesar.
I have simply ordered a box of maniacs.
They can be sent back.
25 They can die, I need feed them nothing, I am the owner.

I wonder how hungry they are.
I wonder if they would forget me
If I just undid the locks and stood back and turned into a tree.
There is the laburnum, its blond colonnades,
30 And the petticoats of the cherry.

They might ignore me immediately
In my moon suit and funeral veil.
I am no source of honey
So why should they turn on me?
35 Tomorrow I will be sweet God, I will set them free.

The box is only temporary.

1. What does the early speculation that the box might be "the coffin
of a midget / Or a square baby" suggest about the kind of imaginative
details to be expected? Cite other details that bear out your answer.
2. Is the poem merely about a beekeeper's receiving a box of bees, or
do you have another interpretation? Explain your answer.

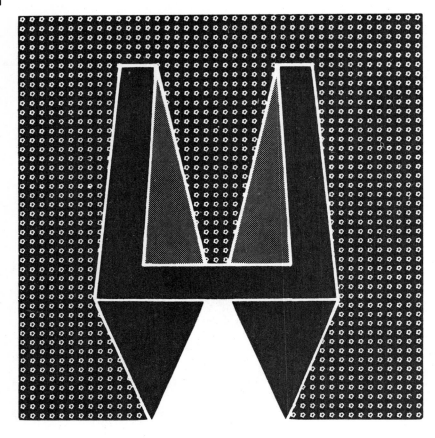

And death shall have no dominion.

DYLAN THOMAS

IT WAS COLD IN THE HOUSE

LISA GRENELLE

After father died it was cold in the house,
cold outside.
Nowhere any softness to finger.
Toad beneath the stoop
5   had a wet rag feel.
Other living were hard and large:
horse in the stable, sheep in the grass.
The tall, talk-talk people
stomp up and down the stairs.
10 block door and hall.

Only in the cellar warmth of kittens
cuddle in a crooked corner.
One painted sun-color creeps
across a round shadow
15 to nestle in my hand.
Water tasting like sweet milk
drops from my eyes
on a soft giving paw.
I didn't feel cold anymore

interpretation

In this poem a child feels death as primarily coldness in other living creatures, even in the adults who might offer comfort. Explain the shift in feeling that comes in the second stanza. What words and phrases indicate this change?

BELLS FOR JOHN WHITESIDE'S DAUGHTER

JOHN CROWE RANSOM

There was such speed in her little body,
And such lightness in her footfall,
It is no wonder her brown study
Astonishes us all.

5 Her wars were bruited in our high window.
We looked among orchard trees and beyond,
Where she took arms against her shadow,
Or harried unto the pond

The lazy geese, like a snow cloud
10 Dripping their snow on the green grass,
Tricking and stopping, sleepy and proud,
Who cried in goose, Alas,

For the tireless heart within the little
Lady with rod that made them rise
15 From their noon apple-dreams and scuttle
Goose-fashion under the skies!

But now go the bells, and we are ready,
In one house we are sternly stopped
To say we are vexed at her brown study,
20 Lying so primly propped.

interpretation

1. In this elegy for a young girl, a heavy subject seems to have been given a light touch. The child is remembered as prodding the geese from their "noon apple-dreams" and sending them running, crying "in goose, Alas." What other details contribute to this mood?

2. What phrases describe the young girl in death? Contrast this particular language with that used to describe the child in life, and comment on the effect.

ON THE DEATH OF A CHILD

D. J. ENRIGHT

The greatest griefs shall find themselves inside the smallest cage.
It's only then that we can hope to tame their rage,

The monsters we must live with. For it will not do
To hiss humanity because one human threw
5 Us out of heart and home. Or part

At odds with life because one baby failed to live.
Indeed, as little as its subject, is the wreath we give—

The big words fail to fit. Like giant boxes
Round small bodies. Taking up improper room,
10 Where so much withering is, and so much bloom.

<hr>

interpretation

1. "The big words fail to fit." What are "big words"? What does the poet mean?
2. In "Bells for John Whiteside's Daughter" does the poet avoid "big words"? Does Ransom seem to follow the advice given in this poem?

<hr>

From THE LAUGHING HYENA AND OTHER POEMS by D. J. Enright (1953). Reprinted by permission of Routledge & Kegan Paul Ltd.

ODE ON THE DEATH OF A FAVORITE CAT   THOMAS GRAY

Drowned in a Tub of Gold Fishes

'Twas on a lofty vase's side,
Where China's gayest art had dyed
   The azure flowers, that blow;
Demurest of the tabby kind,
5 The pensive Selima reclined,
   Gazed on the lake below.

Her conscious tail her joy declared;
The fair round face, the snowy
   beard,
   The velvet of her paws,
10 Her coat, that with the tortoise vies,
Her ears of jet, and emerald eyes,
   She saw; and purred applause.

Still had she gazed; but 'midst
   the tide
Two angel forms were seen to
   glide,
15   The Genii of the stream:
Their scaly armor's Tyrian hue
Through richest purple to the view
   Betrayed a golden gleam.

The hapless Nymph with
   wonder saw:
20 A whisker first and then a claw,
   With many an ardent wish,
She stretched in vain to reach
   the prize.
What female heart can gold
   despise?
   What Cat's averse to fish?

Presumptuous Maid! with looks 25
   intent
Again she stretched, again she bent,
   Nor knew the gulf between.
(Malignant Fate sat by, and
   smiled)
The slipp'ry verge her feet
   beguiled,
   She tumbled headlong in. 30

Eight times emerging from the
   flood
She mewed to ev'ry wat'ry God,
   Some speedy aid to send.
No Dolphin came, no Nereid[1]
   stirred:
Nor cruel Tom, nor Susan heard. 35
   A Fav'rite has no friend!

From hence, ye Beauties,
   undeceived,
Know, one false step is ne'er
   retrieved,
   And be with caution bold.
Nor all that tempts your 40
   wand'ring eyes
And heedless hearts, is lawful
   prize;
   Not all, that glisters, gold.

interpretation

1. We would probably never call a large, elegantly painted Chinese vase a "tub," but Gray does. Picture, then, the favorite cat lying on the rim of the vase and looking down at her reflection in the water. With what feeling does she regard her reflection? What distracts her? What disaster follows?

2. Gray calls his poem an ode. How does it differ in tone from the traditional ode? (See ODE in *Handbook of Terms and Techniques.*)

1. *Dolphin...Nereid.* A dolphin saved the Greek musician Arion when he was cast overboard by sailors. Nereids are sea-nymphs.

CAT DYING IN AUTUMN

IRVING LAYTON

I put the cat outside to die,
Laying her down
Into a rut of leaves
Cold and bloodsoaked;
5 Her moan
Coming now more quiet
And brief in October's economy
Till the jaws
Opened and shut on no sound.

10 Behind the wide pane
I watched the dying cat
Whose fur like a veil of air
The autumn wind stirred
Indifferently with the leaves;
15 Her form (or was it the wind?)
Still breathing—
A surprise of white.

And I was thinking
Of melting snow in spring
Or a strip of gauze 20
When a sparrow
Dropped down beside it
Leaning his clean beak
Into the hollow;
Then whirred away, his wings, 25
You may suppose, shuddering.

Letting me see
From my house
The twisted petal
That fell 30
Between the ruined paws
To hold or play with,
And the tight smile
Cats have for meeting death.

interpretation

1. Both Thomas Gray and Irving Layton write of the death of a cat, but to very different effects. Describe and differentiate the attitudes of the two poets toward their subject.

2. Gray's ode concludes with something like a lesson. What is it? Is there any such lesson at the end of "Cat Dying in Autumn"?

From COLLECTED POEMS by Irving Layton reprinted by permission of The Canadian Publishers, McClelland and Stewart Limited, Toronto.

SONNET TO MY MOTHER   GEORGE BARKER

Most near, most dear, most loved and most far,
Under the window where I often found her
Sitting as huge as Asia, seismic with laughter,
Gin and chicken helpless in her Irish hand,
5 Irresistible as Rabelais[1] but most tender for
The lame dogs and hurt birds that surround her,—
She is a procession no one can follow after
But be like a little dog following a brass band.
She will not glance up at the bomber or condescend
10 To drop her gin and scuttle to a cellar,
But lean on the mahogany table like a mountain
Whom only faith can move, and so I send
O all my faith and all my love to tell her
That she will move from mourning into morning.

THE RITES FOR COUSIN VIT   GWENDOLYN BROOKS

Carried her unprotesting out the door.
Kicked back the casket-stand. But it can't hold her,
That stuff and satin aiming to enfold her,
The lid's contrition nor the bolts before.
5 Oh oh. Too much. Too much. Even now, surmise,
She rises in the sunshine. There she goes,
Back to the bars she knew and the repose
In love-rooms and the things in people's eyes.
Too vital and too squeaking. Must emerge.
10 Even now she does the snake-hips with a hiss,
Slops the bad wine across her shantung, talks
Of pregnancy, guitars and bridgework, walks
In parks or alleys, comes haply on the verge
Of happiness, haply hysterics. Is.

interpretation

1. What did the protagonists of these two sonnets have in common?
2. What attitude toward death is inherent in the descriptions of the mother and Cousin Vit? Quote lines to back up your answer.
3. Both of these poems are considered sonnets. How do they differ from the traditional sonnet?

1. *Rabelais* (rab′ə lā), a sixteenth-century French author, famous for robust humor and satire.

AUNT HELEN

T. S. ELIOT

Miss Helen Slingsby was my maiden aunt,
And lived in a small house near a fashionable square
Cared for by servants to the number of four.
Now when she died there was silence in heaven
5   And silence at her end of the street.
The shutters were drawn and the undertaker wiped his feet—
He was aware that this sort of thing had occurred before.
The dogs were handsomely provided for,
But shortly afterwards the parrot died too.
10 The Dresden clock continued ticking on the mantelpiece,
And the footman sat upon the dining-table
Holding the second housemaid on his knees—
Who had always been so careful while her mistress lived.

THOUGHT FOR A SUNSHINY MORNING

DOROTHY PARKER

It costs me never a stab nor squirm
To tread by chance upon a worm.
"Aha, my little dear," I say,
"Your clan will pay me back one day."

TRACT

WILLIAM CARLOS WILLIAMS

I will teach you my townspeople
how to perform a funeral
for you have it over a troop
of artists—
5 unless one should scour the world—
you have the ground sense necessary.

See! the hearse leads.
I begin with a design for a hearse.
For Christ's sake not black—
10 nor white either—and not polished!
Let it be weathered—like a farm wagon—
with gilt wheels (this could be
applied fresh at small expense)
or no wheels at all:
15 a rough dray to drag over the ground.
Knock the glass out!
My God!—glass, my townspeople!
For what purpose? Is it for the dead
to look out or for us to see
20 how well he is housed or to see
the flowers or the lack of them—
or what?
To keep the rain and snow from him?

He will have a heavier rain soon:
25 pebbles and dirt and what not.
Let there be no glass—
and no upholstery, phew!
and no little brass rollers
and small easy wheels on the bottom—
30 my townspeople what are you thinking of?

A rough plain hearse then
with gilt wheels and no top at all.
On this the coffin lies
by its own weight.

No wreaths please—
35 especially no hot house flowers.
Some common memento is better,
something he prized and is known by:
his old clothes—a few books perhaps—
God knows what! You realize
40 how we are about these things
my townspeople—
something will be found—anything
even flowers if he had come to that.
So much for the hearse.

45 For heaven's sake though see to the driver!
Take off the silk hat! In fact
that's no place at all for him—
up there unceremoniously
dragging our friend out to his own dignity!
50 Bring him down—bring him down!
Low and inconspicuous! I'd not have him ride
on the wagon at all—damn him—
the undertaker's understrapper!
Let him hold the reins
55 and walk at the side
and inconspicuously too!

Then briefly as to yourselves:
Walk behind—as they do in France,
seventh class, or if you ride
60 Hell take curtains! Go with some show
of inconvenience; sit openly—
to the weather as to grief.
Or do you think you can shut grief in?
What—from us? We who have perhaps
65 nothing to lose? Share with us
share with us—it will be money
in your pockets.
                    Go now
I think you are ready.

Interpretation

1. A *tract* is usually a short paper on a political or religious subject. Why do you think this poem is entitled "Tract"?
2. Why do you think the speaker seems angry with his fellow townspeople? What is his attitude toward the dead?
3. Explain lines 65–67: "Share with us / share with us—it will be money / in your pockets."

THERE'S BEEN A DEATH, IN THE OPPOSITE HOUSE

EMILY DICKINSON

There's been a Death, in the Opposite House,
As lately as Today—
I know it, by the numb look
Such Houses have—alway—

5   The Neighbors rustle in and out—
The Doctor—drives away—
A Window opens like a Pod—
Abrupt—mechanically—

Somebody flings a Mattress out—
10   The Children hurry by—
They wonder if it died—on that—
I used to—when a Boy—
The Minister—goes stiffly in—
As if the House were His—
15   And He owned all the Mourners—now—
And little Boys—besides—

And then the Milliner—and the Man
Of the Appalling Trade—
To take the measure of the House—

20   There'll be that Dark Parade—

Of Tassels—and of Coaches—soon—
It's easy as a Sign—
The Intuition of the News—
In just a Country Town—

---

interpretation

1. Who is the speaker? What words and phrases give you an insight into the speaker's point of view and attitude toward death?

2. What is the "Dark Parade"? In what way is the "Dark Parade" a "Sign" or "The Intuition of the News"?

3. Emily Dickinson often uses slant rhyme. (See entry for RHYME in *Handbook of Terms and Techniques*.) Find examples of slant rhyme in this poem. What are the advantages of this kind of rhyme?

From THE COMPLETE POEMS OF EMILY DICKINSON, ed. by Thomas H. Johnson. Published by Little, Brown & Co.

THE MOON AND THE YEW TREE

SYLVIA PLATH

This is the light of the mind, cold and planetary.
The trees of the mind are black. The light is blue.
The grasses unload their griefs on my feet as if I were God,
Prickling my ankles and murmuring of their humility.
5 Fumey, spiritous mists inhabit this place
Separated from my house by a row of headstones.
I simply cannot see where there is to get to.

The moon is no door. It is a face in its own right,
White as a knuckle and terribly upset.
10 It drags the sea after it like a dark crime; it is quiet
With the O-gape of complete despair. I live here.
Twice on Sunday, the bells startle the sky—
Eight great tongues affirming the Resurrection.
At the end, they soberly bong out their names.

15 The yew tree points up. It has a Gothic shape.
The eyes lift after it and find the moon.
The moon is my mother. She is not sweet like Mary.[1]
Her blue garments unloose small bats and owls.
How I would like to believe in tenderness—
20 The face of the effigy, gentled by candles,
Bending, on me in particular, its mild eyes.

I have fallen a long way. Clouds are flowering
Blue and mystical over the face of the stars.
Inside the church, the saints will be all blue,
25 Floating on their delicate feet over the cold pews,
Their hands and faces stiff with holiness.
The moon sees nothing of this. She is bald and wild.
And the message of the yew tree is blackness—blackness and silence.

interpretation

1. Where do you visualize the speaker as the poem opens?
2. Stanzas 2–4 appear to develop a tension between the outdoor scene and the nearby church, between the moon and Mary, between nature (in its more threatening aspects) and religion. With which side does the speaker identify?
3. Compare the endings of the Dickinson and Plath poems. Which seems more hopeful, which more bleak?

1. *Mary*, the mother of Jesus.

AND DEATH SHALL HAVE NO DOMINION

DYLAN THOMAS

And death shall have no dominion.
Dead men naked they shall be one
With the man in the wind and the west moon;
When their bones are picked clean and the clean bones gone,
5   They shall have stars at elbow and foot;
Though they go mad they shall be sane,
Though they sink through the sea they shall rise again;
Though lovers be lost love shall not;
And death shall have no dominion.

10   And death shall have no dominion.
Under the windings of the sea
They lying long shall not die windily;
Twisting on racks when sinews give way,
Strapped to a wheel, yet they shall not break;
15   Faith in their hands shall snap in two,
And the unicorn evils run them through;
Split all ends up they shan't crack;
And death shall have no dominion.

And death shall have no dominion.
20   No more may gulls cry at their ears
Or waves break loud on the seashores;
Where blew a flower may a flower no more
Lift its head to the blows of the rain;
Though they be mad and dead as nails,
25   Heads of the characters hammer through daisies;
Break in the sun till the sun breaks down,
And death shall have no dominion.

interpretation

Each stanza of this poem asserts in a different way that because life endures, even though in different forms, death will not conquer. In the first stanza we find images of the cosmic dispersal of life. In the second stanza the poet affirms that life and its elements endure even through torture. And in the third stanza we find images of a kind of physical resurrection of life as it appears in new forms.

Discuss the meaning of the poem as it comes into focus in line 25: "Heads of the characters hammer through daisies."

From THE POEMS OF DYLAN THOMAS. Copyright 1943, 1946 by New Directions Publishing Corporation. Reprinted by permission of New Directions Publishing Corporation, J. M. Dent & Sons Ltd., Publishers and the Trustees for the Copyrights of the late Dylan Thomas.

DEATH, BE NOT PROUD

JOHN DONNE

Death, be not proud, though some have callèd thee
Mighty and dreadful, for thou art not so;
For those whom thou think'st thou dost overthrow
Die not, poor Death, nor yet canst thou kill me.
5   From rest and sleep, which but thy pictures be,
Much pleasure; then from thee much more must flow,
And soonest our best men with thee do go,
Rest of their bones, and soul's delivery.
Thou art slave to fate, chance, kings, and desperate men,
10   And dost with poison, war, and sickness dwell,
And poppy[1] or charms can make us sleep as well
And better than thy stroke; why swell'st[2] thou then?
One short sleep past, we wake eternally,
And death shall be no more; Death, thou shalt die.

interpretation

Both Thomas and Donne appear defiant in their attitudes toward death.
Yet the reasons for their defiance seem different. Explore and explain.

1. *poppy*, the source of certain narcotic drugs. 2. *swell'st*, puff up with pride.

VIGIL STRANGE I KEPT ON THE FIELD ONE NIGHT   WALT WHITMAN

Vigil strange I kept on the field one night;
When you my son and my comrade dropped at my side that day,
One look I but gave which your dear eyes returned with a look I shall
      never forget,
One touch of your hand to mine O boy, reached up as you lay on the
      ground,
5 Then onward I sped in the battle, the even-contested battle,
Till late in the night relieved to the place at last again I made my way,
Found you in death so cold dear comrade, found your body son of
      responding kisses, (never again on earth responding,)
Bared your face in the starlight, curious the scene, cool blew the
      moderate night-wind,
Long there and then in vigil I stood, dimly around me the battle-field
      spreading,
10 Vigil wondrous and vigil sweet there in the fragrant silent night,
But not a tear fell, not even a long-drawn sigh, long, long I gazed,
Then on the earth partially reclining sat by your side leaning my chin
      in my hands,
Passing sweet hours, immortal and mystic hours with you dearest
      comrade—not a tear, not a word,
Vigil of silence, love and death, vigil for you my son and my soldier,
15 As onward silently stars aloft, eastward new ones upward stole,
Vigil final for you brave boy, (I could not save you, swift was your
      death,
I faithfully loved you and cared for you living, I think we shall
      surely meet again,)
Till at latest lingering of the night, indeed just as the dawn appeared,
My comrade I wrapped in his blanket, enveloped well his form,
20 Folded the blanket well, tucking it carefully over head and carefully
      under feet,
And there and then and bathed by the rising sun, my son in his grave,
      in his rude-dug grave I deposited,
Ending my vigil strange with that, vigil of night and battle-field dim,
Vigil for boy of responding kisses, (never again on earth responding,)
Vigil for comrade swiftly slain, vigil I never forget, how as day
      brightened,
25 I rose from the chill ground and folded my soldier well in his blanket,
And buried him where he fell.

interpretation

1. This poem is an imagined experience which grew out of Whitman's
experiences in the Civil War. How does the repetition of words, phrases,
and clauses affect your emotional response to the death described?
What is your response to the poetic diction?

2. Would you describe the poem as affirmative or negative, as optimistic
or pessimistic?

AN ELEGY IS PREPARING ITSELF

DONALD JUSTICE

There are pines that are tall enough
Already. In the distance,
The whining of saws; and needles,
Silently slipping through the chosen cloth.
5 The stone, then as now,
Perfectly weightless. And certain words
That will come together to mourn,
Waiting in their dark clothes, apart.

1. What is an elegy? (See *Handbook of Terms and Techniques.*) Explain the function of the pine trees, the saws, the needles, and the stone in the preparation.
2. What are the "certain words" that wait "apart"? Why are they in "dark clothes"?

From *The New Yorker*, (March 3, 1973). Reprinted by permission; © 1973 The New Yorker Magazine, Inc.

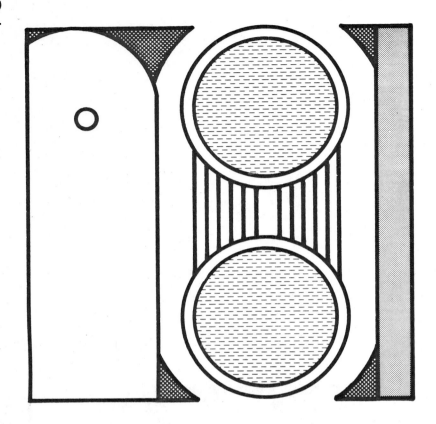

12

And yet we hold the road.

LOUIS MACNEICE

LOVE 20¢ THE FIRST QUARTER MILE

KENNETH FEARING

All right. I may have lied to you and about you, and made a few
    pronouncements a bit too sweeping, perhaps, and possibly forgotten
    to tag the bases here or there,
And damned your extravagance, and maligned your tastes, and libeled
    your relatives, and slandered a few of your friends,
O.K.,
Nevertheless, come back.

5 Come home. I will agree to forget the statements that you issued so
    copiously to the neighbors and the press,
And you will forget that figment of your imagination, the blonde from
    Detroit;
I will agree that your lady friend who lives above us is not crazy, bats,
    nutty as they come, but on the contrary rather bright,
And you will concede that poor old Steinberg is neither a drunk, nor
    a swindler, but simply a guy, on the eccentric side, trying to get along.
(Are you listening, you bitch, and have you got this straight?)

10 Because I forgive you, yes, for everything.
I forgive you for being beautiful and generous and wise,
I forgive you, to put it simply, for being alive, and pardon you, in short,
    for being you.

Because tonight you are in my hair and eyes,
And every street light that our taxi passes shows me you again, still you,
15 And because tonight all other nights are black, all other hours are cold
    and far away, and now, this minute, the stars are very near and bright.

Come back. We will have a celebration to end all celebrations.
We will invite the undertaker who lives beneath us, and a couple of
    boys from the office, and some other friends.
And Steinberg, who is off the wagon, and that insane woman who lives
    upstairs, and a few reporters, if anything should break.

Interpretation

1. What is the function of the title in terms of the poem's setting and
mood?
2. This is a dramatic monologue. (See *Handbook of Terms and Techniques*.) To whom is the speaker talking, and why? Point out words
and phrases that give us some clue to the speaker's personality.
3. Although the poem is clear and direct and tells us a great deal, what
is the question it leaves unanswered?

Reprinted from NEW AND SELECTED POEMS by Kenneth Fearing. Copyright © 1956 by Kenneth
Fearing. Reprinted by permission of Indiana University Press.

VACATION TRIP

WILLIAM STAFFORD

The loudest sound in our car
was Mother being glum;

little chiding valves,
a surge of detergent oil,
5   all that deep chaos,
the relentless accurate fire,
the drive shaft wild to arrive,

and, tugging along behind in its great big balloon,
that looming piece of her mind—

10   "I wish I hadn't come."

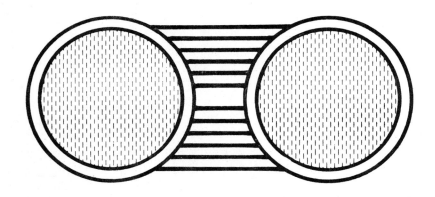

BIOGRAPHY OF SOUTHERN RAIN

KENNETH PATCHEN

Rain's all right. The boys who physic
through town on freights won't kick
if it comes; they often laugh then, talking
about the girl who lived down the block,
5   and how her hair was corn-yellow gold
that God could use for money. But rain,
like memory, can come in filthy clothes too.

The whole upstairs of space caved in that night;
as though a drunken giant had stumbled over the sky —
10   and all the tears in the world came through.
It was that. Like everyone hurt crying at once.
Trees bent to it, their arms a gallows for all
who had ever died in pain, or were hungry, since
the first thief turned to Christ,[1] cursing . . .

15   Then, out of the rain, a girl's voice—her hand
on my arm. "Buddy, help me get this train."
Her voice was soft . . . a cigarette after coffee.
I could hear the clickdamnitclick of the wheels;
saw the headlight writing something on the rain.
20   Then I saw her face—its bleeding sores—I didn't
ask her if she had ever been in love
or had ever heard of Magdalen and Mary[2]
or why she wanted to leave that town.

Do you see what I mean about the rain?

---

interpretation

1. Contrast is an important element in this poem. For example, in what ways is the girl mentioned in stanza 1 contrasted with the girl in stanza 3? What other contrasts can you find?
2. The poet makes extensive use of figurative language. (See *Handbook of Terms and Techniques*.) Find examples and explain their function.
3. What is the purpose of the Biblical allusions?

From COLLECTED POEMS by Kenneth Patchen. Copyright 1942 by New Directions Publishing Corporation. Reprinted by permission of New Directions Publishing Corporation.

1. *first thief . . . Christ,* one of the two malefactors crucified along with Christ. This thief challenged Christ, commanding him, if he were God, to save them all. (Luke 23:39) **2.** *Magdalen and Mary.* Mary Magdalene (in the Bible) was a reformed prostitute who became a follower of Jesus. Mary was the mother of Jesus.

THE FAMILIES ALBUM

MICHAEL S. HARPER

Goggled mother with her children
stomp on the tar road,
their dresses black:
sugar maple, white pine,
5 apple tree, sumac,
young birch, red oak,
pine, cedar, deer moss
watch the archival[1] print
in their death march,
10 for they lived here,
as they live with us now,
in these slanted pine floors
they tried to straighten,
in these squared windows
15 unsquared, in wallpaper torn
down, in the bare beams
of the addition plastered,
in a mother's covered eye
diseased by too much light,
20 too much blood which struck
her husband dead, too much
weed to make the farm work,
too many crooked doorways
on a dirt road tarred over.

25 This old house which was hers
made her crooked back a shingle,
her covered eye this fireplace oven,
her arms the young pine beams
now our clapboard siding;
30 the covered well runs in this dirt
basement, her spring watering her grave
where the fruit, vegetables, woodpile, lie.

commentary

"The Families Album" is part seven of a nine part poem "Photographs: Negatives: History As Apple Tree," a cycle which tries to incorporate the details of photography, the history of the place, and by extension the country, the making of myth out of history to expostulate and promulgate an idea of history contrary to the history as told by the indigenous

From PHOTOGRAPHS: NEGATIVES: HISTORY AS APPLE TREE by Michael Harper. Reprinted by permission of Scarab Press.

1. *archival*, pertaining to or contained in archives or records.

people, a personal history of a family, the loss of children, and the birth of an expected child, and of a black man's presence in a context which forces him to confront the time and place of the writing of the poem, and his connection with the true history of the place and his function in it, by conjuring up, by his own body, the roots of the tree and the land on which he walks and is responsible for, since the land belongs to no single person, and cannot be owned, as his people were and were not owned, though they were "defined" as property. It is also a love poem for his, the poet's, wife, a tribute to a forthcoming daughter born after the loss of two sons, and a tribute to the suffering and humanizing of the poet through the lens of his wife, in her own medium, the picture, the land, the apple tree.

"The Families Album" is about a family in an album, a photographic record of a family, and extended family, the human family. The particulars are important only as suggestion of a larger truth, the human investment in tending the hearth as center to a household, in a field of sixteen acres. The house is actually set upon an Indian burial ground, though the original occupants do not know it, though they do; the woman in the poem has glaucoma, and the walking on the road is a ceremony of mourning, and of rejuvenation in the lives of her children. They are part of the environment as the trees are part of this burial ground, and one is looking at an album of human history through the technique of the lens. The house is photographed as well, a misshapen house built piecemeal, as a misplaced ethic of human enterprise, a puritanism (that version codified in the vision of John Winthrop), manifest destiny, the notion of progress, displacement of indigenes; the straight road of the grid of technology and therefore dominion, and the crooked road of the spiritual path to enlightenment by connection with time and place, and one's duties and responsibilities to one's environment, rather than one's "freedom" to migrate and dispossess, and by amnesia move away from what one had seen and done. Out of death comes life, life begins in the process of dying as one lives; it is a cosmic enterprise. An album is also a reminder—record of one's commitment to one's ancestors; and the lens corrects their misapprehensions, fears, blindnesses, as it illuminates the profundity of their lives. The sachem is only a vehicle to the truth the land knows, the trees know, and which the people know but do not know: a man is a reflection of his environment, and the environment is a reflection of the man. Men know their responsibility and duty to other men, through nature, and by contact with men; the women do the spiritual tending by the process of tending the hearth, the space of children, the spiritual landscape, and the people that occupy that space, with other living and dead "becomings." Most of all, the internal and external landscape is a balance, a unity: man is the caretaker. The dream of every poem is to become a true myth. Every man is an artform; to be beautified is man's aesthetics. The process is man's utterance, the poem: "The Families Album."

Michael Harper

THE TRAIN RUNS LATE TO HARLEM

CONRAD KENT RIVERS

Each known mile comes late.
Faces that leave with me earlier,
Return, sit and wait.
We made eight gruesome hours today.
5   And lunch; lunch we barely ate,
Watching today tick away.

One bravado is going to crash
One of those pine paneled suites
Where the boss sits, laying before
10 Him mankind's pleas. Old Boss
In his wild sophisticated way,
He'll quote from Socrates or Plato,
Then confess to be one of us.

I'll take Sunday's long way home,
15 Ride those waves;
Book passage around the world.
New house: boarding school for my
Kids, free rides at Riverside, buy
Out Sherman's barbecue,
20 Lift my people from poverty,
Until my train pops 133rd square
In her tiger's mouth
Returning me, returning me.

interpretation

The speaker is on a subway train bound for Harlem, where he lives.
But he is also traveling outside of actual space and time. How is this
double journey revealed in the poem?

SPEED

MAY SWENSON

In 200 miles
a tender painting
on the wind-

shield, not yet done,
5 in greeny yellows,
crystalline pinks,

a few smeared
browns. Fuselages
split on impact,

10 stuck, their juices
instantly dried. Spat-
tered flat out-

lines, superfine
strokes, tokens of
15 themselves flying,

frail engines
died in various
designs: mainly arrow-

shapes, wings gone,
bellies smitten   20
open, glaze and tincture

the wipers can't
erase. In 400 miles
a palette, thick

impasto[1]; in 600   25
a palimpsest[2] the sun
bakes through. Stained

glass, not yet done
smiting the wind-
borne, speeds on.   30

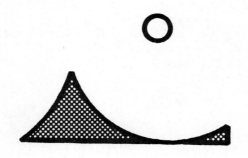

interpretation

1. What is the poem about?
2. How do the words *painting, impasto, palimpsest,* and *stained glass*
contribute to the development of the idea?

1. *impasto,* a thick application of paint or pigment. **2.** *palimpsest,* a surface such as parchment from
which an original writing or drawing has been erased to make room for another.

THE WIPER

LOUIS MACNEICE

Through purblind[1] night the wiper
Reaps a swathe of water
On the screen[2]; we shudder on
　　And hardly hold the road,
5　All we can see a segment
Of blackly shining asphalt
With the wiper moving across it
　　Clearing, blurring, clearing.

But what to say of the road?
10　The monotony of its hardly
Visible camber,[3] the mystery
　　Of its far invisible margins,
Will these be always with us,
The night being broken only
15　By lights that pass or meet us
　　From others in moving boxes?

Boxes of glass and water,
Upholstered, equipped with dials
Professing to tell the distance
20　　We have gone, the speed we are going,
But never a gauge nor needle
To tell us where we are going
Or when day will come, supposing
　　This road exists in daytime.

1. *purblind,* nearly blind; dim-sighted. 2. *screen,* British term for windshield. 3. *camber,* a slight
arching or upward curve in the middle.

25 For now we cannot remember
   Where we were when it was not
   Night, when it was not raining,
      Before this car moved forward
   And the wiper backward and forward
30 Lighting so little before us
   Of a road that, crouching forward,
      We watch move always towards us,

   Which through the tiny segment
   Cleared and blurred by the wiper
35 Is sucked in under the axle
      To be spewed behind us and lost
   While we, dazzled by darkness,
   Haul the black future towards us
   Peeling the skin from our hands;
40   And yet we hold the road.

interpretation

MacNeice's poem may be said to function on two levels—the literal and the symbolic. The speeding car, the highway, the passing lights of other automobiles, and the rainy night are presented in concrete detail. But they are at the same time given symbolic significance; that is, they stand for something, suggest something, over and beyond their literal or familiar meanings. The poem thus implies more than it actually states.

What does the journey through darkness and rain suggest? Discuss lines and images that support your interpretation.

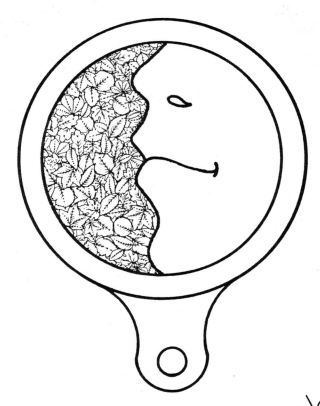

13

...And I saw in the turning so clearly
a child's forgotten mornings...

DYLAN THOMAS

POEM IN OCTOBER

DYLAN THOMAS

It was my thirtieth year to heaven
Woke to my hearing from harbor and neighbor wood
  And the mussel pooled and the heron
     Priested shore
5   The morning beckon
With water praying and call of seagull and rook
And the knock of sailing boats on the net webbed wall
    Myself to set foot
     That second
10   In the still sleeping town and set forth.

My birthday began with the water—
Birds and the birds of the winged trees flying my name
  Above the farms and the white horses
     And I rose
15   In the rainy autumn
And walked abroad in a shower of all my days.
High tide and the heron dived when I took the road
    Over the border
     And the gates
20 Of the town closed as the town awoke.

A springful of larks in a rolling
Cloud and the roadside bushes brimming with whistling
  Blackbirds and the sun of October
     Summery
25   On the hill's shoulder,
Here were fond climates and sweet singers suddenly
Come in the morning where I wandered and listened
    To the rain wringing
     Wind blow cold
30 In the wood faraway under me.

continued

Pale rain over the dwindling harbor
And over the sea wet church the size of a snail
With its horns through mist and the castle
Brown as owls
35   But all the gardens
Of spring and summer were blooming in the tall tales
Beyond the border and under the lark full cloud.
There could I marvel
My birthday
40   Away but the weather turned around.

It turned away from the blithe country
And down the other air and the blue altered sky
Streamed again a wonder of summer
With apples
45   Pears and red currants
And I saw in the turning so clearly a child's
Forgotten mornings when he walked with his mother
Through the parables
Of sun light
50   And the legends of the green chapels

And the twice told fields of infancy
That his tears burned my cheeks and his heart moved in mine.
These were the woods the river and sea
Where a boy
55   In the listening
Summertime of the dead whispered the truth of his joy
To the trees and the stones and the fish in the tide.
And the mystery
Sang alive
60   Still in the water and singingbirds.

And there could I marvel my birthday
Away but the weather turned around. And the true
Joy of the long dead child sang burning
In the sun.
65   It was my thirtieth
Year to heaven stood there then in the summer noon
Though the town below lay leaved with October blood.
O may my heart's truth
Still be sung
70   On this high hill in a year's turning.

Here is a superb example of the *personal lyric*. Although it is less difficult than it may at first appear, the poem is sufficiently difficult to warrant some comment on style, structure, and technique.

In writing of his poetry, Thomas has said: "What I like to do is to treat words as a craftsman does his wood or stone or what-have-you, to hew, carve, mould, coil, polish and plane them into patterns, sequences, sculptures, fugues of sound expressing some lyrical impulse, some spiritual doubt or conviction, some dimly-realised truth I must try to reach and realise."[1]

We follow the poet through the Welsh countryside as he goes to visit his boyhood home on his thirtieth birthday. Once there, he stands on a hill, recalling the "forgotten mornings" of childhood, his mother, and the "joy of the long dead child" who is Dylan Thomas himself.

So much for the paraphrasable content. But the essential meaning of the poem is dependent upon verbal music, evocative concrete images, and figures of speech. All these carry the meaning. They are not mere ornamentation but organic parts of the whole. It is through image and metaphorical language that Thomas communicates, for example, his belief in the beauty, innocence, and holiness of the natural world of birds, beasts, flowers, children. His response is both sensuous and religious. Thus, the herons along the shore stand like priests ("the heron / Priested shore"). The water is "praying." He speaks of "the parables / of sun light / And the legends of the green chapels." And the (divine) "mystery" sings "alive" to the child. In the repeated phrase, "my thirtieth year to heaven," Thomas both affirms his concept of life as a spiritual journey and implies the transiency of life—his own in particular.

Auditory and visual images abound; every stanza is replete with sensuous details. Alliteration occurs throughout the poem, and Thomas has employed both slant and true rhyme. These devices, together with the vowel sounds and the fluent, somewhat free rhythms, produce a richly textured music.

Robert Hayden

---

[1] From "Notes on the Art of Poetry" by Dylan Thomas. Published by *The Texas Quarterly* of 1961. Copyright © 1961 by Trustees of the Copyrights of Dylan Thomas.

WRIT ON THE EVE OF MY 32ND BIRTHDAY

A slow thoughtful spontaneous poem

GREGORY CORSO

I am 32 years old
and finally I look my age, if not more.
Is it a good face what's no more a boy's face?
It seems fatter. And my hair,
5 it's stopped being curly. Is my nose big?
The lips are the same.
And the eyes, ah the eyes get better all the time.
32 and no wife, no baby; no baby hurts,
    but there's lots of time.
I don't act silly any more.
10 And because of it I have to hear from so-called friends:
"You've changed. You used to be so crazy so great."
They are not comfortable with me when I'm serious.
Let them go to the Radio City Music Hall.
32; saw all of Europe, met millions of people;
    was great for some, terrible for others.
15 I remember my 31st year when I cried:
"To think I may have to go another 31 years!"
I don't feel that way this birthday.
I feel I want to be wise with white hair in a tall library
    in a deep chair by a fireplace.
Another year in which I stole nothing.
20 8 years now and haven't stole a thing!
I stopped stealing!
But I still lie at times,
and still am shameless yet ashamed when it comes
    to asking for money.
32 years old and four hard real funny sad bad wonderful
    books of poetry
25 —the world owes me a million dollars.

From LONG LIVE MAN by Gregory Corso. Copyright © 1962 by New Directions Publishing Corporation. Reprinted by permission of New Directions Publishing Corporation.

I think I had a pretty weird 32 years.
And it weren't up to me, none of it.
No choice of two roads; if there were,
    I don't doubt I'd have chosen both.
I like to think *chance* had it I play the bell,
30 The clue, perhaps, is in my unabashed declaration:
"I'm good example there's such a thing as called soul."
I love poetry because it makes me love
    and presents me life.
And of all the fires that die in me,
there's one burns like the sun;
35 it might not make day my personal life,
    my association with people,
    or my behaviour toward society,
but it does tell me my soul has a shadow.

interpretation

1. The subtitle reads: "A slow thoughtful spontaneous poem." What clues does this give you to the mood and tone of the poem?
2. Do you consider this a good poem or a bad poem? Why?

SHORT ODE TO THE CUCKOO

W. H. AUDEN

No one now imagines you answer idle questions
—*How long shall I live? How long remain single?*
Will butter be cheaper?—nor does your shout make
  husbands uneasy.

5 Compared with arias by the great performers
such as the merle,[1] your two-note act is kid-stuff:
our most hardened crooks are sincerely shocked by
  your nesting habits.

Science, Aesthetics, Ethics, may huff and puff but they
10 cannot extinguish your magic: you marvel
the commuter as you wondered the savage.
  Hence, in my diary,

where I normally enter nothing but social
engagements and, lately, the death of friends, I
15 scribble year after year when I first hear you,
  of a holy moment.

Interpretation

1. What does Auden mean by saying the cuckoo's "shout" does not "make husbands uneasy"? (As an aid to your interpretation look up the word *cuckold* in the dictionary.) Why are the "most hardened crooks" shocked by the cuckoo's nesting habits?
2. Note the poet's use of the word *marvel* (line 10) and *wondered* (line 11). In what way does it differ from conventional usage?
3. What effect do "kid stuff" and "huff and puff" have on the tone of the poem? How does the tone differ from that of the traditional ode? (See *Handbook of Terms and Techniques*.)
4. Why do you think the poet considers the first sound of the cuckoo "a holy moment"?

1. *merle*, the common European blackbird.

HIS LAST AUTUMN

(for Andrew Young, 1885–1971)

LESLIE NORRIS

He had never known such an autumn.
At his slow feet were apples
Redder than sun, and small flowers,
Their names no longer thought of,

5 Grew afresh in his recovered innocence.
His eyes had taken colour of the speedwell.[1]
Looking at the sea, he felt its
Lifting pull as he dived, years deep,

Where slant light picked the rocks
10 With brilliants. It was the distant
Road of his boyhood we drove along
On sunny afternoons, it was the laid

Dust of his past that rose beneath
Our wheels. Tranquilly the weather
15 Lingered, warm day after warm day.
He was dead when the cold weather came.

Interpretation

1. How old was the man who was celebrating his last autumn? Find examples of metaphorical language the poet uses to explain that the old man lives in the past.
2. In what way is the weather related to the theme of the poem?

---

1. *speedwell*, a plant with blue flowers.

DURING WIND AND RAIN

THOMAS HARDY

They sing their dearest songs—
He, she, all of them—yea,
Treble and tenor and bass,
    And one to play;
5 With the candles mooning each face. . . .
    Ah, no; the years O!
How the sick leaves reel down in throngs!

They clear the creeping moss—
Elders and juniors—aye,
10 Making the pathways neat
    And the garden gay;
And they build a shady seat. . . .
    Ah, no; the years, the years;
See, the white storm-birds wing across!

15 They are blithely breakfasting all—
Men and maidens—yea,
Under the summer tree,
    With a glimpse of the bay,
While pet fowl come to the knee. . . .
20   Ah, no; the years O!
And the rotten rose is ript from the wall.

They change to a high new house,
He, she, all of them—aye,
Clocks and carpets and chairs
25   On the lawn all day,
And brightest things that are theirs. . . .
    Ah, no; the years, the years;
Down their carved names the rain-drop ploughs.

In 1910 Emma [Hardy's first wife], now a woman of seventy, began writing some memories of her early life. The book was given the title *Some Recollections*. At the beginning we read of Emma's childhood in Plymouth at No. 9 Bedford Terrace. The house stood so high that Emma and her sister could lie in bed on moonlight nights and see the fishing boats in Plymouth Sound. There can be no doubt that Hardy had this house, which he visited after Emma's death, in mind when he wrote one of his finest poems—"During Wind and Rain." When we know that Emma, in addition to mentioning the high new house, also refers in *Some Recollections* to her mother and father singing their old songs together as in their youth (stanza 1), to a shady seat in the garden (stanza 2), to being able to see the bay from the house in Bedford Terrace and to a mania for keeping "handsome fowl" (stanza 3), it is obvious that the genesis of this poem lies deep in *Some Recollections*.

Hardy's manuscript of this poem differs in several ways from the later version. In the last line of stanza 1 his first thought was:

How the sickened leaves drop down in throngs!

but he altered this to:

How the sick leaves reel down in throngs!

Once again we see the craftsman at work: "sickened leaves" has connotations of disgust which were not intended. They are sick, not sickened, and it is the sickness of old age from which they suffer. And *reel* is a far better description of the fall of a leaf and a far more imaginative description of the movement of an old and sick person than *drop*.

In the third stanza there is a further alteration in the last line. Hardy first wrote:

And the wind-whipt creeper lets go the wall.

But whatever he crossed out, nothing could better the final form:

And the rotten rose is ript from the wall . . .

with its hard alliteration on the *r* sound, its onomatopoetic *ript*, and the suggestion of a powerful force at its work of destruction.

Perhaps the poetic process at work in Hardy is best seen in the last line of the poem where in the manuscript Hardy first wrote:

On their chiselled names the lichen grows . . .

but then crossed out *On* and *lichen grows*, and altered the line to:

Commentary from THOMAS HARDY—THE MAKING OF POETRY by James Gibson. © 1971 by James Gibson. Reprinted by permission of Macmillan, London and Basingstoke.

Down their carved names the rain-drop ploughs.

Here the word *Down* is far stronger in sense and sound than *On* and
it adds yet one more heavy sound to a line which is full of them, and
the idea of the rain-drop ploughing its way into the tombstone and becoming a symbol of time effacing our names and our memory is far
more effective in emphasising the oblivion that faces us all than is the
idea of the lichen growing. Rhythmically, too, "the rain-drop ploughs"
is better than "the lichen grows" in that it provides three heavy syllables
on which to end—"the rain-drop ploughs," and the finality of the poem
is made stronger by this.

James Gibson

LET NO CHARITABLE HOPE

ELINOR WYLIE

Now let no charitable hope
Confuse my mind with images
Of eagle and of antelope:
I am in nature none of these.

5 I was, being human, born alone;
I am, being woman, hard beset;
I live by squeezing from a stone
The little nourishment I get.

In masks outrageous and austere
10 The years go by in single file;
But none has merited my fear,
And none has quite escaped my smile.

interpretation

1. The first stanza of the poem may be read as the speaker's denial of
the good qualities attributed to her. What impression is conveyed by
using the word *Now* at the very beginning of the poem? Why do you
think hope is spoken of as "charitable"? What types of mind do the
eagle and the antelope signify?
2. How would you characterize the speaker's attitude toward life?

THE FACE IN THE MIRROR

ROBERT GRAVES

Grey haunted eyes, absent-mindedly glaring
From wide, uneven orbits; one brow drooping
Somewhat over the eye
Because of a missile fragment still inhering,
5   Skin deep, as a foolish record of old-world fighting.

Crookedly broken nose—low tackling caused it;
Cheeks, furrowed; coarse grey hair, flying frenetic;
Forehead, wrinkled and high;
Jowls, prominent; ears, large; jaw, pugilistic;
10   Teeth, few; lips, full and ruddy; mouth, ascetic.

I pause with razor poised, scowling derision
At the mirrored man whose beard needs my attention,
And once more ask him why
He still stands ready, with a boy's presumption,
15   To court the queen in her high silk pavilion.

THE VETERAN

DOROTHY PARKER

When I was young and bold and strong,
Oh, right was right, and wrong was wrong!
My plume on high, my flag unfurled,
I rode away to right the world.
5   "Come out, you dogs, and fight!" said I,
And wept there was but once to die.

But I am old; and good and bad
Are woven in a crazy plaid.
I sit and say, "The world is so;
10   And he is wise who lets it go.
A battle lost, a battle won—
The difference is small, my son."

Inertia rides and riddles me;
The which is called Philosophy.

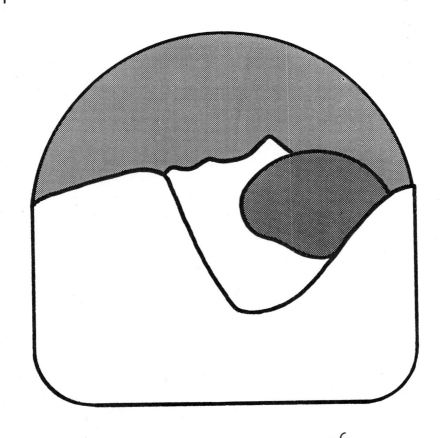

I see, stooping among her
orchard trees/the old,
sound Earth, gathering her
windfalls in...

A. D. HOPE

SPRING IS LIKE A PERHAPS HAND

E. E. CUMMINGS

Spring is like a perhaps hand
(which comes carefully
out of Nowhere)arranging
a window,into which people look(while
5   people stare
arranging and changing placing
carefully there a strange
thing and a known thing here)and

changing everything carefully

10   spring is like a perhaps,
Hand in a window
(carefully to
and fro moving New and
Old things,while
15   people stare carefully
moving a perhaps
fraction of flower here placing
an inch of air there)and

without breaking anything.

interpretation

1. What does Cummings mean by *perhaps?* Why is the word appropriate here?
2. What particular kind of window is referred to?
3. What characteristics of spring are suggested?

END OF MAY

MONA VAN DUYN

Atop each stem
an iris or two has turned in
on itself with no regrets and
    given up
color. Pink, yellow, and red,
5 the rose petals are spread
so wide they already tend
toward total drop.
Peony litter covers the ground.
On earlier days,
10 friends and neighbors in pairs
    have been summoned
to have a drink and see the
    bloom,
have admired everything and
    gone.

I sit in my suntan oil alone—
almost alone; a jay
15 tries to flap me away
from his drinking trough.
His coarse, demanding rebukes
pierce my ears. He chirks
news of impending drouth.

20 But under my feet as I tan
is no longer a brick patio,
rather a light brown

paisley made of seed wings
from the silver maple, which
    can sow
faster than I could sew   25
this fine fabric into something.
And in the air,
like a great snow,
are flakes alive with purpose.
The cottonwood huffs and puffs 30
them everywhere.

On oil that sheathes me from sun
they cling to bare parts of person.
All the long, late
day, my arms and legs are furred 35
with such a will to beget
I think I can almost afford
to forget it's only skin-deep.
It's like taking dope.

It's too late, I tell the tree, 40
*you've settled on somebody
    seedless.*
Equivocally, it nods its head.
But I have been overheard.
Maybe for you but not for me,
the seedy old world says. 45

---

interpretation

1. Contrast is an important element in this poem. What contrast is developed in the first stanza? What things are being contrasted in the following stanzas?

2. What seems to be the speaker's mood, and what has evoked it?

3. *Seedy* means both "shabby" and "containing many seeds." Which of these meanings does the poet intend? Would both be suitable here?

From MERCIFUL DISGUISES: Published and Unpublished Poems by Mona Van Duyn. Copyright © 1972 by Mona Van Duyn. Reprinted by permission of Atheneum Publishers. Appeared originally in *The New Yorker*.

MY PARTY THE RAIN

WILLIAM STAFFORD

Loves upturned faces, laves everybody,
applauds tennis courts, pavements; its fingers
ache and march through the forest numbering
limbs, animals, Boy Scouts; it recognizes
5 every face, the blind, the criminal,
beggar or millionaire, despairing child,
minister cloaked; it finds all the dead
by their stones or mounds, or their deeper listening
for the help of such rain, a census that cares
10 as much as my party, neutral in politics.

It proposes your health, Governor, at the Capitol;
licks every stone, likes the shape of our state.
Let wind in high snow this year
legislate its own mystery; our lower winter
15 rain feathers in over miles of trees
to explore. A cold, cellophane layer,
silver wet, it believes what it touches,
and goes on, persuading one thing at a time,
fair, clear, honest, kind—
20 a long session, Governor. Who knows the end?

Interpretation

1. In what sense or senses is the word *party* used?
2. What are some of the ways in which the democratic impartiality of
the rain is expressed?
3. In line 2 the speaker declares that the rain "applauds tennis courts."
Comment on both the meaning and the effectiveness of this image.
4. How do you interpret the last line? With what tone is it spoken?

From *The Atlantic*, (Nov. 1968). Copyright © 1968, by The Atlantic Monthly Company, Boston, Mass.
Reprinted with permission of the author.

THIS FEVERS ME

RICHARD EBERHART

This fevers me, this sun on green,
On grass glowing, this young spring.
The secret hallowing is come,
Regenerate sudden incarnation,
5   Mystery made visible
In growth, yet subtly veiled in all,
Ununderstandable in grass,
In flowers, and in the human heart,
This lyric mortal loveliness,
10 The earth breathing, and the sun.
The young lambs sport, none udderless.
Rabbits dash beneath the brush.
Crocuses have come; wind flowers
Tremble against quick April.
15 Violets put on the night's blue,
Primroses wear the pale dawn,
The gold daffodils have stolen
From the sun. New grass leaps up;
Gorse yellows, starred with day;
20 The willow is a graceful dancer
Poised; the poplar poises too.
The apple takes the seafoam's light,
And the evergreen tree is densely bright.
April, April, when will he
25 Be gaunt, be old, who is so young?
This fevers me, this sun on green,
On grass glowing, this young spring.

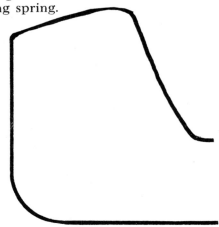

From COLLECTED POEMS, 1930–1960 by Richard Eberhart. © 1960 by Richard Eberhart. Reprinted by permission of Oxford University Press and Chatto and Windus Ltd.

When I was a young man of twenty-three just out of Dartmouth I wanted to give my father's ideas a try. He wanted me to become a businessman. It was 1927. I took a job in the basement of the Men's Store at Marshall Field's in Chicago. After about half a year I became very restless and wanted to work my way around the world on tramp freighters. Seeing that I was determined, my father, whom I admired greatly, gave me his blessing and some letters to persons in China and Manila, in case I should need help. When I got to Cambridge University, my destination by way of the Pacific and Indian oceans, I soon dreamed of a long poem which should explore the growth of my mind. It was patterned after Wordsworth's *Prelude*. I sat in hall at St. John's College every day under his benign portrait gaze.

The passage "This Fevers Me" is the beginning of the long poem which was entitled *A Bravery of Earth,* my first book. It needs little comment as it is a direct expression of the beauty of the world as felt when young.

Richard Eberhart

WITH HIS EYES

SIMON J. ORTIZ

> I take my son outside
> and show him a tree,
> have him touch leaves,
> this is a leaf, see,
> 5   it is green, it's got lines,
> and it is shaped this way,
> touch.
> He touches, the leaf
> and branch tremble with his touch,
> 10   fat little hand roughly
> and gently grasping what I show him.
> Make him stand, bare feet
> to the ground, feel
> that dirt, brown dirt and gravel,
> 15   solid clay, it won't grow seed
> too well, have to have sand
> and leaves, sticks, manure,
> and then it will grow things.
> That's what I tell him.
> 20   With his eyes, he tells me:
> leaves and standing on the ground.

From NAKED IN THE WIND by Simon J. Ortiz. Reprinted by permission of Quetzal/Vihio Press.

AN INTERLUDE

ALGERNON CHARLES SWINBURNE

In the greenest growth of the Maytime,
   I rode where the woods were wet,
Between the dawn and the daytime;
   The spring was glad that we met.

5 There was something the season wanted,
   Though the ways and the woods smelt sweet;
The breath at your lips that panted,
   The pulse of the grass at your feet.

You came, and the sun came after,
10   And the green grew golden above;
And the flag-flowers lightened with laughter,
   And the meadow-sweet shook with love.

Your feet in the full-grown grasses
   Moved soft as a weak wind blows;
15 You passed me as April passes,
   With face made out of a rose.

By the stream where the stems were slender,
   Your bright foot paused at the sedge;
It might be to watch the tender
20   Light leaves in the springtime hedge,

On boughs that the sweet month blanches
   With flowery frost of May:
It might be a bird in the branches,
   It might be a thorn in the way.

25 I waited to watch you linger
   With foot drawn back from the dew,
Till a sunbeam straight like a finger
   Struck sharp through the leaves at you.

And a bird overhead sang *Follow*,
30   And a bird to the right sang *Here;*
And the arch of the leaves was hollow,
   And the meaning of May was clear.

From COLLECTED EDITION OF SWINBURNE'S POEMS.

I saw where the sun's hand pointed,
  I knew what the bird's note said;
35 By the dawn and the dewfall anointed,
  You were queen by the gold on your head.

As the glimpse of a burnt-out ember
  Recalls a regret of the sun,
I remember, forget, and remember
40 What Love saw done and undone.

I remember the way we parted,
  The day and the way we met;
You hoped we were both broken-hearted,
  And knew we should both forget.

45 And May with her world in flower
  Seemed still to murmur and smile
As you murmured and smiled for an hour;
  I saw you turn at the stile.

A hand like a white wood-blossom
50 You lifted, and waved, and passed,
With head hung down to the bosom,
  And pale, as it seemed, at last.

And the best and the worst of this is
  That neither is most to blame
55 If you've forgotten my kisses
  And I've forgotten your name.

Interpretation

1. Why is the poem called "An Interlude"?
2. Scan a stanza or two of this poem. (See RHYTHM in the *Handbook of Terms and Techniques*.) Do you see any relationship between the subject matter and the rhythm? Discuss.
3. Chart the rhyme scheme. What two kinds of rhyme occur in each quatrain? (See RHYME in the *Handbook of Terms and Techniques*.)
4. This is a very musical lyric. What devices are used to achieve its songlike quality?

REQUIEM FOR SONORA

RICHARD SHELTON

1

a small child of a wind
stumbles toward me down the arroyo[1]
lost and carrying no light
tearing its sleeves
5 on thorns of the palo verde[2]
talking to itself
and to the dark shapes it touches
searching for what it has not lost
and will never find
10 searching
and lonelier
than even I can imagine

the moon sleeps
with her head on the buttocks of a young hill
15 and you lie before me
under moonlight as if under water
oh my desert
the coolness of your face

2

men are coming inland to you
20 soon they will make you the last resort
for tourists who have
nowhere else to go

what will become of the coyote
with eyes of topaz
25 moving silently to his undoing
the ocotillo[3]
flagellant of the wind
the deer climbing with dignity
further into the mountains
30 the huge and delicate saguaro[4]

what will become of those who cannot learn
the terrible knowledge of cities

Included in CALENDAR (Baleen Press) and OF ALL THE DIRTY WORDS (University of Pittsburgh Press). Reprinted by permission; © 1971 The New Yorker Magazine, Inc.

1. *arroyo*, a small, dry gully. 2. *palo verde* (pä′lō ver′dā; pä′lō verd), a thorny tree or shrub found in dry areas of the southwestern United States and Mexico. 3. *ocotillo* (ō′kə tēl′yō; *Sp.* ô′kô tē′y ô), a resinous wood such as the pine, with thorns and scarlet flowers. 4. *saguaro* (sä gwä′rō), a treelike cactus which may attain a height of sixty feet.

3

years ago I came to you as a stranger
and have never been worthy
35   to be called your lover or to speak your name
loveliest
most silent sanctuary
more fragile than forests
more beautiful than water

40   I am older and uglier
and full of the knowledge
that I do not belong to beauty
and beauty does not belong to me
I have learned to accept
45   whatever men choose to give me
or whatever they choose to withhold
but oh my desert
yours is the only death I cannot bear

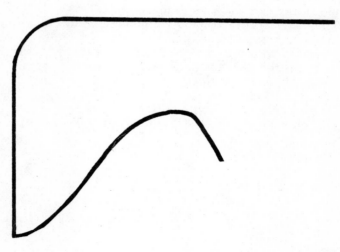

interpretation

1. What is Sonora? How do you know?
2. In writing about Sonora the poet makes extensive use of figurative language. Select and identify some of the figures of speech. (See *Handbook of Terms and Techniques*.) What do these add to the description of Sonora?
3. To whom is the poem addressed? Why does the speaker call it a *requiem*?
4. Is "Requiem for Sonora" at all concerned with ecology?

TO AUTUMN

JOHN KEATS

1

Season of mists and mellow fruitfulness,
  Close bosom-friend of the maturing sun;
Conspiring with him how to load and bless
  With fruit the vines that round the thatch-eaves run;
5 To bend with apples the mossed cottage trees,
    And fill all fruit with ripeness to the core;
      To swell the gourd, and plump the hazel shells
With a sweet kernel; to set budding more,
  And still more, later flowers for the bees,
10   Until they think warm days will never cease,
      For Summer has o'er-brimmed their clammy cells.

2

Who hath not seen thee oft amid thy store?[1]
  Sometimes whoever seeks abroad may find
Thee sitting careless on a granary floor,
15 Thy hair soft-lifted by the winnowing wind;
Or on a half-reaped furrow sound asleep,
  Drowsed with the fume of poppies, while thy hook[2]
    Spares the next swath and all its twinèd flowers:
And sometime like a gleaner thou dost keep
20   Steady thy laden head across a brook;
  Or by a cider-press, with patient look,
    Thou watchest the last oozings, hours by hours.

---

1. *store,* possessions accumulated and stored for future use. 2. *hook,* a large curved knife for cutting
grass or grain.

3

Where are the songs of Spring? Ay, where are they?
Think not of them, thou hast thy music too—
25   While barrèd clouds bloom the soft-dying day,
And touch the stubble-plains with rosy hue;
Then in a wailful choir the small gnats mourn
Among the river sallows,³ borne aloft
Or sinking as the light wind lives or dies;
30   And full-grown lambs loud bleat from hilly bourn⁴;
Hedge-crickets sing; and now with treble soft
The redbreast whistles from a garden-croft,⁵
And gathering swallows twitter in the skies.

interpretation

1. "To Autumn" is rich in imagery that engages our senses of sight, touch, taste, hearing, and smell. (See IMAGERY in *Handbook of Terms and Techniques*.) Point out examples of each kind of image. Are there instances in which you find that the same image calls into play two or more of your senses simultaneously? Discuss.
2. List the different ways in which autumn is personified. Describe the visual image presented by the personification in lines 19-20.
3. What evidence can you find to suggest that the first stanza focuses upon early autumn, that it is the height of autumn in the second stanza, and that by the third stanza it has become late autumn?
4. Why is "To Autumn" considered an ode? (See *Handbook of Terms and Techniques*.)

---

3. *sallows*, willows. **4.** *bourn*, place or domain. **5.** *garden-croft*, small area enclosed by a fence or a hedge.

SONGS from *Love's Labour's Lost*

WILLIAM SHAKESPEARE

SPRING

1

When daisies pied[1] and violets blue,
   And lady-smocks[2] all silver-white,
And cuckoo-buds[3] of yellow hue
   Do paint the meadows with delight,
5 The cuckoo then, on every tree,
Mocks married men; for thus sings he,
        Cuckoo![4]
Cuckoo, cuckoo!—O word of fear,
Unpleasing to a married ear!

10 When shepherds pipe on oaten straws,[5]
   And merry larks are ploughmen's clocks,
When turtles[6] tread, and rooks, and daws,
   And maidens bleach their summer smocks
The cuckoo then, on every tree,
15 Mocks married men; for thus sings he,
        Cuckoo!
Cuckoo, cuckoo!—O word of fear,
Unpleasing to a married ear!

---

1. *pied*, of various colors. **2.** *lady-smocks*, English wildflower, also known as the cuckoo flower or ragged robin. **3.** *cuckoo-buds*, another English wildflower, also known as crow's foot. **4.** *Cuckoo!* In Shakespeare's time, the call or song of the cuckoo was associated with the word *cuckold*, a term applied to a married man whose wife has been unfaithful to him. **5.** *oaten straws*, whistles or pipes fashioned from hollow oat stems. **6.** *turtles*, turtledoves or English wild doves.

WINTER

2

When icicles hang by the wall,
20   And Dick the shepherd blows his nail.[1]
And Tom bears logs into the hall,
  And milk comes frozen home in pail,
When blood is nipped and ways be foul,
Then nightly sings the staring owl,
25   To-whit!
To-who!—a merry note,
While greasy Joan doth keel[2] the pot.

When all aloud the wind doth blow,
  And coughing drowns the parson's saw,
30 And birds sit brooding in the snow,
  And Marian's nose looks red and raw,
When roasted crabs[3] hiss in the bowl,
Then nightly sings the staring owl,
        To-whit!
35 To-who!—a merry note,
While greasy Joan doth keel the pot.

interpretation

1. Cite details that demonstrate Shakespeare's firsthand knowledge of English country life.
2. How would you interpret line 11 in the spring song: "And merry larks are ploughmen's clocks"?
3. Winter is often associated in poetry with desolation, old age, death. How does the winter song avoid such associations?
4. Discuss the element of humor in both songs. How is it achieved?
5. Both songs rely heavily upon refrain. (See *Handbook of Terms and Techniques*.) Describe as fully as you can the function of the refrains in both poems.

---

1. *blows his nail*, breathes on his fingers to warm them. **2.** *keel*, stir. **3.** *crabs*, crabapples.

WIND

TED HUGHES

This house has been far out at sea all night,
The woods crashing through darkness, the booming hills,
Winds stampeding the fields under the window
Floundering black astride and blinding wet

5   Till day rose; then under an orange sky
The hills had new places, and wind wielded
Blade-like, luminous black and emerald,
Flexing like the lens of a mad eye.

At noon I scaled along the house-side as far as
10 The coal-house door. I dared once to look up—
Through the brunt wind that dented the balls of my eyes
The tent of the hills drummed and strained its guyrope,[1]

The fields quivering, the skyline a grimace,
At any second to bang and vanish with a flap:
15 The wind flung a magpie away and a black-
Back gull bent like an iron bar slowly. The house

Rang like some fine green goblet in the note
That any second would shatter it. Now deep
In chairs, in front of the great fire, we grip
20 Our hearts and cannot entertain book, thought,

Or each other. We watch the fire blazing,
And feel the roots of the house move, but sit on,
Seeing the window tremble to come in,
Hearing the stones cry out under the horizons.

interpretation

1. Explain in your own words the situation the poet describes.
2. The experience is made vivid through concrete, sensory details and figures of speech. Find examples of personification, hyperbole, metaphor, and simile. (See *Handbook of Terms and Techniques*.)

1. *guyrope*, a rope attached to an object to steady it.

SNOW MAKES ME SAD

RICHARD BRAUTIGAN

Flying East today first to Chicago,
then North Carolina snow makes me sad
below in the mountains of the West.
It is a white sadness that rises
5   from California, Nevada, Utah
and Colorado to visit the airplane,
to sit here beside me like a snowy 1943
map of my childhood.

SNOW

LOUIS MACNEICE

The room was suddenly rich and the great bay-window was
Spawning snow and pink roses against it
Soundlessly collateral and incompatible:
World is suddener than we fancy it.

5   World is crazier and more of it than we think,
Incorrigibly plural. I peel and portion
A tangerine and spit the pips and feel
The drunkenness of things being various.

And the fire flames with a bubbling sound for world
10 Is more spiteful and gay than one supposes—
On the tongue on the eyes on the ears in the palms of your hands—
There is more than glass between the snow and the huge roses.

Interpretation

1. Visualize a room in which a bowl of roses is set in a bay window
while outside the snow swirls against the window. Why does the speaker
regard the roses and the snow as "collateral" and "incompatible"?
2. From his feeling that the room is "suddenly rich," the speaker goes
on to muse about the fullness and variety of the world. What details
does he use to build up this sense that the world is "incorrigibly plural"
(line 6)? What senses are involved in his discovery?

STANDARDIZATION

A. D. HOPE

When, darkly brooding on this Modern Age,
the journalist with his marketable woes
fills up once more the inevitable page
of fatuous, flatulent, Sunday-paper prose;

5 whenever the green aesthete starts to whoop
with horror at the house not made with hands
and when from vacuum cleaners and tinned soup
another pure theosophist[1] demands

rebirth in other, less industrial stars
10 where huge towns thrust up in synthetic stone
and films, and sleek miraculous motor cars
and celluloid and rubber are unknown;

when from his vegetable Sunday-school
emerges with the neatly maudlin phrase
15 still one more Nature poet, to rant or drool
about the "standardization of the race";

I see, stooping among her orchard trees
the old, sound Earth, gathering her windfalls in,
broad in the hams and stiffening at the knees
20 pause, and I see her grave, malicious grin.

For there is no manufacturer competes
with her in the mass production of shapes and things.
Over and over she gathers and repeats
the cast of a face, a million butterfly wings.

25 She does not tire of the pattern of a rose.
Her oldest tricks still catch us with surprise.
She cannot recall how long ago she chose
the streamlined hulls of fish, the snail's long eyes,

1. *theosophist*, a philosopher who claims, through spiritual self-development, to have a special knowledge of the divine nature.

Love which still pours into its ancient mould
30 the lashing seed that grows to a man again,
from whom by the same processes unfold
unending generations of living men.

She has standardized his ultimate needs and pains.
Lost tribes in a lost language mutter in
35 his dreams: his science is tethered to their brains,
his guilt merely repeats Original Sin.

And beauty standing motionless before
her mirror sees behind her, mile on mile,
a long queue in an unknown corridor,
40 anonymous faces plastered with her smile.

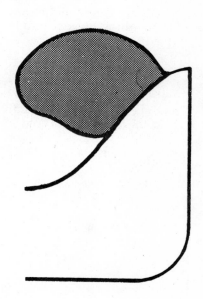

interpretation

1. What two types of standardization are being compared?
2. What is the poet's attitude toward those who criticize modern industrialization? Point out words and phrases that clearly indicate his feelings.
3. Do you think that the argument he presents in favor of standardization is sound? Discuss.

BAVARIAN GENTIANS[1]

D. H. LAWRENCE

Not every man has gentians in his house
in Soft September, at slow, sad Michaelmas.[2]

Bavarian gentians, big and dark, only dark
darkening the day-time, torch-like with the smoking blueness of
    Pluto's gloom,[3]
5 ribbed and torch-like, with their blaze of darkness spread blue
down flattening into points, flattened under the sweep of white day
torch-flower of the blue-smoking darkness, Pluto's dark-blue daze,
black lamps from the halls of Dis, burning dark blue,
giving off darkness, blue darkness, as Demeter's pale lamps[4] give
    off light,
10 lead me then, lead the way.

Reach me a gentian, give me a torch!
let me guide myself with the blue, forked torch of this flower
down the darker and darker stairs, where blue is darkened on
    blueness
even where Persephone goes, just now, from the frosted September
15 to the sightless realm where darkness is awake upon the dark
and Persephone herself is but a voice
or a darkness invisible enfolded in the deeper dark
of the arms Plutonic, and pierced with the passion of dense gloom,
among the splendour of torches of darkness, shedding darkness on
    the lost bride and her groom.

From THE COMPLETE POEMS OF D. H. LAWRENCE ed. by Vivian de Sola Pinto and F. Warren
Roberts. Copyright © 1964, 1971 by Angelo Ravagli & C. M. Weekley, Executors of the Estate of
Frieda Lawrence Ravagli. Reprinted by permission of The Viking Press, Inc., Laurence Pollinger
Ltd., and the Estate of the late Mrs. Frieda Lawrence.

1. *gentians*, deep blue flowers, usually fringed and resembling open-mouthed trumpets. 2. *Michael-mas*, the feast of the archangel Michael, September 29. 3. *Pluto's gloom*. Pluto, or Dis, in classical mythology, was the ruler of Hades, the abode of the dead. 4. *Demeter's* (di mē′tərz) *pale lamps*. Pluto fell in love with Persephone (pər sef′ə nē), daughter of Demeter, goddess of agriculture and fruitfulness. Pluto absconded with his beloved to Hades, and when Demeter discovered the abduction, she searched with torches for her daughter. Finally an agreement was reached by which Pluto would release Persephone for the spring and summer months. Only during these months when Persephone lived above the ground would Demeter allow plants to grow.

The greatest of his [Lawrence's] mythological poems is certainly "Bavarian Gentians." The immediate suggestion for this poem seems to have come from some gentians which he saw at Rottach in Bavaria, where he was staying in September 1929, just before he left for the South of France, where he died in the following March. The sight of the dark blue flowers seems to have evoked the memory of his exploration of the Etruscan tombs in April 1927, as described by his friend Earl Brewster who accompanied him on that occasion:

> From the jewelled splendour of these dark tombs we came forth into the brightness of an April day and a blue sky broken by hurrying clouds: the fields through which we walked were gay with red poppies: our guide unlocked the door leading to another tomb and we would descend again to behold the joyous scenes with which the Etruscans, of such a distant world, chose to adorn the homes of their dead.

As Mr. Hassall[1] has written: "Even the physical act of entering these tombs . . . had become for Lawrence a symbol of death with that noble lack of bitterness or protest which is so lovely an element in his last poems."

Here Lawrence does not, as in his early poems, try to give the reader an immediate apprehension of the life of the flowers; he uses them mythologically, turning them into miraculous torches from the halls of Dis, lighting us down stairs that lead to the underworld, where the spring goddess goes to the embrace of Hades, the "arms Plutonic," and we are made to feel that she is the *anima,* the soul of man going to the embrace of death, which is not terrible but august and godlike. This is a use of mythology not as decoration or allegory, but, like that of Keats in *The Fall of Hyperion,* as a means to lead the reader to "a world of wonder and reverence."

Vivian de Sola Pinto and F. Warren Roberts

From the Introduction to THE COMPLETE POEMS OF D. H. LAWRENCE edited by Vivian de Sola Pinto and F. Warren Roberts. Copyright © 1964, 1971 by Angelo Ravagli & C. M. Weekley. Reprinted by permission of The Viking Press, Inc., Laurence Pollinger Ltd., and the Estate of the late Mrs. Frieda Lawrence.

1. *Mr. Hassall.* Christopher Hassall wrote an article titled "D. H. Lawrence and the Etruscans."

APOSTROPHE TO THE OCEAN

from *Childe Harold's Pilgrimage*

GEORGE GORDON, LORD BYRON

There is a pleasure in the pathless woods,
There is a rapture on the lonely shore,
There is society where none intrudes
By the deep Sea, and music in its roar:
5   I love not Man the less, but Nature more,
From these our interviews, in which I steal
From all I may be, or have been before,
To mingle with the Universe, and feel
What I can ne'er express, yet cannot all conceal.

10   Roll on, thou deep and dark blue Ocean, roll!
Ten thousand fleets sweep over thee in vain;
Man marks the earth with ruin, his control
Stops with the shore; upon the watery plain
The wrecks are all thy deed, nor doth remain
15   A shadow of man's ravage, save his own,
When, for a moment, like a drop of rain,
He sinks into thy depths with bubbling groan,
Without a grave, unknelled, uncoffined, and unknown.

His steps are not upon thy paths, thy fields
20   Are not a spoil for him,—thou dost arise
And shake him from thee; the vile strength he wields
For earth's destruction thou dost all despise,
Spurning him from thy bosom to the skies,
And send'st him, shivering in thy playful spray
25   And howling, to his Gods, where haply lies
His petty hope in some near port or bay,
And dashest him again to earth:—there let him lay.

The armaments which thunderstrike the walls
Of rock-built cities, bidding nations quake
30   And monarchs tremble in their capitals,
The oak leviathans,[1] whose huge ribs make
Their clay creator the vain title take
Of lord of thee and arbiter of war,—
These are thy toys and, as the snowy flake,
35   They melt into thy yeast of waves which mar
Alike the Armada's pride[2] or spoils of Trafalgar.[3]

---

1. *oak leviathans*, warships built with timbers of oak. A leviathan is a whale or other huge sea creature.
2. *Armada's pride*. The Spanish Armada, a fleet of warships sent by Spain against England, was defeated by the English navy in 1588, after which many of the remaining vessels were destroyed by a great storm at sea. **3.** *spoils of Trafalgar* (trə fal′gər; Sp. trä′fäl gär′). After the British defeated the combined French and Spanish fleets at Trafalgar in 1805, many of the captured warships were destroyed by a storm.

Thy shores are empires, changed in all save thee;—
Assyria, Greece, Rome, Carthage,[4] what are they?
Thy waters washed them power while they were free,
40 And many a tyrant since; their shores obey
The stranger, slave or savage; their decay
Has dried up realms to deserts;—not so thou;
Unchangeable save to thy wild waves' play,
Time writes no wrinkle on thine azure brow;
45 Such as creation's dawn beheld, thou rollest now.

Thou glorious mirror, where the Almighty's form
Glasses itself in tempests; in all time,
Calm or convulsed,—in breeze, or gale, or storm,
Icing the pole, or in the torrid clime
50 Dark-heaving;—boundless, endless, and sublime,—
The image of Eternity,—the throne
Of the Invisible; even from out thy slime
The monsters of the deep are made; each zone
Obeys thee; thou goest forth, dread, fathomless, alone.

55 And I have loved thee, Ocean! and my joy
Of youthful sports was on thy breast to be
Borne like thy bubbles, onward. From a boy
I wantoned with thy breakers,—they to me
Were a delight; and if the freshening sea
60 Made them a terror, 'twas a pleasing fear;
For I was as it were a child of thee,
And trusted to thy billows far and near,
And laid my hand upon thy mane,—as I do here.

interpretation

1. Describe the speaker's attitude toward the ocean. What is the tone?
Is it sustained consistently throughout? Do you feel that it occasionally
becomes excessive or tiresome? Discuss.
2. What view of humanity, in relation to the ocean, emerges from the
poem?
3. List the images with which this poem depicts the ocean. Do these
images sometimes conflict with one another? For example, do you feel
that the image of the ocean's "mane" (in the last line) clashes with the
ocean's being addressed as a "glorious mirror" (line 46)? Discuss.
4. How many lines are there in each stanza? What is the rhyme scheme?
How does the meter of the last line in each stanza differ from the meter
of the preceding lines? (See RHYME and RHYTHM in *Handbook of Terms
and Techniques.*) The stanza form Byron uses, which Spenser originated
for *The Faerie Queene* and which Keats used in *The Eve of St. Agnes,*
is called a Spenserian stanza.

4. *Assyria . . . Carthage*, sites of powerful empires of the past.

from **A CONTINUAL INTEREST IN THE SUN AND SEA**

KEITH GUNDERSON

A GAME CALLED
TRYING TO DISCERN
THE INDIVIDUAL JOURNEY: or try to keep your eye on
a single wave coming in
pick any wave coming in

go on,
go on,
pick one:

now

try to keep
your eye on
your eye on
your
eye
on
on

it

is   it

still
the very wave
you'd
picked?

(for those who do not
live near the sea
use a leaf
or a flake
of snow
fall-
ing

interpretation

1. This is a concrete poem. (See *Handbook of Terms and Techniques*.) What visual image is the poet creating? What does the use of repetition add?
2. What does a falling leaf or a flake of snow have in common with a wave?

THE PRESENCE

MAXINE KUMIN

Something went crabwise[1]
across the snow this morning.
Something went hard and slow
over our hayfield.
5 It could have been a raccoon
lugging a knapsack,
it could have been a porcupine
carrying a tennis racket,
it could have been something
10 supple as a red fox
dragging the squawk and spatter
of a crippled woodcock.
Ten knuckles underground
those bones are seeds now
15 pure as baby teeth
lined up in the burrow.

I cross on snowshoes
cunningly woven from
the skin and sinews of
20 something else that went before.

interpretation

1. What suggests to the speaker the images of the "raccoon / lugging a knapsack" and a "porcupine / carrying a tennis racket"? What probably did cross the snow?
2. What idea occurs to the speaker as she crosses the snow on snowshoes? What prompts this thought?

1. *crabwise*, sidewise.

15

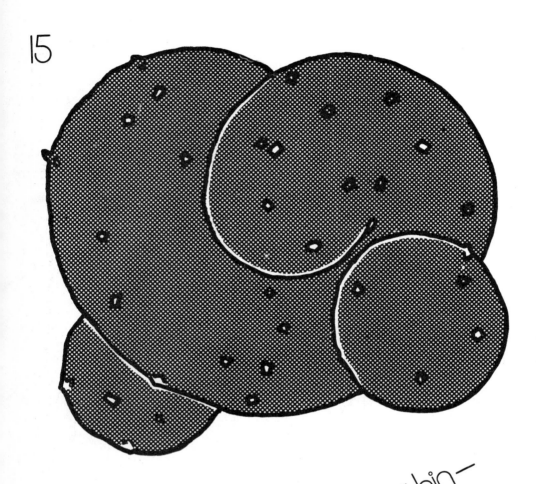

And Something's odd—within—

EMILY DICKINSON

RIZPAH[1]

ALFRED, LORD TENNYSON

1

Wailing, wailing, wailing, the wind over land and sea—
And Willy's voice in the wind, "O mother, come out to me!"
Why should he call me tonight, when he knows that I cannot go?
For the downs are as bright as day, and the full moon stares at the
    snow.

2

5 We should be seen, my dear; they would spy us out of the town.
The loud black nights for us, and the storm rushing over the down,
When I cannot see my own hand, but am led by the creak of the
    chain,[2]
And grovel and grope for my son till I find myself drenched with the
    rain.

3

Anything fallen again? nay—what was there left to fall?
10 I have taken them home, I have numbered the bones, I have hidden
    them all.
What am I saying? and what are *you*? do you come as a spy?
Falls? what falls? who knows? As the tree falls so must it lie.

4

Who let her in? how long has she been? you—what have you heard?
Why did you sit so quiet? you never have spoken a word.
15 O—to pray with me—yes—a lady—none of their spies—
But the night has crept into my heart, and begun to darken my eyes.

5

Ah—you, that have lived so soft, what should *you* know of the night,
The blast and the burning shame and the bitter frost and the fright?
I have done it, while you were asleep—you were only made for the
    day.
20 I have gathered my baby together—and now you may go your way.

---

1. *Rizpah.* In the Bible, Rizpah was the concubine of King Saul. She kept vigil for months over the
bodies of her sons who were hanged on the hill of Gibeah in expiation for Saul's crimes against the
Gibeonites. (II Samuel 21:1-14) **2.** *creak of the chain.* In eighteenth-century England it was customary
to hang the bodies of criminals in chains after their execution.

6

Nay—for it's kind of you, madam, to sit by an old dying wife.
But say nothing hard of my boy, I have only an hour of life.
I kissed my boy in the prison, before he went out to die.
"They dared me to do it," he said, and he never has told me a lie.
25 I whipped him for robbing an orchard once when he was but a child—
"The farmer dared me to do it," he said; he was always so wild—
And idle—and couldn't be idle—my Willy—he never could rest.
The King should have made him a soldier, he would have been one
        of his best.

7

But he lived with a lot of wild mates, and they never would let him
        be good;
30 They swore that he dare not rob the mail, and he swore that he would;
And he took no life, but he took one purse, and when all was done
He flung it among his fellows—"I'll none of it," said my son.

8

I came into court to the judge and the lawyers. I told them my tale,
God's own truth—but they killed him, they killed him for robbing
        the mail.
35 They hanged him in chains for a show—we had always borne a good
        name—
To be hanged for a thief—and then put away—isn't that enough shame?
Dust to dust—low down—let us hide! but they set him so high
That all the ships of the world could stare at him, passing by.
God'ill pardon the hell-black raven and horrible fowls of the air,
40 But not the black heart of the lawyer who killed him and hanged
        him there.

9

And the jailer forced me away. I had bid him my last good-bye;
They had fastened the door of his cell. "O mother!" I heard him cry.
I couldn't get back though I tried, he had something further to say,
And now I never shall know it. The jailer forced me away.

10

45 Then since I couldn't but hear that cry of my boy that was dead,
They seized me and shut me up; they fastened me down on my bed.
"Mother, O mother!"—he called in the dark to me year after year—
They beat me for that, they beat me—you know that I couldn't but hear;
And then at the last they found I had grown so stupid and still
50 They let me abroad again—but the creatures had worked their will.

214

11

Flesh of my flesh was gone, but bone of my bone was left—
I stole them all from the lawyers—and you, will you call it a theft?—
My baby, the bones that had sucked me, the bones that had laughed
    and had cried—
Theirs? O, no! they are mine—not theirs—they had moved in my side.

12

55 Do you think I was scared by the bones? I kissed 'em, I buried 'em all—
I can't dig deep, I am old—in the night by the churchyard wall.
My Willy'ill rise up whole when the trumpet of judgment'ill sound,
But I charge you never to say that I laid him in holy ground.

13

They would scratch him up—they would hang him again on the
    cursed tree.
60 Sin? O, yes, we are sinners, I know—let all that be,
And read me a Bible verse of the Lord's goodwill toward men—
"Full of compassion and mercy, the Lord"—let me hear it again;
"Full of compassion and mercy—long-suffering." Yes, O, yes!
For the lawyer is born but to murder—the Saviour lives but to bless.
65 *He'll* never put on the black cap except for the worst of the worst,
And the first may be last—I have heard it in church—and the last
    may be first.
Suffering—O, long-suffering—yes, as the Lord must know,
Year after year in the mist and the wind and the shower and the snow.

14

Heard, have you? what? they have told you he never repented his sin.
70 How do they know it? are *they* his mother? are *you* of his kin?
Heard! have you ever heard, when the storm on the downs began,
The wind that'ill wail like a child and the sea that'ill moan like a man?

15

Election, Election, and Reprobation—it's all very well.
But I go tonight to my boy, and I shall not find him in hell.
75 For I cared so much for my boy that the Lord has looked into my care,
And He means me I'm sure to be happy with Willy, I know not where.

16

And if *he* be lost—but to save *my* soul, that is all your desire—
Do you think that I care for *my* soul if my boy be gone to the fire?
I have been with God in the dark—go, go, you may leave me alone—
80 You never have borne a child—you are just as hard as a stone.

continued

17

Madam, I beg your pardon! I think that you mean to be kind,
But I cannot hear what you say for my Willy's voice in the wind—
The snow and the sky so bright—he used but to call in the dark,
And he calls to me now from the church and not from the gibbet—
     for hark!
85 Nay—you can hear it yourself—it is coming—shaking the walls—
Willy—the moon's in a cloud—Good-night. I am going. He calls.

commentary

According to his manuscript notes, Tennyson based his poem on an incident recounted in an article concerning a Mrs. Phoebe Hessel, which appeared in "some penny magazine called *Old Brighton.*"

". . . After the death of her second husband, William Hessel, by the assistance of some friends she purchased a donkey and travelled with fish and other commodities to the villages about Brighton.

"It was in one of these journeys that she obtained such information as led to the arrest and conviction of Rooke and Howell for robbing the mail, a circumstance which made a considerable sensation at the close of the last century. They were gibbeted on the spot where the robbery was committed, and there is an affecting story connected with Rooke. When the elements had caused the clothes and flesh to decay, his aged mother, night after night, in all weathers, and the more tempestuous the weather the more frequent the visits, made a sacred pilgrimage to the lonely spot at the Downs, and it was noticed that on her return she always brought something away with her in her apron. Upon being watched it was discovered that the bones of the hanging man were the objects of her search, and as the wind and rain scattered them on the ground she conveyed them to her home. There she kept them, and, when the gibbet was stripped of its horrid burden, in the dead silence of the night she interred them in the hallowed enclosure of Old Shoreham Churchyard. What a sad story of a Brighton Rizpah!"

                                    Hallam Tennyson

interpretation

1. "Rizpah" is a dramatic monologue. (See *Handbook of Terms and Techniques.*) Who is the listener? What do you learn about the speaker as she tells her story?
2. Why does the Tennyson commentary speak of the mother as a "Brighton Rizpah"?

From ALFRED LORD TENNYSON: A MEMOIR BY HIS SON by Hallam Tennyson. Copyright 1899 by Macmillan Company.

RINGING THE BELLS

ANNE SEXTON

And this is the way they ring
the bells in Bedlam[1]
and this is the bell-lady
who comes each Tuesday morning
5 to give us a music lesson
and because the attendants make you go
and because we mind by instinct,
like bees caught in the wrong hive,
we are the circle of the crazy ladies
10 who sit in the lounge of the mental house
and smile at the smiling woman
who passes us each a bell,
who points at my hand
that holds my bell, E flat,
15 and this is the gray dress next to me
who grumbles as if it were special
to be old, to be old,
and this is the small hunched squirrel girl
on the other side of me
20 who picks at the hairs over her lip,
who picks at the hairs over her lip all day,
and this is how the bells really sound,
as untroubled and clean
as a workable kitchen,
25 and this is always my bell responding
to my hand that responds to the lady
who points at me, E flat;
and although we are no better for it,
they tell you to go. And you do.

interpretation

1. What is the situation described? Why do you think the poet uses repetition in describing it?
2. There are some rather striking figures of speech in lines 8, 15, and 22–24. Identify each of them and explain why they are appropriate in this particular poem.

From TO BEDLAM AND PART WAY BACK by Anne Sexton. Copyright © 1960 by Anne Sexton. Reprinted by permission of Houghton Mifflin Company.

1. *Bedlam*, a madhouse, insane asylum. [*Archaic*]

The man "in the house of Bedlam" was the internationally famous American poet, Ezra Loomis Pound (1885-1972). In 1946 he was arrested for treason, having broadcast Fascist propaganda over the Italian radio during World War II. He never stood trial, because psychiatrists declared him insane, and he was committed to St. Elizabeth's Hospital in Washington, D.C. He was released, after twelve years, largely through the efforts of other American poets, among them Elizabeth Bishop, William Carlos Williams, and Robert Frost. Pound returned to Italy, where he remained until his death.

VISITS TO ST. ELIZABETHS (1950)

ELIZABETH BISHOP

This is the house of Bedlam.

This is the man
that lies in the house of Bedlam.

This is the time
5 of the tragic man
that lies in the house of Bedlam.

This is a wristwatch
telling the time
of the talkative man
10 that lies in the house of Bedlam.

This is a sailor
wearing the watch
that tells the time
of the honored man
15 that lies in the house of Bedlam.

This is the roadstead all of board
reached by the sailor
wearing the watch
that tells the time
20 of the old, brave man
that lies in the house of Bedlam.

These are the years and the walls of the ward,
the winds and clouds of the sea of board
sailed by the sailor
25   wearing the watch
that tells the time
of the cranky man
that lies in the house of Bedlam.

This is a Jew in a newspaper hat
30   that dances weeping down the ward
over the creaking sea of board
beyond the sailor
winding his watch
that tells the time
35   of the cruel man
that lies in the house of Bedlam.

This is a world of books gone flat.
This is a Jew in a newspaper hat
that dances weeping down the ward
40   over the creaking sea of board
of the batty sailor
that winds his watch
that tells the time
of the busy man
45   that lies in the house of Bedlam.

This is a boy that pats the floor
to see if the world is there, is flat,
for the widowed Jew in the newspaper hat
that dances weeping down the ward
50   waltzing the length of a weaving board
by the silent sailor
that hears his watch
that ticks the time
of the tedious man
55   that lies in the house of Bedlam.

These are the years and the walls and the door
that shut on a boy that pats the floor

to feel if the world is there and flat.
This is a Jew in a newspaper hat
60 that dances joyfully down the ward
into the parting seas of board
past the staring sailor
that shakes his watch
that tells the time
65 of the poet, the man
that lies in the house of Bedlam.

This is a soldier home from the war.
These are the years and the walls and the door
that shut on a boy that pats the floor
70 to see if the world is round or flat.
This is a Jew in a newspaper hat
that dances carefully down the ward,
walking the plank of a coffin board
with the crazy sailor
75 that shows his watch
that tells the time
of the wretched man
that lies in the house of Bedlam.

interpretation

1. Miss Bishop has adopted the old form of "The House That Jack Built," which employs cumulative repetition. What effect does repetition have on the length of the stanzas? What does it contribute to tone and meaning?

2. In stanza 2 "the man / that lies in the house of Bedlam" is introduced; in the second last line of all subsequent stanzas he is characterized. Note the words used to describe him. Do they give you a coherent idea of the man? Explain.

THE FIRST DAY'S NIGHT HAD COME

EMILY DICKINSON

The first Day's Night had come—
And grateful that a thing
So terrible—had been endured—
I told my Soul to sing—

5 She said her Strings were snapt—
Her Bow—to Atoms blown—
And so to mend her—gave me work
Until another Morn—

And then—a Day as huge
10 As Yesterdays in pairs,
Unrolled its horror in my face—
Until it blocked my eyes—

My Brain—begun to laugh—
I mumbled—like a fool—
15 And tho' 'tis Years ago—that Day—
My Brain keeps giggling—still.

And Something's odd—within—
That person that I was—
And this One—do not feel the same—
20 Could it be Madness—this?

---

interpretation

1. The speaker does not tell us what the experience—the terrible thing—was; but she describes its fearful consequences. It has left her a divided person—has brought on what amounts to schizophrenia. Describe the ways in which the poet expresses this sense of a divided self.
2. Why, do you think, is personification appropriate as the basic figure of speech in this poem?
3. Comment on the use of the word *giggling* in line 16. It is a simple enough word, but what are its connotations in the present context?

SONNET ON NIGHTMARES

J. S. MANIFOLD

When bright Orion[1] has declined
His aim obliquely from the Pole,
And darkness taken full control
Of earth and sleeping humankind,

5 Stampeding from the wastes behind,
The skewbald nightmare and her foal
Plunge their great hoofs and caracole[2]
Against the fences of the mind.

Hold, screaming wire and splintering rail!
10 Panic, not malice, drives the beast;
She dare not linger to break in,

For, racing closer on her tail,
She sniffs the horsemen of the East
Who patch their tents with nightmare-skin.

Originally published by Overland Publishers. Reprinted by permission of the author.

1. *Orion* (ô rī′ən; ō rī′ən), a constellation, represented as a hunter in illustrations of zodiacal signs.
2. *caracole* (kar′ə kōl), prance or turn in zigzag fashion.

"Sonnet on Nightmares" was written during the Cold-War or McCarthy-ite period when it seemed that the Western democracies were bent on stamping out the same civil liberties which they had successfully defended in 1939–45. Metaphorically, the bright stars were setting and darkness was taking full control.

In such darkness one might expect the nightmare of Fascism to return. I think that *skewbald* may have reference to the black, white and red banner of the Nazi party, though a skewbald (mare) is really black, white, and bay or chestnut.

So I implore "the fences of the mind," which shut out irrationality and brute violence, to hold firm. "The beast," the nightmare, is violent because it is panic-stricken; it is scared of the coming daylight, the first rays of the sun. Presently, any minute now, night will be gone, leaving nothing of the nightmare except little dark "patches" of cloud scattered on the "tent" of the sunlit sky.

At the same time I see the first rays of the sun as "horsemen of the East" belting across the sky on little scurrying Mongol ponies. No, they're not (consciously) modern Chinese cavalry—though that would make sense too—but rather the horsemen of Attila or Genghis Khan, coming from the *Morgenland* to chastise the corruption of Christianity. They would have no more awe of nightmares than they had of the anathemas of the Church, and would cheerfully put the shreds of a dismembered nightmare to some such casual use as "patching a tent."

I still find sonnet-form, which forces one to compress, a valuable discipline. In this case I have deliberately compressed still further by reducing the line-length from the standard five feet to four feet. French poets commonly do this, but it is not a common practice in English. Of course poetry is always more compact than prose, like those funny little dried flowers from Japan that we used to buy as children: put them in water and they swell up to life-size.

John Manifold

MY LAST DUCHESS

Ferrara[1]

ROBERT BROWNING

That's my last Duchess painted on the wall,
Looking as if she were alive. I call
That piece a wonder, now; Fra Pandolf's[2] hands
Worked busily a day, and there she stands.
5   Will't please you sit and look at her? I said
"Fra Pandolf" by design, for never read
Strangers like you that pictured countenance,
The depth and passion of its earnest glance,
But to myself they turned (since none puts by
10 The curtain I have drawn for you, but I)
And seemed as they would ask me, if they durst,
How such a glance came there: so, not the first
Are you to turn and ask thus. Sir, 'twas not
Her husband's presence only, called that spot
15 Of joy into the Duchess' cheek; perhaps
Fra Pandolf chanced to say, "Her mantle laps
Over my lady's wrist too much," or "Paint
Must never hope to reproduce the faint
Half-flush that dies along her throat": such stuff
20 Was courtesy, she thought, and cause enough
For calling up that spot of joy. She had
A heart—how shall I say?—too soon made glad,
Too easily impressed: she liked whate'er
She looked on, and her looks went everywhere.
25 Sir, 'twas all one! My favour at her breast,
The dropping of the daylight in the West,
The bough of cherries some officious fool
Broke in the orchard for her, the white mule
She rode with round the terrace—all and each
30 Would draw from her alike the approving speech,
Or blush, at least. She thanked men,—good! but thanked
Somehow—I know not how—as if she ranked
My gift of a nine-hundred-years-old name
With anybody's gift. Even had you skill

---

1. *Ferrara*, a city in northern Italy. During the Renaissance it was a center of art and culture. **2.** *Fra Pandolf*, an imaginary Renaissance painter.

35 In speech—(which I have not)—to make your will
Quite clear to such an one, and say "Just this
Or that in you disgusts me; here you miss,
Or there exceed the mark"—and if she let
Herself be lessoned so, nor plainly set
40 Her wits to yours, forsooth, and made excuse,
—E'en then would be some stooping; and I choose
Never to stoop. Oh, sir, she smiled, no doubt,
Whene'er I passed her; but who passed without
Much the same smile? This grew; I gave commands;
45 Then all smiles stopped together. There she stands
As if alive. Will't please you rise? We'll meet
The company below, then. I repeat,
The Count your master's known munificence
Is ample warrant that no just pretence
50 Of mine for dowry will be disallowed;
Though his fair daughter's self, as I avowed
At starting, is my object. Nay, we'll go
Together down, sir. Notice Neptune,[3] though,
Taming a sea-horse, thought a rarity,
55 Which Claus of Innsbruck[4] cast in bronze for me!

interpretation

1. What motivates the Duke's monologue? To whom is he speaking, and why?
2. What sort of person is the Duke?
3. Comment on the character of the Duchess. What, apparently, caused her death?
4. Comment on the symbolic significance of the statue of Neptune taming a seahorse mentioned in lines 53–55. What further insight into the Duke's personality does it provide?
5. This dramatic monologue is written in rhymed iambic pentameter couplets; yet the effect is conversational. How has the poet achieved this effect?

3. *Neptune,* Roman god of the sea. 4. *Claus of Innsbruck,* an imaginary Renaissance sculptor.

16

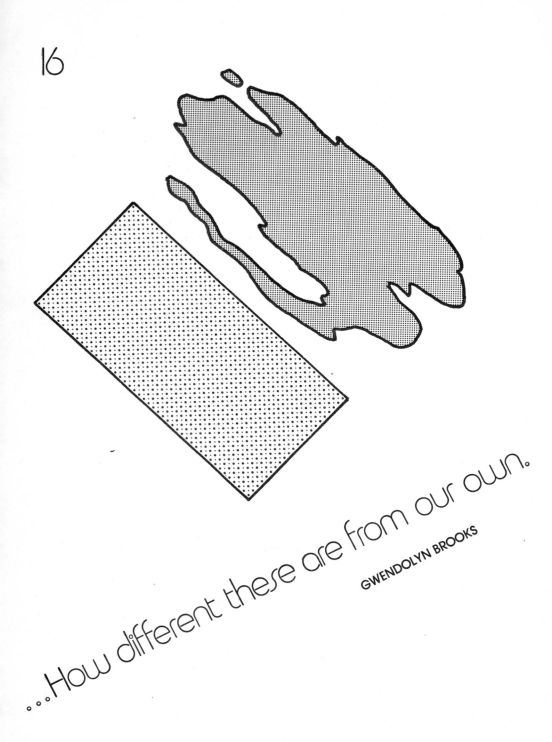

...How different these are from our own.

GWENDOLYN BROOKS

THE CASE FOR THE MINERS

SIEGFRIED SASSOON

Something goes wrong with my synthetic brain
When I defend the Strikers and explain
My reasons for not blackguarding[1] the Miners.
"What do you know?" exclaim my fellow-diners
5   (Peeling their plovers eggs[2] or lifting glasses
Of mellowed *Château Rentier*[3] from the table),
"What do you know about the working classes?"

I strive to hold my own; but I'm unable
To state the case succinctly. Indistinctly
10 I mumble about World-Emancipation,
Standards of Living, Nationalization
Of Industry; until they get me tangled
In superficial details; goad me on
To unconvincing vagueness. When we've wrangled
15 From soup to savoury, my temper's gone.

"Why should a miner earn six pounds a week?
Leisure! They'd only spend it in a bar!
Standard of life! You'll never teach them Greek
Or make them more contented than they are!"
20 That's how my port-flushed friends discuss the Strike.
And that's the reason why I shout and splutter.
And that's the reason why I'd almost like
To see them hawking matches in the gutter.

Interpretation

1. What event provides a background for the poem?
2. Characterize the people with whom the speaker argues. What do the details reveal about the kind of life they lead?
3. Check the rhyme scheme in the various stanzas. What differences do you find? What is the dominant meter? What effect does the combination of regularity and irregularity have on the poem as a whole? (See RHYME and RHYTHM in *Handbook of Terms and Techniques*.)

From COLLECTED POEMS by Siegfried Sassoon. All rights reserved. Reprinted by permission of The Viking Press, Inc., and G. T. Sassoon.

1. *blackguarding*, reviling or abusing foully. 2. *plovers eggs*, eggs of a shore-inhabiting bird, considered a great table delicacy. 3. *Château Rentier* (shä tô′ räN tyä′), a distinguished Bordeaux wine. *Château* indicates the castle or mansion of the estate on which the vineyard is located.

*It was an important moment in the history of blacks in the United States
when, in 1903, W. E. B. DuBois, a young black intellectual, made a
speech attacking Booker T. Washington, an important black leader and the
founder of Tuskegee Institute, for his advice to blacks to accept their
inferior social and political status in return for economic improvement.
Although Washington contributed much to the advancement of blacks, it was
DuBois' more militant ideas that were to win the future.*

BOOKER T. AND W. E. B.

DUDLEY RANDALL

"It seems to me," said Booker T.,
"It shows a mighty lot of cheek
To study chemistry and Greek
When Mister Charlie needs a hand
5 To hoe the cotton on his land,
And when Miss Ann looks for a cook,
Why stick your nose inside a book?"

"I don't agree," said W. E. B.,
"If I should have the drive to seek
10 Knowledge of chemistry or Greek,
I'll do it. Charles and Miss can look
Another place for hand or cook.
Some men rejoice in skill of hand,
And some in cultivating land,
15 But there are others who maintain
The right to cultivate the brain."

"It seems to me," said Booker T.,
"That all you folks have missed the boat
Who shout about the right to vote,
20 And spend vain days and sleepless nights
In uproar over civil rights.
Just keep your mouths shut, do not grouse,
But work, and save, and buy a house."

From POEM COUNTERPOEM, © 1966 by Margaret Danner and Dudley Randall. Reprinted by
permission of Broadside Press.

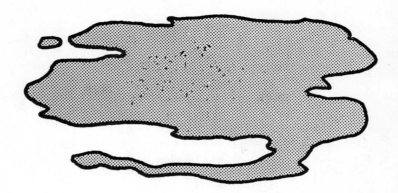

"I don't agree," said W. E. B.,
25 "For what can property avail
If dignity and justice fail.
Unless you help to make the laws,
They'll steal your house with trumped-up clause.
A rope's as tight, a fire as hot,
30 No matter how much cash you've got.
Speak soft, and try your little plan,
But as for me, I'll be a man."

"It seems to me," said Booker T.—

"I don't agree,"
35 Said W. E. B.

interpretation

A "quarrel" is going on in Randall's poem. How would you characterize it? Is it friendly, violent, intense? How do the rhythm and rhyme
affect the reader's reaction to the speeches and to the situation drama-
tized in the poem? Read the poem aloud for your analysis.

W. E. B. DuBOIS AT HARVARD

JAY WRIGHT

In Harvard Square,
the designing locks
swing to your pace.
The bells push you
5   toward the teasing dons.[1]
Bright boys begin to trill
their lamentable lessons.
It is too early for you.
All night, again, all night,
10   you've been at your
fledgling history,
passing through the old songs,
through the old laments.
But here, in Harvard Square,
15   the prosody[2] of those dark voices
is your connection.
In any square,
the evening bell
may be your release.

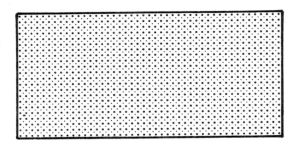

Interpretation

1. What impression of W. E. B. do you gain from "W. E. B. DuBois at Harvard"? Point out some of the details that help create this impression.
2. Contrast the tone of "Booker T. and W. E. B." with that of "W. E. B. DuBois at Harvard." How does the tone of the poem affect the impression of DuBois the reader receives?

From THE HOMECOMING SINGER by Jay Wright. Copyright © 1971. Reprinted by permission of Corinth Books.

1. *don,* a tutor or teaching assistant, or professor at a university. 2. *prosody,* the science of versification that examines meter, rhyme, and all areas of metrical structure. Here, the word probably refers to intonations and patterns of speech.

A POLISHED PERFORMANCE

D. J. ENRIGHT

Citizens of the polished capital
  Sigh for the towns up country,
And their innocent simplicity.

People in the towns up country
5   Applaud the unpolished innocence
Of the distant villages.

Dwellers in the distant villages
  Speak of a simple unspoilt girl,
Living alone, deep in the bush.

10 Deep in the bush we found her,
  Large and innocent of eye,
Among gentle gibbons[1] and mountain ferns.

Perfect for the part, perfect,
  Except for the dropsy
15 Which comes from polished rice.

In the capital our film is much admired,
  Its gentle gibbons and mountain ferns,
Unspoilt, unpolished, large and innocent of eye.

commentary

I was living in Bangkok at the time, and used to hear a lot about how "unspoilt," how spiritually superior, the people living in the country were—all this from city-dwellers who had no intention of leaving the fleshpots of Bangkok for the hardships of the country. There was a good deal of poverty, especially in Northeastern Thailand, and a sad lack of medical facilities . . . With this in mind, and reading a report that a film unit was on its way up north to film those "unspoilt" parts, I wrote the poem—wondering how the film director would handle the human element. Really the poem is a short gloss on the common saying, "Distance lends enchantment."

D. J. Enright

From THE TYPEWRITER REVOLUTION, (British title: SELECTED POEMS). © D. J. Enright. Reprinted by permission of Open Court Publishing Company and Chatto & Windus Ltd.

1. *gibbon*, a small, arboreal ape.

BEVERLY HILLS, CHICAGO

"and the people live till they have white hair" E. M. Price

GWENDOLYN BROOKS

The dry brown coughing beneath their feet,
(Only a while, for the handyman is on his way)
These people walk their golden gardens.
We say ourselves fortunate to be driving by today.

5   That we may look at them, in their gardens where
The summer ripeness rots. But not raggedly.
Even the leaves fall down in lovelier patterns here.
And the refuse, the refuse is a neat brilliancy.

When they flow sweetly into their houses
10 With softness and slowness touched by that everlasting gold,
We know what they go to. To tea. But that does not mean
They will throw some little black dots into some water and add
            sugar and the juice of the cheapest lemons that are sold,

While downstairs that woman's vague phonograph bleats, "Knock
      me a kiss."
And the living all to be made again in the sweatingest physical
      manner
15 Tomorrow. . . . Not that anybody is saying that these people have no
      trouble.
Merely that it is trouble with a gold-flecked beautiful banner.

Nobody is saying that these people do not ultimately cease to be. And
Sometimes their passings are even more painful than ours.
It is just that so often they live till their hair is white.
20 They make excellent corpses, among the expensive flowers. . . .

Nobody is furious. Nobody hates these people.
At least, nobody driving by in this car.
It is only natural, however, that it should occur to us
How much more fortunate they are than we are.

25 It is only natural that we should look and look
At their wood and brick and stone
And think, while a breath of pine blows,
How different these are from our own.

We do not want them to have less.
30 But it is only natural that we should think we have not enough.
We drive on, we drive on.
When we speak to each other our voices are a little gruff.

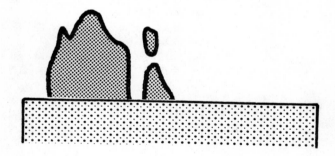

Interpretation

Poor people drive through an upper-class neighborhood, and how do
they see it? "Even the leaves fall down in lovelier patterns here." Can
this be? How? How can trouble be "trouble with a gold-flecked beautiful banner"? Why, at the end of the poem, are the voices in the car "a
little gruff"?

NEVERTHELESS

MARIANNE MOORE

> you've seen a strawberry
>   that's had a struggle; yet
>   was, where the fragments met,
>
> a hedgehog or a star-
> 5   fish for the multitude
>   of seeds. What better food
>
> than apple seeds—the fruit
>   within the fruit—locked in
>   like counter-curved twin
>
> 10 hazelnuts? Frost that kills
>   the little rubber-plant-
>   leaves of *kok-saghyz*-stalks, can't
>
> harm the roots; they still grow
>   in frozen ground. Once where
> 15   there was a prickly-pear-
>
> leaf clinging to barbed wire,
>   a root shot down to grow
>   in earth two feet below;
>
> as carrots form mandrakes
> 20   or a ram's-horn root some-
>   times. Victory won't come
>
> to me unless I go
>   to it; a grape tendril
>   ties a knot in knots till

25 knotted thirty times—so
      the bound twig that's under-
      gone and over-gone, can't stir.

    The weak overcomes its
      menace, the strong over-
30   comes itself. What is there

    like fortitude! What sap
      went through that little thread
      to make the cherry red!

commentary

Imagine that someone has just remarked on the fragility and vulnerability of things, and the poet replies by agreeing mildly, and then
saying, "Nevertheless. . . ." This title must be read as the first word
of the poem: Nevertheless, there are examples of extraordinary fortitude
in the face of adversity. A strawberry that hasn't had enough water or
protection from the sun survives by knotting its seeds into a cluster
that resembles a hedgehog or a starfish. The apple locks its seeds into
a hazelnut-shaped container at the center of the fruit. The roots of
rubber plants survive the frost that kills the leaves. A prickly-pear
leaf caught on a barbed-wire fence sends down a root to the ground
below. Carrots without sufficient nourishment or favorable soil may
grow into grotesque shapes, but they survive. A grape tendril knots
itself a multitude of times in order to keep the grape plant sturdy. All
of these are examples of "victory" won in the face of defeat, of the weak
overcoming threats of extinction, of strength surviving the dangers of
its own strength. The final example is an example of common "fortitude"—the strength and determination that forced the sap through
those very delicate veins in the cherry to make it red.

                                                    James E. Miller, Jr.

THE WELL DRESSED MAN WITH A BEARD

WALLACE STEVENS

> After the final no there comes a yes
> And on that yes the future world depends.
> No was the night. Yes is this present sun.
> If the rejected things, the things denied,
> 5 Slid over the western cataract, yet one,
> One only, one thing that was firm, even
> No greater than a cricket's horn, no more
> Than a thought to be rehearsed all day, a speech
> Of the self that must sustain itself on speech,
> 10 One thing remaining, infallible, would be
> Enough. Ah! douce campagna¹ of that thing!
> Ah! douce campagna, honey in the heart,
> Green in the body, out of a petty phrase,
> Out of a thing believed, a thing affirmed:
> 15 The form on the pillow humming while one sleeps,
> The aureole above the humming house . . .
>
> It can never be satisfied, the mind, never.

---

interpretation

1. Would you say this poem makes an affirmative or a negative statement about life? Cite phrases or lines to support your answer.
2. The speaker demands only "one thing that was firm." Does this have to be an important thing? Why do you think it is referred to as "honey in the heart"?
3. What resemblances do you find between this poem and Marianne Moore's "Nevertheless"?
4. "The Well Dressed Man with a Beard" is written in blank verse. (See *Handbook of Terms and Techniques.*) What devices does the poet use to give the form variety? Would you describe the overall effect as oratorical, conversational, singsong? Or would you use some other word to describe it?

---

1. *douce campagna* (düs′ käm pä′nyə), sweet country.

HOMAGE

KENNETH FEARING

They said to him, "It is a very good thing that you have done, yes,
    both good and great, proving this other passage to the Indies.
    Marvelous," they said. "Very. But where, Señor, is the gold?"

They said: "We like it, we admire it very much, don't misunder-
5   stand us, in fact we think it's almost great. But isn't there,
    well, a little too much of this Prince of Denmark? After all,
    there is no one quite like you in your lighter vein."
"Astonishing," they said. "Who would have thought you had it in
    you, Orville?" They said, "Wilbur, this machine of yours is
10   amazing, if it works, and perhaps some day we can use it to
    distribute eggs, or to advertise."

And they were good people, too. Decent people.
They did not beat their wives. They went to church. And they kept
    the law.

BEGINNERS

WALT WHITMAN

How they are provided for upon the earth, (appearing at intervals,)
How dear and dreadful they are to the earth,
How they inure to themselves as much as to any—
    what a paradox appears their age,
How people respond to them, yet know them not,
5   How there is something relentless in their fate all times,
How all times mischoose the objects of their adulation and reward,
And how the same inexorable price must still be paid for the same
    great purchase.

interpretation

1. How are Columbus, Shakespeare, and the Wright brothers of the
first poem related to the "beginners" of the second poem?
2. Describe the differences in tone between the two poems. Comment
on Fearing's use of "Homage" as a title.

"Homage" reprinted from NEW AND SELECTED POEMS by Kenneth Fearing. Copyright © 1956
by Kenneth Fearing. Reprinted by permission of Indiana University Press.

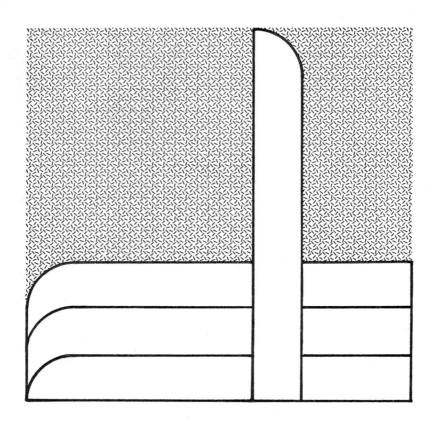

He knew a path that wanted walking...

ROBERT FROST

A MAN'S A MAN FOR A' THAT

ROBERT BURNS

Is there, for honest poverty,
   That hings his head, an' a' that?
The coward slave, we pass him by,
   We dare be poor for a' that!
5   For a' that, an' a' that,
      Our toils obscure, an' a' that;
     The rank is but the guinea's stamp[1];
     The man's the gowd[2] for a' that.

What tho' on hamely fare we dine,
10   Wear hodden gray,[3] an' a' that?
Gie fools their silks, and knaves their wine,
   A man's a man for a' that!
     For a' that, an' a' that,
      Their tinsel show, an' a' that;
15   The honest man, tho' e'er sae poor,
     Is king o' men for a' that.

Ye see yon birkie,[4] ca'd a lord,
   Wha struts, an' stares, an' a' that?
Tho' hundreds worship at his word,
20   He's but a coof[5] for a' that!
     For a' that, an' a' that,
      His riband, star, an' a' that;
     The man o' independent mind,
     He looks and laughs at a' that.

continued

---

1. *guinea's stamp*, the imprint of the King's head on a coin as a statement of its value. **2.** *gowd*, gold. **3.** *hodden gray*, coarse gray woolen cloth, undyed. **4.** *birkie*, young fellow. **5.** *coof*, fool.

25 A prince can mak a belted knight,
    A marquis, duke, an' a' that;
    But an honest man's aboon[6] his might,
    Guid faith he mauna fa'[7] that!
      For a' that, an' a' that,
30   Their dignities, an' a' that;
    The pith o' sense, an' pride o' worth,
    Are higher rank than a' that.

    Then let us pray that come it may,
    As come it will for a' that,
35 That sense and worth, o'er a' the earth,
    May bear the gree,[8] an' a' that;
      For a' that, an' a' that,
      It's coming yet, for a' that,
    That man to man, the warld o'er,
40   Shall brothers be for a' that!

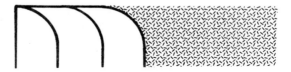

interpretation

1. Robert Burns wrote in the latter eighteenth century when lords and princes played a prominent role and there was clear social stratification. Does this aspect of his poem have meaning today?
2. Burns makes use of a refrain. How does he vary the refrain? What is its function?

6. *aboon*, above. 7. *mauna fa'*, must not claim or get. 8. *bear the gree*, have the prize.

Toussaint L'Ouverture (tü saɴ′ lü ver tür′), the black man who liberated
Haiti, was born in 1743 in what was then the French colony of St. Dominique.
A slave who learned to read and write, he was the military leader of
the slaves during their revolt against their French masters. In 1801 he became
ruler of the entire island of Haiti and set up a good administration.
Napoleon, emperor of France, sent troops to reconquer Haiti and reestablish
slavery. Toussaint resisted, was arrested by treachery, and sent to France
in June 1802. He died there, a prisoner, the following year.

TO TOUSSAINT L'OUVERTURE

WILLIAM WORDSWORTH

> Toussaint, the most unhappy man of men!
> Whether the whistling Rustic tend his plough
> Within thy hearing, or thy head be now
> Pillowed in some deep dungeon's earless den;—
> 5   O miserable Chieftain! where and when
> Wilt thou find patience! Yet die not; do thou
> Wear rather in thy bonds a cheerful brow:
> Though fallen thyself, never to rise again,
> Live, and take comfort. Thou hast left behind
> 10   Powers that will work for thee; air, earth, and skies;
> There's not a breathing of the common wind
> That will forget thee; thou hast great allies;
> Thy friends are exultations, agonies,
> And love, and man's unconquerable mind.

---

interpretation

1. What indications do you find that this poem was written while Toussaint was alive?
2. In what does the poet tell Toussaint to "take comfort"?

SONNET: POLITICAL GREATNESS

PERCY BYSSHE SHELLEY

Nor happiness, nor majesty, nor fame,
Nor peace, nor strength, nor skill in arms or arts,
Shepherd those herds whom tyranny makes tame;
Verse echoes not one beating of their hearts,
5 History is but the shadow of their shame,
Art veils her glass, or from the pageant starts
As to oblivion their blind millions fleet,
Staining that Heaven with obscene imagery
Of their own likeness. What are numbers knit
10 By force or custom? Man who man would be,
Must rule the empire of himself, in it
Must be supreme, establishing his throne
On vanquished will, quelling the anarchy
Of hopes and fears, being himself alone.

Interpretation

1. What kinds of people does Shelley characterize as "herds" (line 3)?
What impression is conveyed by use of this term?
2. According to the poet, in what does greatness consist?

UPON THIS AGE

EDNA ST. VINCENT MILLAY

Upon this age, that never speaks its mind,
This furtive age, this age endowed with power
To wake the moon with footsteps, fit an oar
Into the rowlocks of the wind, and find
5   What swims before his prow, what swirls behind—
Upon this gifted age, in its dark hour,
Rains from the sky a meteoric shower
Of facts . . . they lie unquestioned, uncombined.
Wisdom enough to leech[1] us of our ill
10 Is daily spun; but there exists no loom
To weave it into fabric; undefiled
Proceeds pure Science, and has her say; but still
Upon this world from the collective womb
Is spewed all day the red triumphant child.

Interpretation

1. Of what age is the poet speaking? Cite images to prove your point.
2. Explain the image of the thread and the loom (lines 9–11). Why do you think the poet characterizes this age as "furtive" (line 2) and in a "dark hour" (line 6)?
3. The sonnets by Wordsworth, Shelley, and this one by Millay all affirm individuality or independence. Compare and contrast these affirmations.
4. Compare the structure of the sonnets. Which follows most closely the traditional sonnet form?

From COLLECTED POEMS, Harper & Row. Copyright 1939, 1967 by Edna St. Vincent Millay and Norma Millay Ellis. Reprinted by permission of Norma Millay Ellis, Literary Executor.

1. *leech*, to cure or heal as by a physician.

I HEAR AMERICA SINGING

WALT WHITMAN

I hear America singing, the varied carols I hear,
Those of mechanics, each one singing his as it should be blithe and
    strong,
The carpenter singing his as he measures his plank or beam,
The mason singing his as he makes ready for work, or leaves off work,
5 The boatman singing what belongs to him in his boat, the deckhand
    singing on the steamboat deck,
The shoemaker singing as he sits on his bench, the hatter singing as
    he stands,
The wood-cutter's song, the ploughboy's on his way in the morning,
    or at noon intermission or at sundown,
The delicious singing of the mother, or of the young wife at work,
    or of the girl sewing or washing,
Each singing what belongs to him or her and to none else,
10 The day what belongs to the day—at night the party of young fellows,
    robust, friendly,
Singing with open mouths their strong melodious songs.

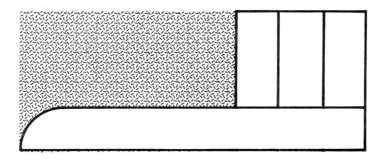

I, TOO, SING AMERICA

LANGSTON HUGHES

I, too, sing America.

I am the darker brother.
They send me to eat in the kitchen
When company comes,
5 But I laugh,
And eat well,
And grow strong.

Tomorrow,
I'll be at the table
10 When company comes.
Nobody'll dare
Say to me,
"Eat in the kitchen,"
Then.

15 Besides,
They'll see how beautiful I am
And be ashamed—

I, too, am America.

interpretation

In what sense might this poem be considered a response to the Whitman poem?

INDEPENDENCE

I will think of the leech-gatherer[1] on the lonely moor.—Wordsworth

NANCY CATO

How the red road stretched before us, mile on mile
Narrowing into the distance, straight as though ruled
On yellow paper, away to the lilac hills
Low on the horizon. Above them the storm-clouds piled
5   In a sky blue as though bruised, yet all ahead
Was glowing in an unearthly wash of light—
Dry roly-poly and saltbush[2] lit to beauty,
The sky a menace, but the wide plains bright.

And there in that lonely place an ancient swagman,
10   Traveller, bagman, sundowner,[3] what you will—
His rolled-up blankets slung aslant his shoulders,
Billy,[4] dangling, his back to the line of hills
And the coming storm; as mysterious in that place
(With his hat set straight and his grey beard blowing)
15   As a small ship glimpsed a moment far from land.
Where did he come from, where could he be going?

I shall never know, for we had to race the rain
That turns the blacksoil plains to a gluey mud
Bogging to the axles. Only a wave of the hand,
20   But still the imagination glows, the blood
Stirs at the memory of that symbolic stranger
Glimpsed in a moment of vision, and swiftly gone:
Man and his independent spirit, alone
On the vast plains, with night and rain coming on.

From THE DARKENED WINDOW, (Published by the Lyre Bird Writers). Reprinted by permission of Angus & Robertson (Publishers) Pty. Ltd.

1. *leech-gatherer,* a character that represents independence in Wordsworth's poem "Resolution and Independence." 2. *roly-poly and saltbush.* Roly-poly is the tumbleweed, and saltbush is the shrub-like plant found in certain arid regions of Australia. 3. *swagman . . . sundowner,* various names for the vagabond of the Australian bush country, who carries his personal belongings in a bundle (swag). 4. *Billy,* a can made of tin or enamel with a lid and usually a handle.

A PEASANT

R. S. THOMAS

Iago Prytherch his name, though, be it allowed,
Just an ordinary man of the bald Welsh hills,
Who pens a few sheep in a gap of cloud.
Docking mangels,[1] chipping the green skin
5 From the yellow bones with a half-witted grin
Of satisfaction, or churning the crude earth
To a stiff sea of clods that glint in the wind—
So are his days spent, his spittled mirth
Rarer than the sun that cracks the cheeks
10 Of the gaunt sky perhaps once in a week.
And then at night see him fixed in his chair
Motionless, except when he leans to gob in the fire.
There is something frightening in the vacancy of his mind.
His clothes, sour with years of sweat
15 And animal contact, shock the refined,
But affected, sense with their stark naturalness.
Yet this is your prototype, who, season by season
Against siege of rain and the wind's attrition,
Preserves his stock, an impregnable fortress
20 Not to be stormed even in death's confusion.
Remember him then, for he, too, is a winner of wars,
Enduring like a tree under the curious stars.

interpretation

1. Thomas gives us a close-up of a Welsh peasant. Pick out images that make the man and his surroundings vivid. In what essential ways does this portrait differ from Nancy Cato's description of the Australian swagman?

2. What do the swagman and the peasant have in common? Compare the ways in which the poets make their points or draw their conclusions.

From SONG AT THE YEAR'S TURNING by R. S. Thomas. Reprinted by permission of Granada Publishing Limited.

1. *mangels*, large beets used for cattle feed.

A LONE STRIKER

ROBERT FROST

The swinging mill bell changed its rate
To tolling like the count of fate,
And though at that the tardy ran,
One failed to make the closing gate.
5 There was a law of God or man
That on the one who came too late
The gate for half an hour be locked,
His time be lost, his pittance docked.
He stood rebuked and unemployed.
10 The straining mill began to shake.
The mill, though many-many-eyed,
Had eyes inscrutably opaque;
So that he couldn't look inside
To see if some forlorn machine
15 Was standing idle for his sake.
(He couldn't hope its heart would break.)

And yet he thought he saw the scene:
The air was full of dust of wool.
A thousand yarns were under pull,
20 But pull so slow, with such a twist,
All day from spool to lesser spool,
It seldom overtaxed their strength;
They safely grew in slender length.
And if one broke by any chance,
25 The spinner saw it at a glance.
The spinner still was there to spin.
That's where the human still came in.
Her deft hand showed with finger rings
Among the harplike spread of strings.
30 She caught the pieces end to end
And, with a touch that never missed,
Not so much tied as made them blend.
Man's ingenuity was good.
He saw it plainly where he stood,
35 Yet found it easy to resist.

He knew another place, a wood,
And in it, tall as trees, were cliffs;
And if he stood on one of these,
'Twould be among the tops of trees,
40 Their upper branches round him wreathing,
Their breathing mingled with his breathing.
If—if he stood! Enough of ifs!
He knew a path that wanted walking;
He knew a spring that wanted drinking;
45 A thought that wanted further thinking;
A love that wanted re-renewing.
Nor was this just a way of talking
To save him the expense of doing.
With him it boded action, deed.

50 The factory was very fine;
He wished it all the modern speed.
Yet, after all, 'twas not divine,
That is to say, 'twas not a church.
He never would assume that he'd
55 Be any institution's need.
But he said then and still would say,
If there should ever come a day
When industry seemed like to die
Because he left it in the lurch,
60 Or even merely seemed to pine
For want of his approval, why,
Come get him—they knew where to search.

interpretation

1. State briefly the situation described in the poem.
2. Frost's lines sometimes seem simpler than they are—often they are ironic, or filled with much more meaning than they appear to state outright; or they suggest allegorical or symbolic elaborations. Explore the ramifications of the following: "There was a law of God or man . . ." (lines 5–8); "That's where the human still came in" (line 27); "He knew a path that wanted walking" (line 43); "He never would assume that he'd / Be any institution's need" (lines 54–55).
3. Does the independence of Frost's worker differ from that of Nancy Cato's swagman and Thomas' peasant? Explain your answer.

18

Who said a watched clock never moves?

LOUIS MACNEICE

THE SLOW STARTER

LOUIS MACNEICE

A watched clock never moves, they said:
Leave it alone and you'll grow up.
Nor will the sulking holiday train
Start sooner if you stamp your feet.
5   He left the clock to go its way;
   The whistle blew, the train went gay.

Do not press me so, she said;
Leave me alone and I will write
But not just yet, I am sure you know
10 The problem. Do not count the days.
   He left the calendar alone;
   The postman knocked, no letter came.

O never force the pace, they said;
Leave it alone, you have lots of time,
15 Your kind of work is none the worse
For slow maturing. Do not rush.
   He took their tip, he took his time,
   And found his time and talent gone.

Oh you have had your chance, It said;
20 Left it alone and it was one.
Who said a watched clock never moves?
Look at it now. Your chance was I.
   He turned and saw the accusing clock
   Race like a torrent round a rock.

interpretation

1. Each of the first three stanzas describes a missed opportunity. Explain what each is, and compare the opportunities.
2. In the last stanza, what is the "It" of line 19? Compare the first line of the poem with the last two lines.

From THE COLLECTED POEMS OF LOUIS MACNEICE, edited by E. R. Dodds, Copyright ©
The Estate of Louis MacNeice 1966. Reprinted by permission of Oxford University Press and Faber
and Faber Ltd.

ANYONE LIVED IN A PRETTY HOW TOWN

E. E. CUMMINGS

anyone lived in a pretty how town
(with up so floating many bells down)
spring summer autumn winter
he sang his didn't he danced his did.

5 Women and men(both little and small)
cared for anyone not at all
they sowed their isn't they reaped their same
sun moon stars rain

children guessed(but only a few
10 and down they forgot as up they grew
autumn winter spring summer)
that noone loved him more by more

when by now and tree by leaf
she laughed his joy she cried his grief
15 bird by snow and stir by still
anyone's any was all to her

someones married their everyones
laughed their cryings and did their dance
(sleep wake hope and then)they
20 said their nevers they slept their dream

stars rain sun moon
(and only the snow can begin to explain
how children are apt to forget to remember
with up so floating many bells down)

25 one day anyone died i guess
(and noone stooped to kiss his face)
busy folk buried them side by side
little by little and was by was

all by all and deep by deep
30 and more by more they dream their sleep
noone and anyone earth by april
wish by spirit and if by yes.

Women and men(both dong and ding)
summer autumn winter spring
35 reaped their sowing and went their came
sun moon stars rain

commentary

E. E. Cummings nearly always rips language apart and puts it back
together again, seemingly in random fashion. But only *seemingly*, because he uses his displaced parts of speech and his disrupted syntax
to get more, not less, meaning. This poem can be read as a simple love
story between a boy (anyone) and a girl (noone) who lived, loved, married, and died in a small town where other people did the same. But
the language suggests a general or allegorical meaning: *anyone* might
be everyman, his "pretty how town" every place, and such subtly shifting refrains as "sun moon stars rain" might represent all time.

Note how the town (at which we might exclaim "how pretty") is described in the second line: "with up so floating many bells down." The
language is very suggestive. Is the town down in a valley, perhaps,
with a church whose bells make sounds that float up into the surrounding heights? But note how the line is repeated and its meaning connected with the children's memory in stanza 6. In this stanza the "up
so floating" line takes on more the characteristics of mental activity,
with experiences standing to the fore and then fading into the past.
Note also the suggestiveness of line 4, in which anyone "sang his didn't"
and "danced his did." Could this mean, perhaps, that *anyone* sang about
the things he did not do, and he danced to the tune of the things he
actually did?

James E. Miller, Jr.

interpretation

Let the suggestiveness of Cummings' language play on your imagination,
and speculate on the meaning of the following lines:

they sowed their isn't they reaped their same (line 7)
and down they forgot as up they grew (line 10)
when by now and tree by leaf (line 13)
said their nevers they slept their dream (line 20)
reaped their sowing and went their came (line 35)

253

IN TIME OF "THE BREAKING OF NATIONS"

THOMAS HARDY

1

Only a man harrowing clods
  In a slow silent walk
With an old horse that stumbles and nods
  Half asleep as they stalk.

2

5 Only thin smoke without flame
  From the heaps of couch-grass;
Yet this will go onward the same
  Though Dynasties pass.

3

Yonder a maid and her wight[1]
10   Come whispering by:
War's annals will fade into night
  Ere their story die.

Interpretation

A man working in the fields, a pile of coarse creeping grass smoldering, a girl and her boyfriend passing—out of these images Hardy fashions a statement of what endures in contrast with what passes. Why these images? In what sense will they go "onward" while dynasties and wars pass and fade?

1. *wight,* a person; here, a sweetheart.

THE CHESTNUT CASTS HIS FLAMBEAUX[1]

A. E. HOUSMAN

>The chestnut casts his flambeaux, and the flowers
>   Stream from the hawthorn on the wind away,
>The doors clap to, the pane is blind with showers.
>   Pass me the can, lad; there's an end of May.
>
>5 There's one spoilt spring to scant our mortal lot,
>   One season ruined of our little store.
>May will be fine next year as like as not:
>   Oh ay, but then we shall be twenty-four.
>
>We for a certainty are not the first
>10   Have sat in taverns while the tempest hurled
>Their hopeful plans to emptiness, and cursed
>   Whatever brute and blackguard made the world.
>
>It is in truth iniquity on high
>   To cheat our sentenced souls of aught they crave,
>15 And mar the merriment as you and I
>   Fare on our long fool's-errand to the grave.
>
>Iniquity it is; but pass the can.
>   My lad, no pair of kings our mothers bore;
>Our only portion is the estate of man:
>20   We want the moon, but we shall get no more.
>
>If here today the cloud of thunder lours
>   Tomorrow it will hie on far behests;
>The flesh will grieve on other bones than ours
>   Soon, and the soul will mourn in other breasts.
>
>25 The troubles of our proud and angry dust
>   Are from eternity, and shall not fail.
>Bear them we can, and if we can we must.
>   Shoulder the sky, my lad, and drink your ale.

Interpretation

1. Sketch the situation described in the poem.
2. Is Housman's advice in the last line of the poem good advice?

From THE COLLECTED POEMS OF A. E. HOUSMAN. Copyright 1922 by Holt, Rinehart and Winston, Inc. Copyright 1950 by Barclays Bank Ltd. Reprinted by permission of Holt, Rinehart and Winston, Inc., The Society of Authors as the literary representative of the Estate of A. E. Housman; and Jonathan Cape Ltd., publishers of A. E. Housman's COLLECTED POEMS.

1. *chestnut . . . flambeaux.* The chestnut tree bears conically shaped groups of flowers during May. To the poet these flowers suggest flaming torches, or *flambeaux.*

THE GROUNDHOG

RICHARD EBERHART

In June, amid the golden fields,
I saw a groundhog lying dead.
Dead lay he; my senses shook,
And mind outshot our naked frailty.
5 There lowly in the vigorous summer
His form began its senseless change,
And made my senses waver dim
Seeing nature ferocious in him.
Inspecting close his maggots' might
10 And seething cauldron of his being,
Half with loathing, half with a strange love,
I poked him with an angry stick.
The fever arose, became a flame
And Vigour circumscribed the skies,
15 Immense energy in the sun,
And through my frame a sunless trembling.
My stick had done nor good nor harm.
Then stood I silent in the day
Watching the object, as before;
20 And kept my reverence for knowledge
Trying for control, to be still,
To quell the passion of the blood;
Until I had bent down on my knees
Praying for joy in the sight of decay.
25 And so I left; and I returned
In Autumn strict of eye, to see
The sap gone out of the groundhog,
But the bony sodden hulk remained.
But the year had lost its meaning,
30 And in intellectual chains
I lost both love and loathing,
Mured up in the wall of wisdom.
Another summer took the fields again
Massive and burning, full of life,
35 But when I chanced upon the spot
There was only a little hair left,
And bones bleaching in the sunlight
Beautiful as architecture;
I watched them like a geometer,
40 And cut a walking stick from a birch.

It has been three years, now.
There is no sign of the groundhog.
I stood there in the whirling summer,
My hand capped a withered heart,
45 And thought of China and of Greece,
Of Alexander in his tent;
Of Montaigne in his tower,
Of Saint Theresa[1] in her wild lament.

commentary

Eberhart's most moving recognition of the universality of death is in "The Groundhog," a poem based on an actual incident. From the opening lines, emphasis is not on the animal itself but on the poet's reactions to it (lines 1–4). The tone of straightforward report in the first two lines, heightened only by the adjective "golden" and the unobtrusive rhythm, is moved appropriately to the realm of the emotionally meaningful by the inversion of "Dead lay he" in the third line. Although the poem is linked with other Eberhart pieces which see death as change in form rather than as extinction, the emphasis here remains on the process of decay and on the response—almost the lament—this process arouses. The speaker's senses wavered at seeing "nature ferocious" and he reacted "half with loathing, half with a strange love," with revulsion tempered by recognition that what the animal's body was undergoing is the destiny of all living things. His poking at the body "with an angry stick" resulted in a "fever" of energy on the part of the maggots, a fever representing an immense "Vigour" (Eberhart's capital) comparable to, perhaps actually produced by, the sun. The creature's decay was the work of ultimate natural force. The speaker, in contrast, was victim of a "sunless trembling": his reactions were those of a frail living creature aware that he would someday himself be subject to that force. His thrust with the stick had "done nor good nor harm," for human intervention is powerless. The speaker had looked straightforwardly at the most horrifying aspect of death, had kept his "reverence for knowledge," his belief that the process of decay must have a meaning beyond its chemistry. But having failed either to understand or to influence the workings of force, the speaker ultimately went to his knees to pray "for joy in the sight of decay," perhaps for some indication that physical disappearance is not the end of experience. No revelation came, and he left the scene.

continued

From THE ACHIEVEMENT OF RICHARD EBERHART by Bernard F. Engel. Copyright © 1968 by Scott, Foresman and Company.

1. *Alexander . . . Montaigne . . . Saint Theresa.* Alexander the Great (356–323 B.C.) conquered the known world of his era. Montaigne (mon tän′), who lived from 1533 to 1592, was a French writer and philosopher. Saint Theresa of Avila (1515–1582) was a Spanish mystic. These figures represent, respectively, political, intellectual, and spiritual life.

Returning in the autumn, he was still "strict of eye," willing to confront the body without turning away. The "bony sodden hulk" of the animal remained, but "the year had lost its meaning"; in autumn—a season of the spirit as well as of the year—the speaker found himself "in intellectual chains," without the emotional reaction of his summertime visit to the scene. The meaning, we note, lies in "the year," and rises and subsides with the energy of nature. The speaker was as much in the grip of natural energies as the groundhog, though at the moment he was in a different stage of existence.

In the next summer, with nature again "massive and burning," he "chanced" upon the sight once more. Now there was nothing but a little hair and bones, and though he found the skeleton "beautiful as architecture," he saw only as "a geometer"—not, we gather, as an imaginative and philosophical being aware of meanings beyond the object itself. He cut a stick again, now not to attempt intervention but only to walk away. Though the time of this visit was summer, there was nothing in the sight at the moment to inspire further strong feeling. Lines 41 and 42 bring the time forward to the occasion of a fourth visit. Realization of ultimate disappearance brought a climactic access of impassioned feeling (lines 43–48). With the animal's body gone, the speaker could react not to the remains themselves but to the awareness—possible in the summer season of full experience, of full light—that not only the groundhog but also man's empires and leaders must disappear.

The speaker's effort to find relief for his terror causes only a strong awareness of the frailty of all living beings under the power of natural force. Insistence on the recognition of the tension between spirit and flesh makes us feel the reactions of a sensitive man drawn in fascinated desperation to observe an inevitable process. Eberhart allows an interplay of perception and emotion to build the poem without imposition of solutions, or interpretations foreign to the experience.

Bernard F. Engel

SONG
from *Cymbeline*

WILLIAM SHAKESPEARE

Fear no more the heat o' the sun,
   Nor the furious winter's rages;
Thou thy worldly task hast done,
   Home art gone, and ta'en thy wages:
5 Golden lads and girls all must,
As chimney-sweepers, come to dust.

Fear no more the frown o' the great;
   Thou art past the tyrant's stroke;
Care no more to clothe and eat;
10   To thee the reed is as the oak:
The sceptre, learning, physic, must
All follow this, and come to dust.

Fear no more the lightning-flash,
   Nor the all-dreaded thunder-stone;
15 Fear not slander, censure rash;
   Thou hast finished joy and moan:
All lovers young, all lovers must
Consign to thee, and come to dust.

No exorciser harm thee!
20 Nor no witchcraft charm thee!
Ghost unlaid forbear thee!
Nothing ill come near thee!
Quiet consummation have;
And renownèd be thy grave!

interpretation

1. This song from Shakespeare's *Cymbeline* is an incantation, or chant, repeated as a ritual around the body of a dead person, to cast a spell of protection over the departed. What does the poet say is the nature of the life the dead person has escaped?
2. What consolation is offered the dead?

STILL, CITIZEN SPARROW

RICHARD WILBUR

Still, citizen sparrow, this vulture which you call
Unnatural, let him but lumber again to air
Over the rotten office, let him bear
The carrion ballast[1] up, and at the tall

5 Tip of the sky lie cruising. Then you'll see
That no more beautiful bird is in heaven's height,
No wider more placid wings, no watchfuller flight;
He shoulders nature there, the frightfully free,

The naked-headed one. Pardon him, you
10 Who dart in the orchard aisles, for it is he
Devours death, mocks mutability,
Has heart to make an end, keeps nature new.

Thinking of Noah, childheart, try to forget
How for so many bedlam hours his saw
15 Soured the song of birds with its wheezy gnaw,
And the slam of his hammer all the day beset

The people's ears. Forget that he could bear
To see the towns like coral under the keel,
And the fields so dismal deep. Try rather to feel
20 How high and weary it was, on the waters where

He rocked his only world, and everyone's.
Forgive the hero, you who would have died
Gladly with all you knew; he rode that tide
To Ararat[2]; all men are Noah's sons.

interpretation

1. In this poem a central analogy is drawn between the vulture and the Biblical figure, Noah. In stanza 3 we are told that it is the vulture who "Devours death, mocks mutability, / Has heart to make an end, keeps nature new." Can these lines also be applied to Noah?
2. Select images that suggest the motion of the vulture in air. What images make vivid the ark on water? Compare these two sets of images.
3. The poem is addressed to "citizen sparrow." Can you explain this choice?

From CEREMONY AND OTHER POEMS, (British title: POEMS 1943–1956), by Richard Wilbur. Reprinted by permission of Harcourt Brace Jovanovich, Inc. and Faber and Faber Ltd.

1. *carrion ballast*, the weight of decaying flesh. 2. *Ararat*, the mountain in Asia Minor on which Noah's ark landed when the waters of the flood subsided.

DAYS

RALPH WALDO EMERSON

Daughters of Time, the hypocritic Days,
Muffled and dumb like barefoot dervishes,[1]
And marching single in an endless file,
Bring diadems and fagots[2] in their hands.
5   To each they offer gifts after his will,
Bread, kingdoms, stars, and sky that holds them all.
I, in my pleached garden, watched the pomp,
Forgot my morning wishes, hastily
Took a few herbs and apples, and the Day
10 Turned and departed silent. I, too late,
Under her solemn fillet saw the scorn.

interpretation

1. Emerson is probably using the word *hypocritic* in its Greek meaning of "one who plays a part," a pretender. The Days march "single in an endless file" seeming to promise that the now will stretch into forever. Why may the individual consider this "hypocritical"?
2. The Days offer "diadems and fagots." What sort of things might be placed in each category? How would you classify the "herbs and apples" the speaker takes?
3. Why do you think the Day is scornful of his choice?

---

1. *dervishes*, members of a Moslem order who take the vow of poverty and live an austere life as monks or wandering friars. 2. *fagots*, bundles of sticks used for kindling.

IN OCTOBER

MICHAEL HAMBURGER

In October the pregnant woman walked by the river
When autumn's failing green on the water's face
Conjures a world without depth, a landscape of glass.
She saw leaves and their images meet and saw them severed,
5   From the tall trees, glowing, a flicker of red fall down,
Leaves of the weeping willows drop and drown,
Cracking that mirror of green, the immaculate water.
"Tears of time," she thought; "O my son or daughter
Due to be born with the lambs and, like them, slaughtered
10   By the sudden thrust in war, slow waste in peace,
To wonder, to hope for a while, then glimmer passionless.
Man's grief I perpetuate, which else would cease."

Faint, but golden, the sun broke through the haze;
She saw dead leaves assembled on the river's bed,
15   Water-weeds groping for food, their green unshed,
And above, new buds, minute, on the naked boughs.
"Nameless you are," she thought, "my son or daughter,
Nameless as unborn leaves, dead leaves and the water,
A particle, passing but blessed, between always and never.
20   Man's joy I perpetuate, the tree and the river,
Summer's unbroken mirror, the cracking glass
And the stillness that spreads where leaf and image divide."

interpretation

1. Only a slight change in the components of the scene alters the woman's mood. What is her attitude in the first stanza? in the second? What is different about the way the woman sees the autumn scene in stanza 2?
2. How does she apply the scene to herself and her unborn child in each stanza?

From POEMS 1950–1951 by Michael Hamburger. Published by Hand and Flower Press, Aldington, Kent. Reprinted by permission.

ON TIME

JOHN MILTON

Fly, envious Time, till thou run out thy race:
Call on the lazy leaden-stepping Hours,
Whose speed is but the heavy plummet's pace;
And glut thyself with what thy womb devours,
5 Which is no more than what is false and vain,
And merely mortal dross;
So little is our loss,
So little is thy gain!
For, when as each thing bad thou hast entombed,
10 And, last of all, thy greedy self consumed,
Then long Eternity shall greet our bliss
With an individual kiss,
And Joy shall overtake us as a flood;
When everything that is sincerely good,
15 And perfectly divine,
With Truth, and Peace, and Love, shall ever shine
About the supreme throne
Of him, to whose happy-making sight alone
When once our heavenly-guided soul shall climb,
20 Then, all this earthly grossness quit,
Attired with stars we shall for ever sit,
    Triumphing over Death, and Chance, and thee, O Time!

Interpretation

1. Time is presented in this poem as a gluttonous creature who devours all. Trace the elaboration of this image in lines 1-10 and comment on its effectiveness.
2. What defeats Time?
3. How does Milton's affirmation differ from Hamburger's in "In October"?

BEGINNINGS

R. D. FITZGERALD

Not to have known the hard-bitten,
tight-lipped Caesar
clamped down on savage Britain;
or, moving closer,
5   not to have watched Cook[1]
drawing thin lines across
the last sea's uncut book
is my own certain loss;

as too is having come late,
10 the other side of the dark
from that bearded, sedate
Hargrave of Stanwell Park,[2]
and so to have missed, some bright
morning, in the salty, stiff
15 north-easter, a crank with a kite—
steadied above the cliff.

Beginnings once known
are lost. Perpetual day,
wheeling, has grown
20 each year further away
from the original strength
of any action or mind
used, and at length
fallen behind.

25 One might give much
to bring to the hand
for sight and touch
cities under the sand
and to talk and trade
30 with the plain folk met
could we walk with the first who made
an alphabet.

From FORTY YEARS' POEMS. Reprinted by permission of Angus & Robertson (Publishers) Pty. Ltd.

1. *Cook,* Captain James Cook (1728-1779), English navigator and explorer. **2.** *Hargrave of Stanwell Park.* Lawrence Hargrave (1850-1915) was an early experimenter in aeronautics as well as the inventor of the box kite, with which he conducted experiments. His home was at Stanwell Park on the south coast of New South Wales, Australia.

But more than to look back
we choose this day's concern
35 with everything in the track,
and would give most to learn
outcomes of all we found
and what next builds to the stars.
I regret I shall not be around
40 to stand on Mars.

Interpretation

1. Is the speaker more interested in the past or the future?
2. If you had your choice of being present at one past event of your choice or one future event, which would you choose? Why?

NEWS OF THE PHOENIX[1]

A. J. M. SMITH

They say the Phoenix is dying, some say dead.
Dead without issue is what one message said,
But that has been suppressed, officially denied.

I think myself the man who sent it lied.
5 In any case, I'm told, he has been shot,
As a precautionary measure, whether he did or not.

Interpretation

1. What does "Dead without issue" (line 2) say about the Phoenix in the present era?
2. How might the poem be read as a comment on the horrors of the modern age?

From MODERN CANADIAN VERSE. Reprinted by permission of Oxford University Press, Canadian Branch.

1. *Phoenix*, a mythical bird which periodically consumes itself in fire and is reborn from the ashes.

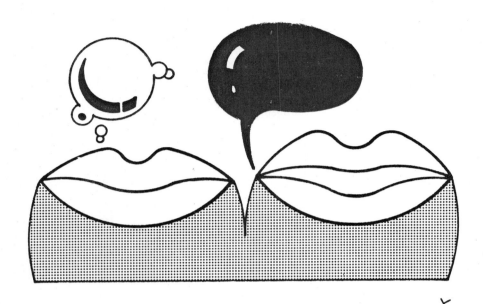

Thou shalt not steal; an empty feat,
When it's so lucrative to cheat...

ARTHUR HUGH CLOUGH

THE LATEST DECALOGUE

ARTHUR HUGH CLOUGH

Thou shalt have one God only; who
Would be at the expense of two?
No graven images may be
Worshipped, except the currency:
5 Swear not at all; for, for thy curse
Thine enemy is none the worse:
At church on Sunday to attend
Will serve to keep the world thy friend:
Honour thy parents; that is, all
10 From whom advancement may befall;
Thou shalt not kill; but need'st not strive
Officiously to keep alive:
Do not adultery commit;
Advantage rarely comes of it:
15 Thou shalt not steal; an empty feat,
When it's so lucrative to cheat:
Bear not false witness; let the lie
Have time on its own wings to fly:
Thou shalt not covet, but tradition
20 Approves all forms of competition.

Interpretation

The Ten Commandments are often spoken of as the *Decalogue*. Compare Clough's decalogue with the Biblical one.

IN WESTMINSTER ABBEY[1]

JOHN BETJEMAN

Let me take this other glove off
  As the *vox humana*[2] swells,
And the beauteous fields of Eden[3]
  Bask beneath the Abbey bells.
5 Here, where England's statesmen lie,
  Listen to a lady's cry.

Gracious Lord, oh bomb the Germans.
  Spare their women for Thy Sake,
And if that is not too easy
10 We will pardon Thy Mistake.
But, gracious Lord, whate'er shall be,
  Don't let anyone bomb me.

Keep our Empire undismembered
  Guide our Forces by Thy Hand,
15 Gallant blacks from far Jamaica,
  Honduras and Togoland;
Protect them Lord in all their fights,
And, even more, protect the whites.

Think of what our Nation stands for,
20 Books from Boots'[4] and country lanes,
Free speech, free passes, class distinction,
  Democracy and proper drains.
Lord, put beneath Thy special care
One-eighty-nine Cadogan Square.[5]

From COLLECTED POEMS by John Betjeman. Reprinted by permission of John Murray (Publishers) Ltd.

1. *Westminster Abbey*, a national sanctuary, church, and burial place, located in the borough of Westminster, London. It is the site of coronations, as well as a place of interment and recognition for national statesmen, soldiers, and writers. 2. *vox humana*, an organ stop whose sound imitates the human voice. 3. *Eden.* In the eighteenth century, certain Englishmen believed that England had been the site of the Biblical Garden of Eden. 4. *Boots*, a British chain store with a lending library. 5. *Cadogan Square*, a square in Kensington, London, with large middle-class houses.

25 Although dear Lord I am a sinner,
   I have done no major crime;
Now I'll come to Evening Service
   Whensoever I have time.
So, Lord, reserve for me a crown,
30 And do not let my shares go down.

I will labour for Thy Kingdom,
   Help our lads to win the war,
Send white feathers to the cowards[6]
   Join the Women's Army Corps,
35 Then wash the Steps around Thy Throne
In the Eternal Safety Zone.

Now I feel a little better,
   What a treat to hear Thy Word,
Where the bones of leading statesmen,
40   Have so often been interr'd.
And now, dear Lord, I cannot wait
Because I have a luncheon date.

---

interpretation

1. What is the character of the speaker? To what social class does she belong?
2. Is she presented as an individual or as a stereotype? What makes you think so?
3. Do you think the poem succeeds or fails as a satire? (See *Handbook of Terms and Techniques*.)
4. What effect do the meter and the rhyme have on the tone?

---

6. *white feathers . . . cowards.* In England, the white feather was a symbol of cowardice and was sent to men of military age who were not serving in the armed forces during wartime.

SATIRES OF CIRCUMSTANCE

THOMAS HARDY

AT TEA

The kettle descants in a cosy drone,
And the young wife looks in her husband's face,
And then at her guest's, and shows in her own
Her sense that she fills an envied place;
5 And the visiting lady is all abloom,
And says there was never so sweet a room.

And the happy young housewife does not know
That the woman beside her was first his choice,
Till the fates ordained it could not be so. . . .
10 Betraying nothing in look or voice
The guest sits smiling and sips her tea,
And he throws her a stray glance yearningly.

AT THE DRAPER'S[1]

"I stood at the back of the shop, my dear,
   But you did not perceive me.
Well, when they deliver what you were shown
   I shall know nothing of it, believe me!"

5   And he coughed and coughed as she paled and said,
   "O, I didn't see you come in there—
Why couldn't you speak?"—"Well, I didn't. I left
   That you should not notice I'd been there.

"You were viewing some lovely things. '*Soon required*
10   *For a widow, of latest fashion*';
And I knew 'twould upset you to meet the man
   Who had to be cold and ashen

"And screwed in a box before they could dress you
   '*In the last new note in mourning*,'
15   As they defined it. So, not to distress you,
   I left you to your adorning."

interpretation

1. "At Tea" and "At the Draper's" are from a series of poems titled
Satires of Circumstance. Sketch briefly the situation described in each
poem. Do you think these poems fit Hardy's group title? Explain your
answer.
2. "At the Draper's" is set up as a dialogue; only one line is spoken
by the narrator. In your opinion does the dialogue form make the poem
more effective?

1. *Draper,* a dealer in cloth and other sewing supplies.

SOLILOQUY OF THE SPANISH CLOISTER

ROBERT BROWNING

1

Gr-r-r—there go, my heart's abhorrence!
Water your damned flower-pots, do!
If hate killed men, Brother Lawrence,
God's blood, would not mine kill you!
5 What? your myrtle-bush wants trimming?
Oh, that rose has prior claims—
Needs its leaden vase filled brimming?
Hell dry you up with its flames!

2

At the meal we sit together;
10 *Salve tibi!*[1] I must hear
Wise talk of the kind of weather,
Sort of season, time of year:
*Not a plenteous cork-crop: scarcely
Dare we hope oak-galls,*[2] *I doubt;*
15 *What's the Latin name for "parsley"?*
What's the Greek name for Swine's Snout?

3

Whew! We'll have our platter burnished,
Laid with care on our own shelf!
With a fire-new spoon we're furnished,
20 And a goblet for ourself,
Rinsed like something sacrificial
Ere 'tis fit to touch our chaps[3]—
Marked with L. for our initial!
(He—he! There his lily snaps!)

4

25 *Saint,* forsooth! While brown Dolores
Squats outside the Convent bank
With Sanchicha, telling stories,
Steeping tresses in the tank,
Blue-black, lustrous, thick like horsehairs,
30 —Can't I see his dead eye glow,
Bright as 'twere a Barbary corsair's?[4]
(That is, if he'd let it show!)

---

1. *Salve tibi* (säl′vä tē′bē), a greeting, "Hail to thee!" [*Latin*] 2. *oak-galls*, swellings on certain oaks, produced by parasitic attacks. The galls are used in curing hides and wines. 3. *chaps*, jaws; lips. 4. *Barbary corsair*, a pirate from the Mediterranean coast of Africa.

5

When he finishes refection,[5]
　　Knife and fork he never lays
35　Cross-wise, to my recollection,
　　As do I, in Jesu's praise.
I the Trinity illustrate,
　　Drinking watered orange-pulp—
In three sips the Arian frustrate[6];
40　　While he drains his at one gulp!

6

Oh, those melons? If he's able
　　We're to have a feast; so nice!
One goes to the Abbot's table,
　　All of us get each a slice.
45　How go on your flowers? None double?
　　Not one fruit-sort can you spy?
Strange!—And I, too, at such trouble,
　　Keep them close-nipped on the sly!

7

There's a great text in Galatians,[7]
50　　Once you trip on it, entails
Twenty-nine distinct damnations,
　　One sure, if another fails;
If I trip him just a-dying,
　　Sure of heaven as sure can be,
55　Spin him round and send him flying
　　Off to hell, a Manichee?[8]

8

Or, my scrofulous[9] French novel
　　On grey paper with blunt type!
Simply glance at it, you grovel
60　　Hand and foot in Belial's[10] gripe;
If I double down its pages
　　At the woeful sixteenth print,
When he gathers his greengages,[11]
　　Ope a sieve[12] and slip it in't?

continued

---

5. *refection*, a meal. **6.** *Arian frustrate*. Arius was a fourth-century heretic who denied the doctrine of the Trinity. The speaker witnesses to the Trinity by drinking his orange juice in three sips. **7.** *Galatians*, one of St. Paul's epistles. The speaker refers to Galatians 3:10-11. **8.** *Manichee*, a heretic who believed in two kingdoms—one good, one evil, the latter including not only the body, but all forms of matter. **9.** *scrofulous*, morally contaminated. **10.** *Belial*, one name for the devil. **11.** *greengages*, plums. **12.** *sieve*, basket.

9

65   Or, there's Satan!—one might venture
      Pledge one's soul to him, yet leave
   Such a flaw in the indenture
      As he'd miss till, past retrieve,
   Blasted lay that rose-acacia
70   We're so proud of! *Hy, Zy, Hine*[13]. . . .
   'St, there's Vespers! *Plena gratia*
      Ave Virgo![14] Gr-r-r—you swine!

interpretation

1. Why does the speaker hate Brother Lawrence with such intensity?
2. In his soliloquy on Brother Lawrence what does the speaker reveal about himself?
3. In what ways has his all-consuming hatred made him ridiculous and grotesque?
4. What does the setting—the cloister of a monastery—contribute to the dramatic impact of this poem?
5. The poem is full of harsh sounds. Point out some of them and discuss their purpose. (See CACOPHONY in *Handbook of Terms and Techniques*.)

---

13. *Hy, Zy, Hine*, nonsense words that perhaps suggest the beginning of a curse. **14.** *Plena gratia, Ave Virgo* (plä′nä grä′tsē ä ä′vä vir′gō), beginning of a prayer, "Hail, Mary, full of grace."

HOW SWEET AND LOVELY DOST THOU MAKE THE SHAME

(Sonnet 95)

WILLIAM SHAKESPEARE

How sweet and lovely dost thou make the shame
Which, like a canker[1] in the fragrant rose,
Doth spot the beauty of thy budding name!
O, in what sweets dost thou thy sins enclose!
5 That tongue that tells the story of thy days,
Making lascivious comments on thy sport,
Cannot dispraise but in a kind of praise;
Naming thy name blesses an ill report.
O, what a mansion have those vices got
10 Which for their habitation chose out thee,
Where beauty's veil doth cover every blot,
And all things turn to fair that eyes can see!
    Take heed, dear heart, of this large privilege;
    The hardest knife ill-used doth lose his edge.

Interpretation

1. Would you consider this a love sonnet, an indictment of a hypocrite, or something else?
2. What type of sonnet is this? Explain your answer by referring to various features of the sonnet itself.

---

1. *canker,* a worm that injures buds and leaves.

...acquainted with the night

ROBERT FROST

THE BURGLAR

SONYA DORMAN

A burglar came, jimmied a window
open in a wall that had no ledge.
This thief dropped tears
in an ashtray, bolted from room to room
5   stamping his hobnails into the rugs,
read one of Emerson's essays and left
the volume open on the floor.
Police found a thumbprint on her furs,
and two expensive rings joined
10 into linked loops, their gems
like heads turned shyly apart.
When all was told and valued, all
he took was the family album.
Perhaps in a Sunday park he explores
15 its dark leaves, reveals
the aunts and cousins, the younger
brother dead but glued there,
immortal, in a birthday smile.
The couple who'd dined out, forgot;
20 fresh paint erased his dubious point
of entry. Somewhere, in gusts
of winter love, he turns a page
and takes a relative or bride.

interpretation

1. What makes this burglar even more mysterious than burglars usually
are?
2. What was he really looking for?
3. Why did he steal the family album?

Originally published in the *Saturday Review*, June 10, 1967. It was subsequently included in Mrs.
Dorman's collection entitled POEMS, published in 1970 by the Ohio State University Press as a National Council on the Arts Selection. Copyright © 1967 by Sonya Dorman.

THE BURGLAR

DAVID WAGONER

Being a burglar, you slip out of doors in the morning
And look at the street by looking at the sky,
Not being taken in by anything blue.
You must look to the left or right to see across.
5   If nothing strikes your eye, if no one comes running,
You've stolen another day.

You must spend it on your toes
At the edges of buildings, doorways, and windows
Wherever no one is watching close enough.
10   Keep your fingers light as smoke.
You may have permission to kiss with one eye open.
Try every door while leaning away from it.

But sundown is serious; it's time to go home
To the house that will draw you under its empty wing.
15   Climbing like ivy up the drains, go through
The furthest window into a dark room.
Wait there to hear how everything has gone.
Then, masking every motion,

Glide to the stairwell.
20   They will be eating dinner: the man and the woman
At opposite ends of a white and silver table;
Between them, food and candles and children.
Their knives and forks go in and out of their mouths;
Whatever they do will aim them toward each other.

25   Now, follow your fingerprints around all corners
From nightlatch to velvet lid, from hasp to stone.
Everything locked, of course, has been locked for you:
You must break in softly, take whatever you find
Whether you understand what it is or not.
30   Breathe in, reach out,

Stealing one gift at a time.
If you grow hungry, thinking of their desserts,
It's time to vanish over the windowsill.
You must go without their dinner into the night,
35   Not saying goodbye, not waiting to scrawl a note
To say you're running away, but running away.

Reprinted by permission of *Chicago Review*; copyright 1966 by *Chicago Review*, a quarterly of art-
work, reviews, drama, essays, poetry, and prose fiction.

This piece is one of a series I wrote (the others were "The Visiting Hour," "The Hold-up," "The Shoplifter," "Magic Night at the Reformatory") about what is called "criminal behavior." In "The Burglar" the poem suggests that many people who are not burglars act like burglars and that the impulse to act that way may well have been formed in childhood: I'm sure many children feel like "second-story men" in their own homes, behaving as burglars do in going through the belongings of other members of the family from whom they feel alienated. And I'm equally sure that many burglars feel like children when they search through the intimate belongings of their victims. Therefore, as in a hushed and suspended dream, the poem tries to combine both the adult and the childhood experiences. Many burglars work at mealtimes, being fairly certain that the upstairs of houses will be deserted then, and I needn't tell you that many children are sent to bed without their suppers and sometimes choose such occasions for running away from home or wishing to. I've tried to blend all these elements in a single narrative sequence.

David Wagoner

1. Compare this burglar with the one in Sonya Dorman's poem.
2. In what ways may both burglars be regarded as symbolic, representing qualities not restricted to them alone?

I AM SUMMONED BY A DOOR

RICHARD BRAUTIGAN

> I am summoned by a door
> but forgotten by the knock
> and left standing here alone
> in a long silent hall, like
> 5 a marble intestine, that knows
>   my name.

HOUSE GUEST

ELIZABETH BISHOP

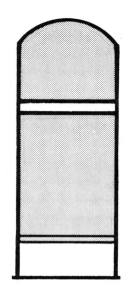

The sad seamstress
who stays with us this month
is small and thin and bitter.
No one can cheer her up.
5 Give her a dress, a drink,
roast chicken, or fried fish—
it's all the same to her.

She sits and watches TV.
No, she watches zigzags.
10 "Can you adjust the TV?"
"No," she says. No hope.
She watches on and on,
without hope, without air.

Her own clothes give us pause,
15 but she's not a poor orphan.
She has a father, a mother,
and all that, and she's earning
quite well, and we're stuffing
her with fattening foods.

20 We invite her to use the binoculars.
We say, "Come see the jets!"
We say, "Come see the baby!"
Or the knife grinder who cleverly
plays the National Anthem
25 on his wheel so shrilly.
Nothing helps.

She speaks: "I need a little
money to buy buttons."
She seems to think it's useless
30 to ask. Heavens, buy buttons,
if they'll do any good,
the biggest in the world—
by the dozen, by the gross!
Buy yourself an ice cream,
35 a comic book, a car!

Her face is closed as a nut,
closed as a careful snail
or a thousand-year-old seed.
Does she dream of marriage?
40   Of getting rich? Her sewing
is decidedly mediocre.

Please! Take our money! Smile!
What on earth have we done?
What has everyone done
45   and when did it all begin?
Then one day she confides
that she wanted to be a nun
and her family opposed her.

Perhaps we should let her go,
50   or deliver her straight off
to the nearest convent—and wasn't
her month up last week, anyway?

Can it be that we nourish
one of the Fates in our bosoms?
55   Clotho,[1] sewing our lives
with a bony little foot
on a borrowed sewing machine,
and our fates will be like hers,
and our hems crooked forever?

Interpretation

Bishop's portrait of the unhappy "house guest" is in some ways prose-like. It presents "the facts in the case" directly, making statements rather than suggesting or implying (except in the final stanza). Yet it is not a piece of prose divided into stanzas, but a poem. In your opinion what qualities or devices make it a poem?

---

1. *Clotho* (klō′thō), in Greek mythology one of the three Fates, goddesses who presided over human destiny. Clotho spun the thread of life. Lachesis (lak′ə sis) determined its length, and Atropos (at′-rə pos) cut it.

TIMES

STEPHEN BERG

No one is here today, the streets
fill with rain, drops echo in long puddles
near the walls. I am talking to you again
but you don't hear.
                In my childhood there's a room
5 where I sit in bed listening to the radio, un-
raveling the edge of a blanket with my lips. The blue
twilight darkness, heavy and soft as wool, trains
jumbled in a box, a tin
horse galloping forever,
10 then sleep—I think about this often.
                      Like now
without anyone. Tell me what your life is like, call.
Sometimes I dial your number in a rich Jersey town
and can't speak. I know what to say,
                      but there are
times when I'm sure I can
15 cross the street and go up and find you
sprawled on the floor studying, playing records,
smiling because I'm there. There are times,
and we grow distant over the years, and live
somebody's life, ask nothing, and live.

interpretation

1. What are the times referred to in the title? Where does the speaker's memory take him?

2. What do you think the speaker has in mind when he says we "live / somebody's life, ask nothing, and live" (lines 18–19)?

3. Has there been anything in your own experience that makes the poem meaningful for you?

From THE DAUGHTERS by Stephen Berg, copyright © 1971, by The Bobbs-Merrill Company, Inc., reprinted by permission of the publisher and the author.

THE GERANIUM

THEODORE ROETHKE

When I put her out, once, by the garbage pail,
She looked so limp and bedraggled,
So foolish and trusting, like a sick poodle,
Or a wizened aster in late September,
5 I brought her back in again
For a new routine—
Vitamins, water, and whatever
Sustenance seemed sensible
At the time: she'd lived
10 So long on gin, bobbie pins, half-smoked cigars, dead beer,
Her shriveled petals falling
On the faded carpet, the stale
Steak grease stuck to her fuzzy leaves.
(Dried-out, she creaked like a tulip.)

15 The things she endured!—
The dumb dames shrieking half the night
Or the two of us, alone, both seedy,
Me breathing booze at her,
She leaning out of her pot toward the window.

20 Near the end, she seemed almost to hear me—
And that was scary—
So when that snuffling cretin of a maid
Threw her, pot and all, into the trash-can,
I said nothing.

25 But I sacked the presumptuous hag the next week,
I was that lonely.

Interpretation

1. Quite often when flowers and animals are personified, the effect is either that of cuteness or of sentimental whimsy and falseness. How do you feel about Roethke's use of personification in this poem?
2. In what form is the poem written? How does this form help to suggest the idea of the poem?

SKUNK HOUR

(For Elizabeth Bishop)

ROBERT LOWELL

Nautilus Island's hermit
heiress still lives through winter in her Spartan cottage;
her sheep still graze above the sea.
Her son's a bishop. Her farmer
5 is first selectman in our village,
she's in her dotage.

Thirsting for
the hierarchic privacy
of Queen Victoria's century,
10 she buys up all
the eyesores facing her shore,
and lets them fall.

The season's ill—
we've lost our summer millionaire,
15 who seemed to leap from an L. L. Bean
catalogue. His nine-knot yawl
was auctioned off to lobstermen.
A red fox stain covers Blue Hill.

And now our fairy
20 decorator brightens his shop for fall,
his fishnet's filled with orange cork,
orange, his cobbler's bench and awl,
there is no money in his work,
he'd rather marry.

25 One dark night,
my Tudor Ford climbed the hill's skull,
I watched for love-cars. Lights turned down,
they lay together, hull to hull,
where the graveyard shelves on the town . . .
30 My mind's not right.

A car radio bleats,
"Love, O careless Love . . ." I hear
my ill-spirit sob in each blood cell,
as if my hand were at its throat . . .
35 I myself am hell,
nobody's here—

only skunks, that search
in the moonlight for a bite to eat.
They march on their soles up Main Street:
40   white stripes, moonstruck eyes' red fire
under the chalk-dry and spar spire
of the Trinitarian Church.

I stand on top
of our back steps and breathe the rich air—
45   a mother skunk with her column of kittens swills the garbage pail.
She jabs her wedge-head in a cup
of sour cream, drops her ostrich tail
and will not scare.

---

commentary

I am not sure whether I can distinguish between intention and interpretation. I think this is what I more or less intended. The first four
stanzas are meant to give a dawdling more or less amiable picture of a
declining Maine sea town. I move from the ocean inland. Sterility howls
through the scenery, but I try to give a tone of tolerance, humor, and
randomness to the sad prospect. The composition drifts, its direction
sinks out of sight into the casual, chancy arrangements of nature and
decay. Then all comes alive in stanzas V and VI. This is the dark night.
. . . My night is not gracious, but secular, puritan, and agnostical. An
Existentialist night. Somewhere in my mind was a passage from Sartre
or Camus about reaching some point of final darkness where the one
free act is suicide. Out of this comes the march and affirmation, an
ambiguous one, of my skunks in the last two stanzas. The skunks are
both quixotic and barbarously absurd, hence the tone of amusement
and defiance. . . .

"Skunk Hour" was written backwards, first the last two stanzas, I
think, and then the next to last two. Anyway, there was a time when I
had the last four stanzas much as they now are and nothing before them.
I found the bleak personal violence repellent. All was too close, though
watching the lovers was not mine, but from an anecdote about Walt
Whitman in his old age. I began to feel that real poetry came, not from
fierce confessions, but from something almost meaningless but imagined. I was haunted by an image of a blue china doorknob. I never used
the doorknob, or knew what it meant, yet somehow it started the cur-
rent of images in my opening stanzas. They were written in reverse
order, and at last gave my poem an earth to stand on, and space to
breathe.

Robert Lowell

From THE CONTEMPORARY POET AS ARTIST AND CRITIC, edited by Anthony B. Ostroff.
Published 1964 by Little, Brown and Company.

MAIL CALL

RANDALL JARRELL

The letters always just evade the hand.
One skates like a stone into a beam, falls like a bird.
Surely the past from which the letters rise
Is waiting in the future, past the graves?
5   The soldiers are all haunted by their lives.

Their claims upon their kind are paid in paper
That establishes a presence, like a smell.
In letters and in dreams they see the world.
They are waiting: and the years contract
10   To an empty hand, to one unuttered sound—

The soldier simply wishes for his name.

interpretation

1. What is the meaning of line 5?
2. Discuss ways in which the letters represent both the past and the future to the soldiers.
3. What is meant by "the years contract / To an empty hand" (lines 9–10)? What is the "one unuttered sound" (line 10)?

ACQUAINTED WITH THE NIGHT

ROBERT FROST

I have been one acquainted with the night.
I have walked out in rain—and back in rain.
I have outwalked the furthest city light.

I have looked down the saddest city lane.
5 I have passed by the watchman on his beat
And dropped my eyes, unwilling to explain.

I have stood still and stopped the sound of feet
When far away an interrupted cry
Came over houses from another street,

10 But not to call me back or say good-by;
And further still at an unearthly height,
One luminary clock against the sky

Proclaimed the time was neither wrong nor right.
I have been one acquainted with the night.

interpretation

1. What reasons can you advance for the speaker's being "acquainted with the night"? Pick out details that influenced your answer.
2. In this poem Frost uses a verse form called *terza rima*. (See *Handbook of Terms and Techniques*.) What is the meter? What is the rhyme scheme? What does it do to move the stanzas forward?

From THE POETRY OF ROBERT FROST, edited by Edward Connery Lathem. Copyright 1923, 1928, © 1969 by Holt, Rinehart and Winston, Inc. Copyright 1951, © 1956 by Robert Frost. Reprinted by permission of Holt, Rinehart and Winston, Inc., the Estate of Robert Frost, and Jonathan Cape Ltd.

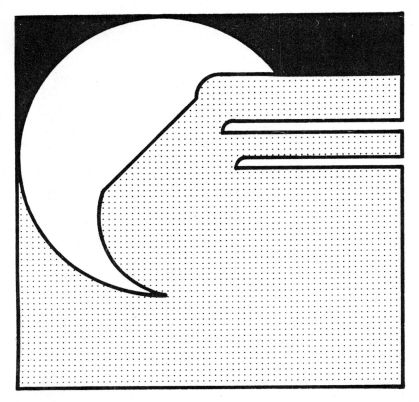

21

You crush all the particles down
into close conformity...
MARIANNE MOORE

A FIRE TRUCK

RICHARD WILBUR

Right down the shocked street with a siren-blast
That sends all else skittering to the curb,
Redness, brass, ladders, and hats hurl past,
    Blurring to sheer verb,

5 Shift at the corner into uproarious gear
And make it around the turn in a squall of traction,
The headlong bell maintaining sure and clear,
    Thought is degraded action!

Beautiful, heavy, unweary, loud, obvious thing!
10 I stand here purged of nuance, my mind a blank.
All I was brooding upon has taken wing,
    And I have you to thank.

As you howl beyond hearing I carry you into my mind,
Ladders and brass and all, there to admire
15 Your phoenix-red simplicity, enshrined
    In that not extinguished fire.

interpretation

Writers choose words both for their denotative and connotative meanings. In the best poems the more precise the diction is, the more evocative it is. (See *Handbook of Terms and Techniques.*) "A Fire Truck,"
besides being enjoyable for its own sake, effectively illustrates this
principle.

1. Try substituting other words or phrases for *(a)* "shocked street"
(line 1), *(b)* "skittering" (line 2), *(c)* "uproarious gear" (line 5), *(d)* "squall
of traction" (line 6), and *(e)* "headlong bell" (line 7). What happens to
the tone and meaning of the lines even when the words you've chosen
are synonyms for Wilbur's?
2. What does "Blurring to sheer verb" (line 4) mean?
3. The phoenix was a mythical bird that periodically burned itself on
a funeral pyre and rose from its own ashes. Why is "phoenix-red" (line
15) especially appropriate in the context of the poem?
4. Describe the meter and the stanza pattern.

THE GOOD RESOLUTION

MONA VAN DUYN

My right hand has suffered an amputation
of its fifth finger, the one with the hot nail,
the one that kept pointing across the room.
While the other four fingers sealed my lips and the thumb
5 asked for a hitchhike to my shoulder, it would point Away.
Now I am self-absorbed and lonesome.

Drifting in great woolly scarves in my head,
like the scene of an English thriller, a fog settles.
My head turns slowly, the fog shifts, and inside
10 its brow, crouched, the sweating maniac is revealed.
He froths and tightens, he starves for the white victim.
Now I am restless and in need of food.

The day extends itself, like a dog's tongue
in dreadful heat, or, like a bay bridge,
15 crosses ten empty islands and still keeps going.
Light dangles from the sky like a wet string.
I try to jerk it down, but it holds fast
and will not drop into interminable evening.

Who would have thought I'd be asking that old chestnut
20 at my age, seriously, Who Am I, demoralized
giant-killer or really furious giant?
One imagines paper dolls from a folded sheet
flipped open to a whole procession of selves, hands joined,
by this time. I can't wait and I won't cheat,

25 and so my simple twins lay hands on each other
and bend each other down to a compromise:
Five times daily let the screws be loosed, the failure
celebrated, and perhaps in the homely future,
tripping with a pursed mouth toward some Damascus,[1]
30 I'll fall to my knees and rise up a non-smoker.

I am poured into five daily boxes, and all
my contents are fingered and re-arranged, arranged
and fingered. The screen I blow is too thin to conceal.
A mouse in the mind, trapped by its tail
35 in front of a mirror, keeps squeaking over and over
it never wanted to know itself *this* well!

Interpretation

1. What is "The Good Resolution" the speaker has made?
2. What is the "fifth finger, the one with the hot nail" (line 2)?
3. Discuss stanzas 2–4. What do they tell us about the persona of the poem?
4. Discuss the meaning of the last three lines. What do they reveal about the speaker's psychological state?
5. What figure of speech is the "fifth finger, the one with the hot nail"? Identify other figures of speech that you consider effective. (See FIG-URATIVE LANGUAGE in *Handbook of Terms and Techniques*.)

---

1. *Damascus,* a city in Syria. The road to Damascus was the site of the dramatic conversion of St. Paul to Christianity.

FULL MOON

ROBERT HAYDEN

No longer throne of a goddess to whom we pray,
no longer the bubble house of childhood's
tumbling Mother Goose man,

The emphatic moon ascends—
5   the brilliant challenger of rocket experts,
the white hope of communications men.

Some I love who are dead
were watchers of the moon and knew its lore;
planted seeds, trimmed their hair,

10   Pierced their ears for gold hoop earrings
as it waxed or waned.
It shines tonight upon their graves.

And burned in the garden of Gethsemane,
its light made holy by the dazzling tears
15   with which it mingled.

And spread its radiance on the exile's path
of Him who was The Glorious One,
its light made holy by His holiness.

Already a mooted goal and tomorrow perhaps
20   an arms base, a livid sector,
the full moon dominates the dark.

<hr>

commentary

The poem moves backwards and forwards in time. In the first stanza
there are negative references to myth and fantasy from the past. In the
second stanza we are in the present, the technological present. In the
third and fourth stanzas we are in the past again, but now it is the poet's
own personal past. The mood, the tone here, I feel, are rather elegiac.
We move farther back in time in the fifth stanza to the night of Christ's

<hr>

agony in the garden. From there we move to the nineteenth century—to a spring night in 1863, to be specific. "The Glorious One" alluded to is Bahá'u'lláh, prophet of the Baha'i Faith, and like Christ a divine manifestation. Both are seen in a moment of crisis. In the final stanza we come back to the present, which seems full of foreboding. The dark referred to in the last line is both the darkness of night and the darkness of the age and our future prospects.

Robert Hayden

ORGAN TRANSPLANT

J. D. REED

I drank,
my arteries filled with fat;
the ventricle went lax
and a clot stopped my heart.

5   Now I sit
in St. Petersburg sunshine.
No whiskey;
wearing a girl's heart.

My blood has adopted a child
10   who shuffles through my chest
carrying a doll.

interpretation

1. In terms of what is known about the effects of heart transplants upon those who receive them, would you say the final stanza is true or untrue to the facts?
2. How important are the "facts" in a poem?

IN GOYA'S GREATEST SCENES[1]

LAWRENCE FERLINGHETTI

In Goya's greatest scenes we seem to see
                                    the people of the world
        exactly at the moment when
            they first attained the title of
                            "suffering humanity"
        They writhe upon the page
                        in a veritable rage
                                    of adversity
        Heaped up
                    groaning with babies and bayonets
                                    under cement skies
                in an abstract landscape of blasted trees
                bent statues bats' wings and beaks
                        slippery gibbets
                cadavers and carnivorous cocks
        and all the final hollering monsters
            of the
                    "imagination of disaster"
            they are so bloody real
                        it is as if they really still existed

    And they do

        Only the landscape is changed

    They still are ranged along the roads
            plagued by legionaires
                        false windmills and demented roosters

1. *Goya's Greatest Scenes.* Francisco de Goya (1746–1828) was a Spanish painter. Among his greatest
works is a series of etchings recording the horrors and brutalities that accompanied the French in-
vasion of Spain under Napoleon.

They are the same people
                              only further from home
            on freeways fifty lanes wide
                    on a concrete continent
30   spaced with bland billboards
                  illustrating imbecile illusions of happiness

            The scene shows fewer tumbrils
                        but more maimed citizens
                                        in painted cars
35   and they have strange licence plates
                and engines
                            that devour America

1. What is the subject of the first stanza?
2. What is meant by "Only the landscape is changed" (line 22)? What examples does the poet give to prove his point?
3. What is the tone of the poem?

DRIVING TO TOWN LATE TO MAIL A LETTER

ROBERT BLY

        It is a cold and snowy night. The main street is deserted.
        The only things moving are swirls of snow.
        As I lift the mailbox door, I feel its cold iron.
        There is a privacy I love in this snowy night.
    5   Driving around, I will waste more time.

From SILENCE IN THE SNOWY FIELDS. Wesleyan University Press, 1962. Copyright © 1962 by Robert Bly, reprinted with his permission.

PRELUDES

T. S. ELIOT

1

The winter evening settles down
With smell of steaks in passageways.
Six o'clock.
The burnt-out ends of smoky days.
5 And now a gusty shower wraps
The grimy scraps
Of withered leaves about your feet
And newspapers from vacant lots;
The showers beat
10 On broken blinds and chimney-pots,
And at the corner of the street
A lonely cab-horse steams and stamps.
And then the lighting of the lamps.

2

The morning comes to consciousness
15 Of faint stale smells of beer
From the sawdust-trampled street
With all its muddy feet that press
To early coffee-stands.
With the other masquerades
20 That time resumes,
One thinks of all the hands
That are raising dingy shades
In a thousand furnished rooms.

3

You tossed a blanket from the bed,
25 You lay upon your back, and waited;
You dozed, and watched the night revealing
The thousand sordid images
Of which your soul was constituted;
They flickered against the ceiling.
30 And when all the world came back
And the light crept up between the shutters

And you heard the sparrows in the gutters,
You had such a vision of the street
As the street hardly understands;
35   Sitting along the bed's edge, where
You curled the papers from your hair,
Or clasped the yellow soles of feet
In the palms of both soiled hands.

4

His soul stretched tight across the skies
40   That fade behind a city block,
Or trampled by insistent feet
At four and five and six o'clock;
And short square fingers stuffing pipes,
And evening newspapers, and eyes
45   Assured of certain certainties,
The conscience of a blackened street
Impatient to assume the world.

I am moved by fancies that are curled
Around these images, and cling:
50   The notion of some infinitely gentle
Infinitely suffering thing.

Wipe your hand across your mouth, and laugh;
The worlds revolve like ancient women
Gathering fuel in vacant lots.

---

interpretation

1. What is a prelude? Why do you think T. S. Eliot entitled this work "Preludes"?

2. "Preludes" makes extensive use of imagery. (See *Handbook of Terms and Techniques.*) Cite images that appeal to the various senses. What effect do these images as a group produce?

3. To what images is the speaker referring in line 49? What is the meaning of lines 48–51?

4. What is the figure of speech with which the poem ends, and how is it related to the theme?

DOLOR

THEODORE ROETHKE

I have known the inexorable sadness of pencils,
Neat in their boxes, dolor of pad and paper-weight,
All the misery of manilla folders and mucilage,
Desolation in immaculate public places,
5   Lonely reception room, lavatory, switchboard,
The unalterable pathos of basin and pitcher,
Ritual of multigraph, paper-clip, comma,
Endless duplication of lives and objects.
And I have seen dust from the walls of institutions,
10 Finer than flour, alive, more dangerous than silica,
Sift, almost invisible, through long afternoons of tedium,
Dropping a fine film on nails and delicate eyebrows,
Glazing the pale hair, the duplicate gray standard faces.

TO A STEAM ROLLER

MARIANNE MOORE

The illustration
is nothing to you without the application.
    You lack half wit. You crush all the particles down
        into close conformity, and then walk back and forth on them.

5   Sparkling chips of rock
are crushed down to the level of the parent block.
    Were not "impersonal judgment in aesthetic
        matters, a metaphysical impossibility," you

might fairly achieve
10 it. As for butterflies, I can hardly conceive
    of one's attending upon you, but to question
        the congruence of the complement is vain, if it exists.

interpretation

1. Both Roethke and Moore use ordinary, utilitarian objects to express an idea. What, in each case, is the poet saying?
2. Do you consider some objects—birds or flowers, for example—more inherently poetic than, say, pencils or steam rollers?

IN SCHRAFFT'S

W. H. AUDEN

> Having finished the Blue-plate Special
> And reached the coffee stage,
> Stirring her cup she sat,
> A somewhat shapeless figure
> 5 Of indeterminate age
> In an undistinguished hat.
>
> When she lifted her eyes it was plain
> That our globular furore,
> Our international rout
> 10 Of sin and apparatus
> And dying men galore,
> Was not being bothered about.
>
> Which of the seven heavens
> Was responsible for her smile
> 15 Wouldn't be sure but attested
> That, whoever it was, a god
> Worth kneeling-to for a while
> Had tabernacled and rested.

interpretation

1. The lady that Auden describes might be considered ordinary, yet unique; vaguely defined, yet vivid. Find details from the poem that justify each of these descriptions.
2. What attitude or tone does Auden adopt toward his subject? (See TONE in *Handbook of Terms and Techniques*.)

AT BREAKFAST

MAY SWENSON

Not quite
spherical
White
Oddly closed
5   and without a lid

A smooth miracle
here in my hand
Has it slid
from my sleeve?

10   The shape
of this box
keels me oval
Heels feel
its bottom
15   Nape knocks
its top

Seated
like a foetus
I look for
20   the dream-seam

What's inside?
A sun?
Off with its head
though it hasn't any
25   or is all head no body
a
One

Neatly
the knife scalps it
I scoop out   30
the braincap
soft
sweetly shuddering

Mooncream
this could be   35
Spoon
laps the larger
crescent
loosens a gilded
nucleus   40
from warm pap
A lyrical food

Opened
a seamless miracle
Ate a sun-germ   45
Good

"At Breakfast" is one of a group of my so-called Riddle Poems; the label "riddle" is applicable simply because the poem's subject—generally some commonly familiar concrete thing—is left unnamed in either the title or the text and is caused gradually to disclose and identify itself through a series of metaphorical or associational clues. In "At Breakfast," the shape, color, and idiosyncrasy of an object is given as tersely and exactly as possible (Stanza 1), then its tactile quality along with its emblematic aura appears (Stanza 2); next, the feel of the thing as if from the inside, its apprehension by cerebral means, is suggested at the same time as the emblem is extended (Stanzas 3 and 4). Next, a related larger metaphor appears, juxtaposed to common use and action (Stanzas 5, 6, and 7). Finally, a terse summation of the developed definition along with the completed action is given; at this point the shape and movement of the poem itself is seen to have become spherical—with the word "opened" in the end stanza answering the word "closed" in the beginning lines.

It is essential, of course, with a device such as this to make not a riddle-pretending-to-be-a-poem but a poem that is also, and as if incidentally, a riddle—and a solvable one. The aim is not to mystify or mislead but to clarify and make recognizable through the reader's own uncontaminated perceptions. By bringing into play the sensual apparatus of the reader, the poem causes the reader to realize the content eye-wise, ear-wise, taste, touch, and muscle-wise *before* beginning to cerebralize. The analyzing intellect ought not to be the first but the last tool that is applied to a poem, for applied alone, as it sometimes is, it can inhibit organic associative responses, can bypass initial curiosity and individual exploration, resulting in little more than a mechanistic contact with the poem.

"To name an object (in a poem) is to suppress three quarters of our pleasure . . . a pleasure which consists in gradually divining . . . ," the French Symbolist poet Mallarmé has said. Which is not to say that my poetic method stems from the Symbolists, or from any other *theory* —not even my own. Art is not the offspring of theory; it is quite the other way around.

May Swenson

SCHIZOPHRENIA ON MADISON AVENUE

CHARLES J. SHAGOURY

Of thee I sing,
I whistle a happy song
Of right or wrong,
My country.

5 But first a word from O beautiful for spacious skies,
For the power of positive thinking, the pause that refreshes,
For the church of your choice, for buy now, pay later.
We are the 99/44/100% pure people, now for the first time one nation,
Under the insurance umbrella, in order to fight
10 Tooth decay and tired blood with justice and liberty,
Forever two-way stretch free, white, and don't delay.
You can be sure if there's one born every minute.
My fellow-Americans, we have nothing to fear,
No other product can make that statement. I pledge
15 Allegiance, give me liberty or give me fast relief,
To brand-name products for the people. These are the times
That try Brand X, the sunshine patriot
Will in his hour of crisis, and don't you wish everybody did,
Shrink hemorrhoids without surgery. Give me
20 Your teeming millions yearning to think young
And clear all eight sinuses, plus a no-risk offer
Of free TV, liberty, and red, white, and blue stamps
Guaranteed forever. Swing low sweet insolent chariot
Coming for the loved one in the land of
25 You know they're safe with no place to hide.

And now a word from our alternate sponsor.

Interpretation

1. What is schizophrenia? Do the organization of the poem, its syntax, and its lack of logical sequence justify the use of this word in the title?
2. What kinds of things make up the body of the poem? What clue do these things give you to the poet's inclusion of "Madison Avenue" in the title?
3. Why may this poem be considered a satire? (See *Handbook of Terms and Techniques*.)
4. Who is the speaker?

From *Trace*, (Summer 1965). Reprinted by permission of Villiers Publications Ltd.

WOOLWORTH'S

DONALD HALL

My whole life has led me here.

Daisies made out of resin,
hairnets and submarines,
sandwiches, diaries, green
5   garden chairs,
and a thousand boxes of cough drops.

Three hundred years ago I was hedging
and ditching in Devon.

I lacked freedom of worship,
10   and freedom to trade molasses
for rum, for slaves, for molasses.

"I will sail to Massachusetts
to build the Kingdom
of Heaven on Earth!"

15   The side of a hill
swung open.
It was Woolworth's!

I followed this vision to Boston.

‹ Interpretation

How would you describe the tone of this poem? Use specific details
or lines to justify your answer.

From THE ALLIGATOR BRIDE Copyright 1950, © 1968, 1969 by Donald Hall. Reprinted by permission of Harper & Row, Publishers, Inc. and Curtis Brown, Ltd.

MONEY

an introductory lecture

HOWARD NEMEROV

This morning we shall spend a few minutes
Upon the study of symbolism, which is basic
To the nature of money. I show you this nickel.
Icons and cryptograms[1] are written all over
5   The nickel: one side shows a hunchbacked bison
Bending his head and curling his tail to accommodate
The circular nature of money. Over him arches
UNITED STATES OF AMERICA, and, squinched in
Between that and his rump, E PLURIBUS UNUM,
10 A Roman reminiscence that appears to mean
An indeterminately large number of things
All of which are the same. Under the bison
A straight line giving him a ground to stand on
Reads FIVE CENTS. And on the other side of our nickel
15 There is the profile of a man with long hair
And a couple of feathers in the hair; we know
Somehow that he is an American Indian, and
He wears the number nineteen-thirty-six.
Right in front of his eyes the word LIBERTY, bent
20 To conform with the curve of the rim, appears
To be falling out of the sky Y first; the Indian
Keeps his eyes downcast and does not notice this;
To notice it, indeed, would be shortsighted of him.
So much for the iconography of one of our nickels,
25 Which is now becoming a rarity and something of
A collectors' item: for as a matter of fact
There is almost nothing you can buy with a nickel,
The representative American Indian was destroyed
A hundred years or so ago, and his descendants'
30 Relations with liberty are maintained with reservations,
Or primitive concentration camps; while the bison,

---

1. *Icons and cryptograms.* An icon is a picture or an image; a cryptogram is something written in code or cipher.

Except for a few examples kept in cages,
Is now extinct. Something like that, I think,
Is what Keats must have meant in his celebrated
35 Ode on a Grecian Urn.
                              Notice, in conclusion,
A number of circumstances sometimes overlooked
Even by experts: (a) Indian and bison,
Confined to obverse and reverse of the coin,
40 Can never see each other; (b) they are looking
In opposite directions, the bison past
The Indian's feathers, the Indian past
The bison's tail; (c) they are upside down
To one another; (d) the bison has a human face
45 Somewhat resembling that of Jupiter Ammon.[2]
I hope that our studies today will have shown you
Something of the import of symbolism
With respect to the understanding of what is symbolized.

interpretation

1. At the beginning and end of the poem, the lecturer speaks of symbolism. What does he mean when he declares that symbolism "is basic / To the nature of money"? Does the "introductory lecture" prove this point? Comment on the last three lines of the poem.
2. Cite several examples of irony. (See *Handbook of Terms and Techniques*.)

---

2. *Jupiter Ammon.* On ancient coins, the head of the Roman god Jupiter was sometimes shown wearing the curling ram's horns associated with the Egyptian deity Ammon.

JUMBLES LIVE LOBSTERS OF RED ONES[1]   KEITH GUNDERSON

Jumbles live lobsters of red ones
in tubs at the FRESH SEAFOOD place
the poor things
they can't feel anything you know
I think they can

On the pier a mackerel
with hardly its mackerel left on it
some kid who is fishing for
mackerel with mackerel

A trot trot
little dog brown
he's here every day I wonder who
maybe he just belongs to the dock
he's here every day

Flicking up some bread and a
gull catching it
flicking up some bread a
gull catching it
flicking up a
gull catching it

-----------------------------snail trails

----------#######bird tracks
" " " " " " "
***********track tracks

marks of the wish-wash   up   back   up
and tide   old eraser
of traces

flung-out hook disguised as a real-live sandcrab
five things in a gunny sack
couldn't tell the difference

a MAN
and a twenty yards after him
WOMAN
and a twenty yards after her after him
DOG
yet all of them walking together
because they are on
a beach

---

1. *"Jumbles live lobsters of red ones"* is an excerpt from *A Continual Interest in the Sun and Sea.* (For a discussion of CONCRETE POETRY, see *Handbook of Terms and Techniques.*)

Not much to say about the excerpt except that it's an attempt to depict in partially representational (or "concrete") ways scenes actually seen along the Southern California coast—in this case on and from the Santa Monica Pier which has a row of shops built on it including a fantastic merry-go-round. The book from which the excerpt is taken is itself the first part of a long work in progress. The second part is just about finished and will be called *Inland Missing the Sea.*

In the line "Jumbles live lobsters of red ones" I attempt to bring off a partial representation of what the line is about (all those lobsters tangled up in each other) by jumbling the syntax (grammar) of the line itself. Here the grammatical arrangement actually accentuates the *sense* of the line. I'm seldom interested in "concrete" or typographically representational tricks in and of themselves—rather, I try to use them to heighten either sense, sound or rhythm of a poem.

Keith Gunderson

SATURDAY

LUIS OMAR SALINAS

It is Saturday . . . day of apples and turnips
on heavy trucks that pass my aunts house
sleeping. My cousin is awake quibbling with
his painful back, this corner of the earth
5   surrenders to the anarchy of cows.

We are off to see the movies and the flesh
of night is torn into small, little children
as angels eat breaded clouds and spiders
tell stories to the rabbits of the neighborhood.

22

Voices are crying an
unknown name in the sky

ARCHIBALD MACLEISH

DE PROFUNDIS[1]

"Man is a tool-making animal." Benjamin Franklin

ALAN BOLD

1

Day after day the soldiers came to see
The hole in the ground. That is, after we
In the village were treated from the blast
That came the first day. Just where the old tree

2

5   Of the village stood, near the coast line where
The waves rocked back and forwards and the air
Bit into human flesh, the flames appeared
And spread towards our houses till the glare

3

Told our own bombers that a strike had been
10   Made. Only a small warning to the green
Hills of our country, they affirmed. In fact,
Few were hurt. It would be being mean

4

With human life to have complained that some
Friends close to us would be ghoulishly dumb
15   For good. In the pamphlets circulated
Around the village, there was a too glum

5

Prediction of the numbers they expected
Dead, or those, so badly mutilated
That their bodies would be burned in oil
20   At a safe distance from a strictly stated

6

Boundary. And while the crumbling white foam
Crumbled in the harbour and the spume
From the trawlers was carried out to sea
The frogmen came with equipment to comb

7

25   The coast line in case there might be some things
To explain a sudden attack. Rings
Of barbed wire now surrounded the deep hole,
The gaping belly where the first soundings

From TO FIND THE NEW. Reprinted by permission of Wesleyan University Press and Chatto & Windus Ltd.

1. *De Profundis*, out of the depths (of despair, sorrow). [*Latin*]

8

Were made. At first the doctors could not say
What caused the burns. At last they said the grey
Faces of those afflicted had been caused
By shock. But when the skin peeled like damp clay

9

From an armature, they began to go
More deeply into their stories. Also,
No country had been identified
As an aggressor; therefore there was no

10

Question of retaliation. Men
Who had seen the blast had drooled, shaken
By the sight, of a huge black creature
Breathing fire that had crashed out from a den

11

Deep in the earth where heat was constantly
Appropriate for its hellish hide. If we
Were frightened by these stories, the scientists
Were worse. "The End of Man's Ascendancy

12

In Sight" the headlines, inches deep, exclaimed
When news got to the press. And then they blamed
The politicians who had "let the rot
Of man go on." Churches said the damned

13

Could be identified and the creature
Was the devil merely overdue,
And that it was certainly time to choose
One's denomination. "You can be sure,"

14

The Pope intoned in St. Peter's Square,
"That those strongest in faith need have no fear.
Others are welcome to our bulging flock
But remember—this is no once a year

15

Offer, it is the chance of a lifetime."
The Archbishop of Canterbury, slime
On his brogues[2] after coming to the scene
Of the incident, began his speech: "'Home

---

2. *brogues*, shoes.

16

Is where one starts from' said our national poet,
And I agree. We did not, could not, know it
But God had decided to make a sign
Before *our* eyes—so that we would believe it."

17

65 In our village, many wearied of those—
Clerics, politicians, generals—whose prose
Blanketed out our air with platitudes
And auguries. But then the monster rose

18

One day from that profound hole in the ground
70 And roared. "For centuries a human sound
Was enough to frighten us from the hard
Surface of the earth. My colleagues have drowned

19

Their sorrows in your lochs[3] or underneath
Your feet. Man *was* supreme. The laurel wreath[4]
75 Was well deserved for that huge brain that made
A heaven on the earth. And now both

20

Our species cannot share it. You have made
A nuclear world of light and pretty red
Flames too hot for you. We will succeed
80 When your own efforts see your species dead."

interpretation

1. Briefly recount the event chronicled in this narrative poem.
2. Who or what is responsible for the surfacing of the monster? Why
had it not appeared before?
3. We may be justified in considering this narrative a kind of "moral
tale." What is the moral? Is it clearly stated or is it implied?

---

3. *lochs,* lakes. [*Scottish*] **4.** *laurel wreath,* symbol of honor. The ancient Greeks and Romans crowned
victors with wreaths of laurel.

EPISTLE TO BE LEFT IN THE EARTH

ARCHIBALD MACLEISH

. . . It is colder now
            there are many stars
                        we are drifting
North by the Great Bear[1]
5   the leaves are falling
The water is stone in the scooped rocks
                     to southward
Red sun grey air
            the crows are
10 Slow on their crooked wings
                  the jays have left us
Long since we passed the flares of Orion[2]
Each man believes in his heart he will die
Many have written last thoughts and last letters
15 None know if our deaths are now or forever
None know if this wandering earth will be found

We lie down and the snow covers our garments
I pray you
             you (if any open this writing)
20 Make in your mouths the words that were our names
I will tell you all we have learned
                   I will tell you everything
The earth is round
            there are springs under the orchards
25 The loam cuts with a blunt knife
              beware of
Elms in thunder
            the lights in the sky are stars
We think they do not see
30   we think also
The trees do not know nor the leaves of the grasses
                   hear us
The birds too are ignorant
            Do not listen
35 Do not stand at dark in the open windows

1. *Great Bear,* Ursa Major, the most prominent northern constellation, seen by ancient astronomers as having the rough outline of a bear. It includes the stars of the Big Dipper. 2. *flares of Orion* (ô rī′ən). The constellation Orion, which is near the equator, is surrounded by a cloudlike, luminous mass.

We before you have heard this
                              they are voices
They are not words at all but the wind rising
Also none among us has seen God
40 (. . . We have thought often
The flaws of sun in the late and driving weather
Pointed to one tree but it was not so.)
As for the nights I warn you the nights are dangerous
The wind changes at night and the dreams come

45 It is very cold
                 there are strange stars near Arcturus[3]

Voices are crying an unknown name in the sky

commentary

I am not sure I agree that commentaries are "valuable in helping students understand" a poem. What they often do is to help a student understand an *explanation* of a poem. But a poem, if it is one, *is* its explanation. And to introduce a commentary between the poem and its reader may very well mean that he will be left with nothing but a bit of extraneous information of no interest to him whatever. Excuse the lecture. It was driven home for me in thirteen years of teaching—trying to teach—poetry at Harvard. What I can do, and will be glad to do, is to correct a few misconceptions I have run into. Since Hiroshima there have been a number of interpreters of this poem who relate it to that disaster. It was first published in *1930* and I am no prophet. Another frequent reading makes the whole thing symbolic in the fashionable sense. Well, any poem means symbolically as well as literally—but only if it is read literally first—and here the literal meaning is essential: the "wandering earth," the dying sun, the ice—"we are drifting / North by the Great Bear." You ask who "we" are? It's a good question. Who *are* we? "I pray you. . . . Make in your mouths the sounds that were our names." But at least we can tell you what we have learned on this dying earth we have loved so well so long. Perhaps that might help?

Archibald MacLeish

---

3. *Arcturus* (ärk tür′əs), the brightest star in the northern sky.

THE FALL OF ROME

(for Cyril Connolly)

W. H. AUDEN

The piers are pummelled by the
   waves;
In a lonely field the rain
Lashes an abandoned train;
Outlaws fill the mountain caves.

5 Fantastic grow the evening gowns;
Agents of the Fisc[1] pursue
Absconding tax-defaulters through
The sewers of provincial towns.

Private rites of magic send
10 The temple prostitutes to sleep;
All the literati[2] keep
An imaginary friend.

Cerebrotonic Cato[3] may
Extol the Ancient Disciplines,
15 But the muscle-bound Marines
Mutiny for food and pay.

Caesar's double-bed is warm
As an unimportant clerk
Writes I DO NOT LIKE MY WORK
On a pink official form.   20

Unendowed with wealth or pity,
Little birds with scarlet legs,
Sitting on their speckled eggs,
Eye each flu-infected city.

Altogether elsewhere, vast   25
Herds of reindeer move across
Miles and miles of golden moss,
Silently and very fast.

---

interpretation

1. In a poem ostensibly about the fall of an ancient city, Auden includes such details as "an abandoned train" (line 3). What is peculiar about a train in this setting? The placing of persons, events, objects, etc., in a historical period to which they do not properly belong is called an *anachronism*. Find other anachronisms in the poem. What bearing do they have on the meaning of the poem?
2. What is the significance of Auden's references to the birds and the reindeer?

---

1. *the Fisc*, Fiscal Agency, a British equivalent of the Internal Revenue Service. **2.** *literati*, men of letters. **3.** *Cerebrotonic Cato*. Cato was an influential Roman senator who tried to preserve the republic against Caesar. He admired discipline and fought to suppress bribery. *Cerebrotonic* is a coined word meaning extremely brainy or cerebral.

THE ETERNAL CITY

A. R. AMMONS

After the explosion or cataclysm, that big
display that does its work but then fails
out with destructions, one is left with the

pieces: at first, they don't look very valuable,
5 but nothing sizable remnant around for
gathering the senses on, one begins to take

an interest, to sort out, to consider closely
what will do and won't, matters having become
not only small but critical: bulbs may have been

10 uprooted: they should be eaten, if edible, or
got back in the ground: what used to be garages,
even the splinters, should be collected for

fires: some unusually deep holes or cleared
woods may be turned to water supplies or
15 sudden fields: ruinage is hardly ever a

pretty sight but it must when splendor goes
accept into itself piece by piece all the old
perfect human visions, all the old perfect loves.

Interpretation

1. What advice does the speaker give to the survivor of a cataclysm?
2. Explain the last lines beginning with the words "ruinage is hardly
ever a / pretty sight . . ." (lines 15-16). What do these lines tell you
about the eternal city and where it is to be found?

ONE MORNING THE WORLD WOKE UP

OSCAR WILLIAMS

One morning the world woke up and there was no news;
No gun was shelling the great ear drum of the air,
No Christian flesh spurted beneath the subtle screws,
No moaning came from the many agony-faced Jews,
5   Only the trees in a gauze of wind trembled and were fair.

No trucks climbed into the groove of an endless road,
No tanks were swaying drunken with death at the hilltop,
No bombs were planting their bushes of blood and mud,
And the aimless tides of unfortunates no longer flowed:
10   A break in the action at last . . . all had come to a stop.

Those trees danced, in their delicate selves half furled
And a new time on the glittering atmosphere was seen;
The lightning stuttering on the closed eyelid of the world
Was gone, and an age of horizons had dawned, soft, pearled,
15   The world woke up to a scene like spring's first green.

Birds chirped in waterfalls of little sounds for hours,
Rainbows, in miniature nuggets, were stored in the dews,
The sky was one vast moonstone of the tenderest blues,
And the meadows lay carpeted in three heights of flowers:
20   One morning the world woke up and there was no news.

EARTH

JOHN HALL WHEELOCK

"A planet doesn't explode of itself," said drily
The Martian astronomer, gazing off into the air—
"That they were able to do it is proof that highly
Intelligent beings must have been living there."

Handbook
of
Terms
and
Techniques

An axe angles
> from my neighbor's ashcan;
It is hell's handiwork,
> the wood not hickory,
The flow of the grain
> not faithfully followed.
The shivered shaft
> rises from a shellheap
5 Of plastic playthings,
> paper plates,
And the sheer shards
> of shattered tumblers
That were not annealed
> for the time needful.
> Wilbur, "Junk"

Note that each line in the excerpt from Wilbur's "Junk" contains words that begin with similar sounds. What initial sound recurs, for example, in line 6? The repetition of sounds in words such as sheer, shards, and shattered is called *alliteration*—the recurrence of similar initial sounds. This term may apply to consonant sounds at the beginning of words (Love's Labour's Lost) or at the beginning of accented syllables (a bout′ the e bul′lient beg′gar). Alliteration may be accomplished in one line of a poem or it may run through several lines. More than one sound can be alliterated in a given line or lines. Although alliteration is usually associated with consonant sounds, the term may also apply to repeated initial vowel sounds. Which line cited above contains vowel alliteration? Some critics have used the term *alliteration* to include any repetition of letter sounds regardless of where they appear in a word.

Just as words have great suggestive powers, so, in combination with other factors, do sounds. A poet strives for the perfect union of meaning and sound and is sensitive to the contribution each can make to the other. However, alliteration can be used simply for musical effect. Which of the following do you think alliteration accomplishes in the preceding passage: musical effect; unification of thought; reinforcement of meaning?

Read the following description of Proserpine, the queen of the underworld, from Swinburne's "The Garden of Proserpine."

> Pale, beyond porch and portal
>   Crowned with calm leaves, she stands
> Who gathers all things mortal
>   With cold immortal hands;
> Her languid lips are sweeter
> Than love's who fears to greet her
> To men that mix and meet her
>   From many times and lands.

Summarize these lines. What mood do they express? Point out examples of alliteration. Explain the relationship, if any, of alliteration to the meaning, tone, mood, music, or movement of the poem.

ALLITERATION: the repetition of identical or nearly identical sounds at the beginning of words or accented syllables.

> The fair breeze blew, the white foam flew,
> The furrow followed free.

---

allusion

RUTH

PHILIP LEVINE

> They would waken
> face to face, the windshield
> crystalled, the car
> so cold they had to get out.
> Beyond the apple orchard
> they saw where the dawn sun
> fell among plowed fields
> in little mounds of shadow
> and a small stream ran black below
> where the rocks slept.
> Her wrists pounding

against it, she rubbed
the water into eyes
and temples, the iron taste
faint on her tongue.
And they'd get going, stopping
for Cokes and gas
and cold candy bars all
through Ohio,
and when the sun failed
north of Toledo,
they were almost there,
the night sky burning
up ahead at River Rouge[1]
like another day.

Another day.
Now he was gone, the children
grown up and gone,
and she back home,
or whatever you could call it,
West Virginia.
A wafer of sunlight
on the pillow, and she rose
and heard the mice startled
beneath the floorboards. Washed
in the sink, lit the stove,
and waited. Another day
falling into the fields, tufted
like a child's quilt.
Beyond the empty yard,
a wall of poplars stared back,
their far sides
still darkness, and beyond,
its teeth dulled with rust,
the harrow tilted
on one frozen wheel, sliding
back to earth.

1. What is the geographical setting of the first stanza of the poem?
2. The words "another day" end the first stanza and are repeated to begin the second stanza. What two purposes related to time and circumstance does this repetition indicate?

---

1. *River Rouge*, a manufacturing town near Detroit.

3. Is any reason given directly in the poem for the title "Ruth," or could the poem just as reasonably have been titled "Margaret," or "Ann," or "Janet"?

4. Ruth is a character in the book of the same name in the Old Testament. Following is the beginning of her story.

> Ruth was a Moabite, a young childless widow. Her
> mother-in-law Naomi, also widowed, decided to return to
> Bethlehem in Judah, her native place. When Ruth decided
> to follow her, Naomi begged her to remain with her own
> people. Ruth replied, "Entreat me not to leave thee
> or to return from following after thee: for whither thou
> goest, I will go. . . ." Ruth followed Naomi to Judah
> and there went into the fields to gather the wheat the
> reapers left behind.

What similarities can you find between the Biblical story and the story in the Levine poem? What differences?

5. Knowledge of the Biblical story of Ruth has a significant impact on the reader's interpretation of this modern poem. Which of the following does this knowledge seem to contribute? (a) information essential to the narrative; (b) timelessness; (c) dignity.

An *allusion* is a reference to a fictional or actual character or event. It may refer to myth, literature, history, religion, or any aspect of ancient or modern culture. (Allusions may appear in prose as well as poetry.) Allusion may be a means of achieving conciseness, since much can be suggested by a single reference. Always the allusion must be appropriate to the dominant intellectual and emotional intent of the work as a whole.

The importance of allusion varies from use to use. Sometimes allusion determines the very meaning of a poem; on other occasions allusion is employed mainly for mood, tone, or atmosphere. If knowledge of an allusion is essential to understanding a work, research is required on the part of the reader. No one reads primarily for the purpose of building up a rich memory source of allusion, but command of allusion is a happy by-product of wide reading.

ALLUSION: a reference to a person, thing, event, or aspect of culture, real or fictional, past or present. The statement, "She met her Waterloo on the final exam," alludes to Napoleon's historic defeat.

The artist can gain special emphasis in a work by placing black against white or large objects against small. A musician sometimes pits harsh sounds against soft sounds or uses a slow tempo as foil to a faster one. Even common adages or expressions use contrast for effect: "Handsome is as handsome does"; "Little pitchers have big ears"; or the phrase "Roses are red, violets are blue" that has launched so much amateur poetry. What contrasts are in the following lines by Kipling?

> For it's Tommy this, an' Tommy that, an' "Chuck 'im out,
> the brute!"
> But it's "Savior of 'is country" when the guns begin
> to shoot.
> Kipling, "Tommy"

In poetry the pitting of unlike things against each other is called *antithesis:* a technique by which a word, clause, sentence, image, or idea is balanced against another for surprise or emphasis. Antithesis operates by opposition of idea and can be reinforced by parallel grammatical structure. Which elements in this definition apply to the Kipling passage?

Note the use of antithesis in the following passage from Thomas Middleton's *Blurt.*

> Love is all in fire, and yet is ever freezing;
> Love is much in winning, yet is more in leesing;
> Love is ever sick, and yet is never dying;
> Love does doat in liking, and is mad in loathing;
> Love indeed is anything, yet indeed is nothing.

ANTITHESIS: a technique in which a word, clause, sentence, image, or idea is balanced against another, often in a parallel structure. Shakespeare uses antithesis in the following line from *Hamlet:*

> With mirth in funeral, and with dirge in marriage.

Excerpt from "Tommy" by Rudyard Kipling from RUDYARD KIPLING'S VERSE: DEFINITIVE EDITION. Reprinted by permission of Doubleday & Company, Inc., Mrs. George Bambridge and A. P. Watt & Son.

Byron addresses the ocean:

> Roll on, thou deep and dark blue Ocean, roll!
> Ten thousand fleets sweep over thee in vain;
> Man marks the earth with ruin, his control
> Stops with the shore; upon the watery plain
> The wrecks are all thy deed. . .
>> Byron, "Apostrophe to the Ocean"

Ezra Pound, writing many years after Walt Whitman's death, addresses that poet:

A PACT

EZRA POUND

> I make a pact with you, Walt Whitman—
> I have detested you long enough.
> I come to you as a grown child
> Who has had a pig-headed father;
> I am old enough now to make friends.
> It was you that broke the new wood,
> Now is a time for carving.
> We have one sap and one root—
> Let there be commerce between us.

Juliet addresses Romeo, whom she believes to be absent:

> O Romeo, Romeo, wherefore art thou Romeo?
> Deny thy father and refuse thy name;
> Or, if thou wilt not, be but sworn my love,
> And I'll no longer be a Capulet. . . .
> 'Tis but thy name that is my enemy.
>> Shakespeare, *Romeo and Juliet*

Each of the preceding passages is an *apostrophe,* a figure of speech in which the absent are addressed as though present, the inanimate as though animate, or the dead as though living. Which example above fits which type of apostrophe?

The apostrophe (like all rhetorical devices) can be easily overused. Occasionally apostrophes deliberately create a humorous effect.

APOSTROPHE: a figure of speech in which an absent or dead person, an inanimate object, or an abstract concept is addressed directly. The following is an apostrophe used for humorous effect.

> Beware, O asparagus, you've stalked my last meal.
> You look like a snake and slip down like an eel.
> I'd prefer drinking a bottle of turpentine,
> Rather than eating a tidbit so serpentine.
> Wanda Fergus

---

assonance

> Cold. Cold. Cold. Cold winds and colder heart,
> The night blows cold from East to West, and love
> Grows cold as England. What fire consoles? . . .
> Thompson, "A Knight of Ghosts and Shadows"

In the above lines, the word *cold* repeatedly appears. What other words in this passage echo the long *o* sound in *cold?* What would you say the repetition of the long *o* sound contributes to mood and meaning in these lines? The recurring long *o* sound in the passage is an example of *assonance*—identical vowel sounds followed by different consonant sounds (gr*ow*s / c*ol*d). Assonance differs from rhyme in that both vowel sounds and the consonant sounds that succeed them are identical in rhyming words (g*old* / c*old*). Assonance, when used skillfully, affects the musical quality of a poem and makes a significant contribution to mood and meaning. It can provide emphasis and a sense of unity in a work. Note how assonance is used in the first line of Shapiro's "The Conscientious Objector" (page 16). Note that assonance in this line contributes to the tone and meaning of the poem.

Examine the passages on the following page. Determine whether assonance generally occurs in stressed or unstressed words or syllables.

> Then a mile of warm sea-scented beach;
> Three fields to cross till a farm appears; . . .
>> Browning, "Meeting at Night"

> The full streams feed on flower of rushes,
> Ripe grasses trammel a traveling foot . . .
>> Swinburne, "When the Hounds of
>> Spring Are on Winter's Traces"

ASSONANCE: repetition of vowel sounds followed by different consonant sounds in stressed words or syllables. Keats uses assonance in the opening lines of "Ode on a Grecian Urn":

> Thou still unravished bride of quietness,
> Thou foster-child of silence and slow time, . . .

---

ballad

Folk Ballad

There is a certain kind of poem called a *ballad*, or perhaps more correctly a *folk ballad*, that is part of the oral tradition, handed down from generation to generation and only recorded in writing many years after its creation. It is of unknown authorship. Here are the first four stanzas from such a poem. Fair Annie of Rough Royal speaks:

> "O who will shoe my small fair foot?
>> And who will glove my hand?
> And who will lace my middle slim
>> With the new made London band?

> "And who will comb my yellow hair,
>> With the new made silver comb?
> And who will father my young son,
>> Till Love Gregor come home?"

"Your father will shoe your small fair foot,
  Your mother will glove your hand;
Your sister will lace your middle slim
  With the new made London band.

"Your brother will comb your yellow hair,
  With the new made silver comb;
And the king of heaven will father your bairn,
  Till Love Gregor come home."
                    Anonymous, "Love Gregor"

1. How many lines does each of these stanzas contain? What is the RHYME scheme of the first stanza? Is its pattern maintained throughout the remaining three stanzas?
2. How many beats are there in the first and third lines; in the second and fourth lines?

As a form, the ballad generally adheres to certain conventions or rules. In answering the questions above you have analyzed the conventional stanza pattern of the ballad. In summary, the ballad stanza is composed of four iambic lines rhyming *a b c b*. The unrhymed first and third lines have four feet, the rhyming second and fourth lines three feet.

In the preceding stanzas, which lines, phrases, and words are repeated? The repetition of lines, phrases, or words is called a REFRAIN. Such repetition may serve to set a scene, provide emphasis, establish tone, or merely entertain.

The story of Fair Annie of Rough Royal (the young woman who asks the questions that open "Love Gregor") goes on at some length. Here is a summary.

Because Annie's lover cannot come to her, she takes her young son and sails to him. When she arrives with the boy at Gregor's home, he is asleep. Though he speaks to her, he thinks he is dreaming and confuses her with "some witch, or wild warlock, / Or mermaid of the flood." He sends her away. The next morning he tells his mother of his "dream," and she admits that Annie was really there. Cursing the old woman for allowing him to send his sweetheart away, Gregor goes to search for Annie. She has already set sail on a rough sea. He calls to her, but "The louder he cried Annie, / The louder roared the sea." Finally, the boat is dashed upon the shore; both Annie and her son are killed. The weeping Gregor is last seen kissing Annie's cold lips and again cursing his mother.

3. Judging from this summary, what do you think is most important—character development, action, tone, setting, or some other aspect? Explain.

The emphasis "Love Gregor" places upon plot and action is another convention of the ballad form; its purpose is to tell a story, usually focusing on a simple dramatic episode or situation. There is little description or attempt at characterization, and the author's tone is objective.

This poem leaves several questions unanswered: why are Gregor and Annie separated? why can't he return home? what might have been his mother's reasons for not allowing Annie into the house? What answers can you advance for these questions? Another characteristic of the ballad is that motivation is almost never explained, but left to the audience to fill in for itself. The ballad moves at a good pace, and to speed things along it omits transitions of time and place and makes much use of succinct dialogue.

Although the preceding qualities characterize the ballad, many ballads do not contain all of them. There are ballads with two- or six-line stanzas and a variety of rhyme schemes and metrical patterns, ballads that make no use of repetition, and ballads that emphasize character or tone.

Literary Ballad

Many of the ancient ballads tell their stories with such dramatic effect and artistry that poets sometimes imitate this traditional form. Such imitations are of known authorship and are called *literary* or *art ballads*. Here is an example.

PROUD MAISIE

SIR WALTER SCOTT

Proud Maisie is in the wood,
    Walking so early;
Sweet Robin sits on the bush,
    Singing so rarely.

"Tell me, thou bonny bird,
    When shall I marry me?"
"When six braw gentlemen
    Kirkward shall carry ye."

"Who makes the bridal bed,
    Birdie, say truly?"
"The gray-headed sexton
    That delves the grave duly.

"The glowworm o'er grave and stone
    Shall light thee steady;
The owl from the steeple sing,
    'Welcome proud lady.'"

1. What questions are asked in this poem? What answers are given?
2. What traits does this literary ballad share with the older, folk-ballad form? Can you find any significant differences between the two forms?

BALLAD: a narrative, originally passed on in the oral tradition. The ballad moves swiftly, and is told simply, directly, and objectively. It often makes use of repetition and dialogue. A ballad whose author is known is called a *literary ballad.*

blank verse

But do not let us quarrel any more.
No, my Lucrezia; bear with me for once:
Sit down and all shall happen as you wish.
You turn your face, but does it bring your heart?
                Browning, "Andrea Del Sarto"

1. Do the preceding lines rhyme?
2. The rhythm of the first line can be indicated as follows. (Stress is indicated by the symbol ⁄ , lack of stress by the symbol ˘ .)

But dó nŏt lét ŭs quár rĕl ăn y̆ móre.

Do the other lines follow this metrical pattern?
    A line with five beats that moves along this way—ta DUM ta DUM ta DUM ta DUM ta DUM—is called *iambic pentameter.* Unrhymed iambic pentameter lines are called *blank verse.* Read the following passages; explain whether or not each of them is blank verse.

You ask why can't Clarissa hold her tongue.
Because she fears her fingers will be stung.
                Hopkins, "Six Epigrams"

Excerpt from "Six Epigrams" from POEMS OF GERARD MANLEY HOPKINS, 4th Edition. Published by Oxford University Press, London.

Cruelty has a Human Heart
And Jealousy a Human Face,
Terror, the Human Form Divine,
And Secrecy, the Human Dress.
    Blake, "A Divine Image"

The world was all before them, where to choose
Their place of rest, and providence their guide:
They hand in hand with wandering steps and slow,
Through Eden took their solitary way.
    Milton, *Paradise Lost*

A line or lines of a blank-verse passage may, at times, depart from a regular iambic pattern. What lines in the following passage deviate from the iambic pentameter pattern?

To-morrow, and to-morrow, and to-morrow,
Creeps in this petty pace from day to day
To the last syllable of recorded time,
And all our yesterdays have lighted fools
The way to dusty death. Out, out, brief candle!
    Shakespeare, *Macbeth*

Such shifts in meter enabled Shakespeare to use blank verse to achieve a great variety of dramatic effects. Although less common in modern poetry, blank verse occasionally appears in contemporary verse. (See "The Ball Poem," page 33, and "The Well Dressed Man with a Beard," page 236.) When used skillfully, blank verse captures and enhances the natural, conversational rhythms of the English language.

BLANK VERSE: unrhymed iambic pentameter.

"What have you done to me! What have we done
To Fate, that she should hate us and destroy us,
Waiting for us to speak. What have we done
So false or foul as to be burned alive
And then be buried alive—as we shall be . . ."
    Robinson, *Tristram*

Excerpt from "Tristram" reprinted with permission of Macmillan Publishing Co., Inc. from COL-LECTED POEMS by Edwin Arlington Robinson. Copyright 1927 by Edwin Arlington Robinson, renewed 1955 by Ruth Nivison and Barbara R. Holt.

cacophony and euphony

Alexander Pope explained that in poetry the "sound must seem an echo to the sense." Read the following lines from his *Essay on Criticism* aloud to determine if Pope heeds his own words.

> Soft is the strain when Zephyr gently blows,
> And the smooth stream in smoother numbers flows;
> But when loud surges lash the sounding shore,
> The hoarse, rough verse should like the torrent roar:
> When Ajax[1] strives some rock's vast weight to throw,
> The line, too, labors, and the words move slow;
> Not so, when swift Camilla[2] scours the plain,
> Flies o'er th' unbending corn, and skims along the main.

Different lines in the preceding passage serve to describe softness, harshness, and speed. Which lines express each of these qualities? Can you find a relationship between Pope's "sense" and his "sounds," between each subject and the words that describe it? What particular sounds, words, or groups of words convey the idea of softness, harshness, speed?

Read the following lines to see if the sound is an echo to the sense.

> Dry clashed his harness in the icy caves
> And barren chasms, and all to left and right
> The bare black cliff clanged round him, as he based
> His feet on juts of slippery crag that rang
> Sharp-smitten with the dint of armed heels—
> And on a sudden, lo, the level lake
> And the long glories of the winter moon!
>   Tennyson, *The Passing of Arthur*

Where does the atmosphere change in the preceding quotation? How is that change reflected in the sound of the poem? Describe the sounds in the first five lines; the final two lines.

Some of the sounds Tennyson uses are harsh, jarring, almost violent ("bare black cliff clanged"). A succession of such sounds is called *cacophony*. What is the "sense" echoed by the cacophony in Tennyson's lines?

Other of Tennyson's sounds are light, harmonious, pleasing to the ear ("lo, the level lake"). A succession of such sounds is called *euphony*. What is the "sense" echoed through euphony in Tennyson's lines?

---

1. *Ajax,* a Greek hero of the Trojan War, noted for his size and strength. **2.** *Camilla,* a swift-footed female warrior who was killed fighting a Trojan band in Italy.

Which term—*cacophony* or *euphony*—would you apply to the sounds in the following passage?

> I love smooth words, like gold enameled fish
> Which circle slowly, with a silken swish . . .
>> Wylie, "Pretty Words"

Try to rewrite Elinor Wylie's lines, making them cacophonous, beginning: I hate harsh words . .

CACOPHONY: a succession of harsh, jarring sounds.

EUPHONY: a combination of agreeable sounds.

Jonson makes use of both cacophony and euphony in these lines from "Explorate":

> They write a verse as smooth, as soft as cream;
> In which there is no torrent, nor scarce scream.

---
caesura

Read these lines aloud:

1. Begin, and cease, and then again begin . . .
>> Arnold, "Dover Beach"

2. To die, to sleep;
   To sleep: perchance to dream: ay, there's the rub; . . .
>> Shakespeare, *Hamlet*

3. To dying ears, when unto dying eyes
   The casement slowly grows a glimmering square;
   So sad, so strange, the days that are no more.
>> Tennyson, *The Princess*

Now read the lines again, stopping for a definite pause when one is indicated by the symbol / /.

1. Begin, / / and cease, / / and then again begin. . .

2. To die, / / to sleep;
   To sleep: / / perchance to dream: / / ay, / / there's the rub; . . .

3. To dying ears, / / when unto dying eyes
   The casement slowly grows a glimmering square;
   So sad, / / so strange, / / the days that are no more.

The first quotation describes the ebb and flow of the tide and the changes that come with time. The second is the reflection of a distraught soul who weighs a painful life against a troubled death. The third is a wistful reminiscence of bygone days. What do the indicated pauses contribute to the lines?

An internal pause in the rhythmic flow of a line of poetry is called a *caesura;* its symbol is / / . Though the caesura is most often indicated by punctuation, it can also be dictated by grammar, natural stops in speech, or emphasis in oral delivery. Occasionally, a caesura is indicated by extra space between words. (See "In the Pocket," page 144.) The placement of the caesura, as well as its length, may vary from reader to reader. A caesura is one of several techniques a poet may use to add variety to regular meters.

Decide where you think the caesuras should be placed in the following lines from Herrick.

> Get up! get up for shame! the blooming morn
> Upon her wings presents the god unshorn.
>   See how Aurora throws her fair
>   Fresh-quilted colors through the air:
>   Get up, sweet slug-a-bed, and see
>   The dew bespangling herb and tree.
>   Herrick, "Corinna's Going A-Maying"

CAESURA: a pause in the rhythmical flow of a line of verse. A caesura can be dictated by a number of factors, among them punctuation, space, grammar, natural stops in speech, and oral delivery. Byron uses caesuras to reinforce his satiric tone in passages such as the following from *Don Juan.*

> She knew the Latin—that is, "The Lord's Prayer,"
> And Greek—the alphabet—I'm nearly sure . . .

UNDER THE BEACH UMBRELLA

JOHN HOLLANDER

Straight
overhead now as white as
it ever gets and fiercer than we
can imagine the sun threatens Not with a hot
white eye but under a cupped palms dark plot to grow
to extend the field of shadow still no wider than our spread
of tented blue canvas Within this dark ring is no pain White beach
burns unbearably beyond a hot line where the edge of the noons blade

is
as
of
an
ax
To
go
by
it
so
as
to
be
in
or
at
or
on
it
is
to
be
of
it
as
we
all
are
even alas out of it within this fragile and shifting circle of shade

1. The connection between the subject matter and the shape of the poem on the preceding page is obvious. What do you think the poet gains by setting up his poem as he does?

Poetry which uses typographical effects (the shape of combined words, letters, or symbols on the page) in addition to or instead of some of the conventions of verse (rhyme, meter, stanza form, etc.) is called *concrete poetry*. The writer of a concrete poem places words on a page in such a manner that the visual effect reinforces the meaning. Though the 1950's saw the development of an international interest in concrete poetry, it is actually a very old form. Following, for example, is a concrete poem written in seventeenth-century England.

EASTER WINGS

GEORGE HERBERT

Lord, who createdst man in wealth and store,[1]
Though foolishly he lost the same,
Decaying more and more
Till he became
Most poor:
With thee
O let me rise
As larks, harmoniously,
And sing this day thy victories:
Then shall the fall further the flight in me.

My tender age in sorrow did begin;
And still with sicknesses and shame
Thou didst so punish sin,
That I became
Most thin.
With thee
Let me combine,
And feel this day thy victory;
For, if I imp[2] my wing on thine,
Affliction shall advance the flight in me.

1. Relate the shape of the above poem to its title and subject matter.
2. Compare this poem and the one printed at the beginning of this exercise. Which do you think was more difficult to write? Why?
3. Does the visual arrangement of words in each poem appear logical, or do you feel either poet has "cheated" at times to make his concrete

---

1. *store*, abundance. 2. *imp*, a term from the sport of falconry in which additional feathers were grafted or "imped" onto a hawk's wing to improve its ability to fly.

poem look right? (Examine, for example, the sentence that contains the "pole" and "stem" of Hollander's poem. Does it make sense?)

CONCRETE POETRY: poetry in which the shape of the printed form is related to its subject.

---

connotation and denotation

The following is the definition of *sea* as it appears in a dictionary.

> **sea** (sē), *n.* **1** the great body of salt water that covers almost three fourths of the earth's surface; the ocean. **2** any large body of salt water, smaller than an ocean, partly or wholly enclosed by land: *the North Sea.* **3** any of various relatively large landlocked bodies of fresh or salt water: *the Sea of Galilee, the Black Sea.* **4** the swell of the ocean: *a heavy sea.* **5** a large, heavy wave. **6** an overwhelming amount or number: *a sea of troubles.* **7** a broad expanse: *a sea of upturned faces.* **8** Often, **Sea.** one of the dark, flat plains of the moon once thought to be seas; mare: *the Sea of Tranquility.*

Does the word *sea* have any personal meanings or associations for you? How do your own meanings for *sea* differ from the dictionary definition? What additional meaning is given to the word *sea* by Gerard Manley Hopkins when he calls it, "The widow-making unchilding unfathering deeps"?

Many of the words we use daily have a double significance: they have a *denotation*, or dictionary definition, and a *connotation*, or a wealth of suggested meanings and associations, some personal, some universal.

> **dan de li on** (dan′dl i′ən), *n.* a common weed of the composite family with deeply notched leaves and bright-yellow flowers that bloom in the spring. [< Middle French *dent de lion* lion's tooth; from its toothed leaves]

What does the word *dandelion* mean to you? Is it a sign of spring, a nuisance, a way to test if you like butter? See what meanings Nemerov finds in the dandelion in the poem on the following page.

Excerpt from "The Wreck of the Deutschland" from POEMS OF GERARD MANLEY HOPKINS, 4th Edition. Published by Oxford University Press, London.

DANDELIONS HOWARD NEMEROV

These golden heads, these common suns
Only less multitudinous
Than grass itself that gluts
The market of the world with green,
They shine as lovely as they're mean,
Fine as the daughters of the poor
Who go proudly in spangles of brass;
Light-headed, then headless, stalked for a salad.

Inside a week they will be seen
Stricken and old, ghosts in the field
To be picked up at the lightest breath,
With brazen tops all shrunken in
And swollen green gone withered white.
You'll say it's nature's price for beauty
That goes cheap; that being light
Is justly what makes girls grow heavy;
And that the wind, bearing their death,
Whispers the second kingdom come.
—You'll say, the fool of piety,
By resignations hanging on
Until, still justified, you drop.
But surely the thing is sorrowful,
At evening, when the light goes out
Slowly, to see those ruined spinsters,
All down the field their ghostly hair,
Dry sinners waiting in the valley
For the last word and the next life
And the liberation from the lion's mouth.[1]

1. Check the preceding dictionary definition and etymology of *dandelion*. Which of its denotative characteristics does Nemerov include in the poem? What characteristics does Nemerov give his dandelions that are not part of the dictionary meaning?
2. What does the Biblical ALLUSION in the last line add to the connotation in the poem? Why is this allusion particularly appropriate, given

1. *liberation . . . mouth.* This line echoes the following words from the Bible: "Notwithstanding the Lord stood with me, and strengthened me . . . and I was delivered out of the mouth of the lion. And the Lord shall deliver me from every evil work, and will preserve *me* unto his heavenly kingdom." (II Timothy 4:17–18) The allusion also suggests the Biblical story of Daniel who was protected by God and spared from death when imprisoned in the lion's den.

the etymology of the word *dandelion* and the portrayal of dandelions as "dry sinners"?

In this poem, the dandelions acquire meanings beyond their dictionary definitions, for here the poet is concerned with the connotations of the word. These connotations lead us away from a literal view of the flower to a nonliteral one.

CONNOTATION: the emotional, imaginative, cultural, or traditional associations surrounding a word, as opposed to its strict, literal dictionary meaning.

DENOTATION: the strict dictionary meaning of a word, presented objectively, without emotional associations. The word *home* has the denotation or dictionary definition of "a dwelling place"; its various connotations, however, may include (or exclude) father and mother, good or bad things to eat, the smell of burning leaves, or garbage cans.

consonance

> The Wind—tapped like a tired Man
> And like a Host—"Come in"
> I boldly answered—entered then
> My Residence within . . .
> > Dickinson, "The Wind Tapped
> > Like a Tired Man"

Although the final words in each line of the preceding stanza do not, strictly speaking, rhyme, they share a common sound. With what consonant sound does each line end? Are the vowel sounds that precede the final consonant sound in *man, in,* and *then* alike or different? Such repetition of identical consonant sounds that are preceded by different vowel sounds is called *consonance*. Wilfred Owen makes frequent use of consonance when he pairs words such as *blade / blood, flash / flesh, heads / lads, teeth / death.* (See "Arms and the Boy," page 30. Note how consonance enhances meaning by suggesting associations between these word pairs.) Shelley uses consonance within a poetic line when he speaks of "an old, mad, blind, despised, and dying king." Consonance is an effective device for creating word music and can reinforce mood and meaning. Consonance, as it is used by Dickinson and Owen,

Excerpt from "The Wind Tapped Like a Tired Man" by Emily Dickinson from THE COMPLETE POEMS OF EMILY DICKINSON, edited by Thomas H. Johnson. Published by Little, Brown and Company.

is synonymous with slant rhyme. (See RHYME.) What examples of consonance can you find in the following lines from Robert Burns? Does the use of consonance here produce any effects?

> And, must I think it! is she gone,
> My secret heart's exulting boast?
> And does she heedless hear my groan?
> And is she ever, ever lost?

CONSONANCE: the repetition of identical consonant sounds that are preceded by different vowel sounds.

> The bold, mad dragon preyed in the wild wood.

---

couplet

> Yes I am proud; I must be proud to see
> Men, not afraid of God, afraid of me.
> Pope, *Epilogue to the Satires*

> See how the flowers, as at parade,
> Under their colours stand displayed:
> Each regiment in order grows,
> That of the tulip, pink, and rose.
> Marvell, "A Garden"

Determine (a) the RHYME scheme and (b) the RHYTHM of each of these quotations.

Couple, of course, means "two," and in poetry a rhymed pattern of two lines is called a *couplet.* Any two consecutive rhymed lines of parallel meter can be considered a couplet.

One special kind of couplet is the *heroic couplet:* two rhymed iambic pentameter lines (see RHYTHM), usually containing a complete thought, and hence with the second line END-STOPPED. Its name derives from the notion that this meter is appropriate for the serious subjects which characterize epic or "heroic" verse. Of the two preceding examples, which one fits this definition? Explain.

COUPLET: a pair of rhyming lines with parallel meter.

> The grave's a fine and private place,
> But none, I think, do there embrace.
> Marvell, "To His Coy Mistress"

denotation See *connotation and denotation.*

---

diction

1. He is fair, fat, and forty.
2. Falstaff sweats to death,
   And lards the lean earth as he walks along.
   > Shakespeare, *Henry IV, Part I*

Which of these two descriptions gives you the more distinctive picture of a large man? Why?

3. My father passed away Tuesday and was laid to rest Thursday.
4. My father died Tuesday and was buried Thursday.

Of examples 3 and 4 which is clearer and more direct?

5. Sam and Jill exchanged their nuptials yesterday.
6. Sam and Jill were married yesterday.
7. Sam and Jill got hitched yesterday.

Under what different circumstances might each of these three accounts of a wedding be appropriately given?

8. He has not yet begun to shave.
9. Alas, poor chin! many a wart is richer.
   > Shakespeare, *Troilus and Cressida*

Which of these two lines gives a better indication of the writer's feelings about his beardless subject? Explain.

10. I was flabbergasted by the kind and courteous treatment shown me by the staff.
11. I was surprised by the kind and courteous treatment shown me by the staff.

The two preceding statements differ only in their verbs. Which verb contributes dignity to the tone of the sentence?

In answering all of the preceding questions, you have been making judgments about the writers' uses of *diction* or choice of words. Because poetry is a condensed form of expression, the poet must choose words having both the DENOTATIONS and CONNOTATIONS that will convey the desired effect. A skillful poet chooses one particular word over others because it best expresses a special mood, meaning, image, or sound.

An effective poet avoids words that are superfluous, or words that weaken, such as clichés (example 1) and euphemisms (example 3). Suppose, for example, Millay had begun her "Elegy" (page 344) with the words: "Let them lay to rest your big eyes / In the Mother Earth firmly and safely." Compare these words to those she actually wrote.

In a successful poem the word choice both creates and is compatible with the tone the poet intends. Formal diction (example 5) or slang (example 7) would be appropriate only if the intention of the poet warrants such diction.

A skillful poet uses words that illustrate his ideas. In example 9 Shakespeare's contrasting of a hairless face with a hairy wart communicates a humorous, perhaps even mocking, attitude. The objective and rather flat "He has not yet begun to shave" (example 8) tells nothing of the writer's feelings.

Once the poet's job is done, the reader's job begins. A poet uses words discriminately, choosing a particular word over others because it best conveys the meaning, establishes the tone, or in effect does what the poet wants it to do. A careful reader becomes aware of the poet's intention and gives almost as much attention to specific details in reading the poem as the poet did in writing it.

A particular kind of diction is termed *poetic diction*. This diction may involve certain words, such as *'twas, doth,* and *o'er,* that occur exclusively in poetry. Poetic diction may be concerned with phrases (*whiskered vermin race* instead of *rats*) or with a reversal of normal word order called *inversion* (*Happy was I* for *I was happy*). Poetic diction grew out of the belief that the language of poetry should be distinguished from the language of prose. These lines from Blake's "Auguries of Innocence" illustrate its use.

> A skylark wounded on the wing
> Doth make a cherub cease to sing.

How might the same thing be said in informal, conversational, or "normal" language? Poetic diction was frequently used and highly regarded until around 1800, when the poet Wordsworth argued that poetry should be written in the natural language of everyday speech. By the twentieth century, poetic diction appeared infrequently in poetry. Such diction appears rarely in modern poetry, and then usually for ironic effect.

Given the preceding general information on diction, comment on the diction of the poem on the next page.

THE BUTCHER

HUGO WILLIAMS

The butcher carves veal for two.
The cloudy, frail slices fall over his knife.

His face is hurt by the parting sinews
And he looks up with relief, laying it on the scales.

He is a rose young man with white eyelashes
Like a bullock. He always serves me now.

I think he knows about my life. How we prefer
To eat in when it's cold. How someone

With a foreign accent can only cook veal.
He writes the price on the grease-proof packet

And hands it to me courteously. His smile
Is the official seal on my marriage.

1. Does Williams use any strongly connotative words? Does he employ any words or phrases figuratively? If so, point out examples.
2. Are there any words you'd change? If so, what are they and how would the change affect the poem?
   The following lines by Josephine Miles are from a poem which relates an encounter between two drivers.

Said, Pull her up a bit will you, Mac, I want to unload there.
Said, Pull her up my rear end, first come first serve.
Said, Give her the gun, Bud, he needs a taste of his own bumper.
                                        Miles, "Reason"

How would you describe the diction used by Miles? Would you term the word choice here "antipoetic"? the subject?

DICTION: the particular choice of words a writer makes in a literary work. The best choice always considers the total contribution a word can make in fulfilling a poet's intention. In the following lines Coleridge describes a ship becalmed; his diction might be considered informal, made up of concrete words producing at least one strong visual image.

> Day after day, day after day,
> We stuck, nor breath nor motion;
> As idle as a painted ship
> Upon a painted ocean.
> Coleridge, "The Rime of
the Ancient Mariner"

dramatic monologue

CONFESSION OVERHEARD IN A SUBWAY

KENNETH FEARING

You will ask how I came to be eavesdropping, in the first place.
The answer is, I was not.
The man who confessed to these several crimes (call him John Doe)
       spoke into my right ear on a crowded subway train, while the
       man whom he addressed (call him Richard Roe) stood at my left.
Thus, I stood between them, and they talked, or sometimes shouted,
       quite literally straight through me.
How could I help but overhear?
Perhaps I might have moved away to some other strap. But the aisles
       were full.
Besides, I felt, for some reason, curious.

"I do not deny my guilt," said John Doe. "My own, first, and after that
       my guilty knowledge of still further guilt.
I have counterfeited often, and successfully.
I have been guilty of ignorance, and talking with conviction. Of
       intolerable wisdom, and keeping silent.

Through carelessness, or cowardice, I have shortened the lives of
     better men. And the name for that is murder.
All my life I have been a receiver of stolen goods."

"Personally, I always mind my own business," said Richard Roe
     "Sensible people don't get into those scrapes."

I was not the only one who overheard this confession.
Several businessmen, bound for home, and housewives and mechanics,
     were within easy earshot.
A policeman sitting in front of us did not lift his eyes, at the mention
     of murder, from his paper.
Why should I be the one to report these crimes?
You will understand why this letter to your paper is anonymous. I will
     sign it: Public-spirited Citizen, and hope that it cannot be
     traced.

1. What inferences can you make about the kind of person the writer of
the letter is?
2. Who is the "you" the speaker is addressing?
3. Do you take John Doe's confession literally; that is, has he actually
murdered someone? Does the speaker seem to take this confession
literally? Explain.

    A poem such as "Confession Overheard in a Subway," in which a
speaker addresses a particular, silent audience, is called a *dramatic
monologue*. The speaker of a dramatic monologue is a fictional character.
Spoken at a critical moment of the speaker's life, the dramatic monologue
serves to reveal aspects of the speaker's personality as well as the circumstances that led to this discourse. The audience addressed is silent
but identifiable. In Fearing's poem, the audience is not present. In most
dramatic monologues, however, including the most famous examples of
this genre by Browning, the audience is present.
    The dramatic monologue differs from the soliloquy in that the latter is
a speech delivered while the speaker is alone, and usually occurs in
drama. A further distinction is that the soliloquy is designed to inform an
audience (not a particular audience) of a character's thoughts or feelings,
while at the same time keeping them from other characters in the play.

DRAMATIC MONOLOGUE: a poem in which a character, during a
critical moment, speaks to a silent but specific audience.

ELEGY   EDNA ST. VINCENT MILLAY

Let them bury your big eyes
In the secret earth securely,
Your thin fingers, and your fair,
Soft, indefinite-colored hair,
All of these in some way, surely,
From the secret earth shall rise;
Not for these I sit and stare,
Broken and bereft completely:
Your young flesh that sat so neatly
On your little bones will sweetly
Blossom in the air.

But your voice . . . never the rushing
Of a river underground,
Nor the rising of the wind
In the trees before the rain,
Not the woodcock's watery call,
Not the note the white-throat utters,
Not the feet of children pushing
Yellow leaves along the gutters
In the blue and bitter fall,
Shall content my musing mind
For the beauty of that sound
That in no new way at all
Ever will be heard again.

Sweetly through the sappy stalk
Of the vigorous weed,
Holding all it held before,
Cherished by the faithful sun,
On and on eternally
Shall your altered fluid run,
Bud and bloom and go to seed:
But your singing days are done;
But the music of your talk
Never shall the chemistry
Of the secret earth restore.
All your lovely words are spoken.
Once the ivory box is broken,
Beats the golden bird no more.

"Elegy" by Edna St. Vincent Millay from COLLECTED POEMS, Harper & Row. Copyright 1921, 1923, 1948, 1951 by Edna St. Vincent Millay and Norma Millay Ellis. Reprinted by permission of Norma Millay Ellis, Literary Executor.

1. What emotion does this poem express? What has caused the speaker's emotion?
2. Does the rhyme scheme follow a regular pattern? Explain.
3. Is there a predominant beat or RHYTHM?

The *elegy* is a lyric of meditation or lament, most often over death, usually the death of a particular individual. In its original Greek form the elegy had a definite structure, but it was adapted into English poetry not as a form but as a quality of emotional expression; thus, it may assume any conventional pattern or may be written in free verse. In most elegies, there is a formality of language and structure which complements the solemnity of death and the sense of personal loss. Many elegies, at their conclusion, shift in tone from despair to a joyous recognition of immortality. Which of the preceding characteristics do you find in Millay's "Elegy"?

ELEGY: a poem of meditation and lament, usually over death, often the death of a particular person.

---

end-stopped line and run-on line

WALLS   ROBERT FRANCIS

A passer-by might just as well be blind.
These walls are walls no passer sees behind.
Or wants or needs to want to see behind.
Let the walls hide what they are there to bind.
Out-of-sight they say is out-of-mind.
The walls are cruel and the walls are kind.

Sophocles long ago
Heard it on the Aegean, and it brought
Into his mind the turbid ebb and flow
Of human misery . . .
    Arnold, "Dover Beach"

In which of the preceding poems does it seem natural to pause at the end of each line? What causes you to pause? In which poem is it difficult to pause at the end of each line?

"Walls" by Robert Francis. Reprinted by permission of Robert Francis and The University of Massachusetts Press from COME OUT INTO THE SUN: NEW AND SELECTED POEMS by Robert Francis, 1965.

A line of verse which ends in a logical pause indicated by punctuation that is actual or implied is called *end-stopped*. Francis' poem consists of a series of end-stopped lines, in this case, sentences. A *run-on line*, on the other hand, continues the thought and structure of a poetic sentence from one line to the next without pause. The use of run-on lines, along with other factors, enables Arnold to portray the continuous "ebb and flow / Of human misery." Note that Francis' use of end-stopped lines helps to reinforce his theme.

Note how Miles uses both run-on and end-stopped lines to vary movement in the following poem.

THE DOCTOR WHO SITS AT THE BEDSIDE OF A RAT

JOSEPHINE MILES

The doctor who sits at the bedside of a rat
Obtains real answers—a paw twitch,
An ear tremor, a gain or loss of weight,
No problem as to which
Is temper and which is true.
What a rat feels, he will do.
Concomitantly then, the doctor who sits
At the bedside of a rat
Asks real questions, as befits
The place, like where did that potassium go, not what
Do you think of Willie Mays or the weather?
So rat and doctor may converse together.

The degree to which lines may be end-stopped varies. Those lines that end with punctuation such as a period, a semicolon, or a question mark might be considered heavily end-stopped. Other lines may be read with a brief pause at the end, determined by other punctuation or by no punctuation at all. Such lines might be considered slightly end-stopped. Most run-on lines should perhaps be read with no line end pause at all. Which lines in Miles' poem do you consider heavily end-stopped? lightly end-stopped? run-on?

END-STOPPED LINE: a line in which thought and structure conclude simultaneously.

Things past belong to memory alone; .
Things future are the property of hope.
Home, *Agis: Lysander*

RUN-ON LINE: a line in which the thought continues beyond the end of the poetic line.

> No longer mourn for me when I am dead
> Than you shall hear the surly sullen bell
> Give warning to the world that I am fled
> From this vile world, with vilest worms to dwell: . . .
> Shakespeare, "Sonnet 71"

epigram

> A little learning is a dangerous thing;
> Drink deep, or taste not the Pierian spring.
> Pope, *An Essay on Criticism*

> How sharper than a serpent's tooth it is
> To have a thankless child!
> Shakespeare, *King Lear*

> Tell them, dear, that if eyes were made for seeing,
> Then Beauty is its own excuse for being.
> Emerson, "The Rhodora"

> The paths of glory lead but to the grave.
> Gray, "Elegy Written
> in a Country Churchyard"

Restate each of the above. In each case, is your restatement as concise and forceful as the original? Any saying which states something true, wise, or witty as briefly and pointedly as possible is called an *epigram*.

EPIGRAM: a short, pointed or witty saying. The following description of an epigram by Coleridge is itself epigrammatic.

> What is an epigram? A dwarfish whole;
> Its body brevity and wit its soul.

euphony See *cacophony and euphony.*

figurative language

ON WATCHING THE CONSTRUCTION OF A SKYSCRAPER

BURTON RAFFEL

> Nothing sings from these orange trees,
> Rindless steel as smooth as sapling skin,
> Except a crane's brief wheeze
> And all the muffled, clanking din
> Of rivets nosing in like bees.

1. What are the "orange trees"? Does the word *orange* here refer to the fruit or the color?
2. In what ways are the "orange trees" and real trees similar? How do they differ?
3. The poet does not directly state that the noise of a crane has replaced the birds' songs; yet such a comparison is implied. Where?
4. To what does the poet compare the sound of rivets?

This is not a poem about trees, but about the steel frameworks, painted in rustproof orange, seen on the construction site of a skyscraper. The descriptions and comparisons are not to be taken literally; that is, a steel framework is not a tree, a crane doesn't wheeze, and rivets are not bees. Yet the poet has used these images *figuratively* to describe the appearance and noises one might encounter when watching the construction of a skyscraper. Try describing this scene in purely literal terms. What does Raffel's description add to yours?

Raffel has appealed to our imagination through his use of *figurative language* (also called *metaphorical language*)—the use of language in nonliteral ways to achieve conciseness, clarity, vividness, and impact. To which senses has he appealed? Words used apart from their literal meanings are called *figures of speech*. The most common figures of speech are the following.

Simile: a stated comparison between two things in different classes, usually indicated by the words *like, as, seems, than,* or *appears.* A simile that occurs in the preceding poem is "rivets nosing in like bees."

Metaphor: an implied comparison between two things. A metaphor is said to be *implied* because the comparison is not directly stated, and there is no connective such as the *like* or *as* in a simile to indicate the comparison. In the preceding poem "these orange trees," with their implied comparison to steel frameworks, is a metaphor.

Personification: the attributing of human qualities to nonhuman things.

> Night's candles are burnt out, and jocund day
> Stands tiptoe on the misty mountain tops.
> Shakespeare, *Romeo and Juliet*

Hyperbole: exaggeration for effect.

> Time shall moult away his wings,
> Ere he shall discover
> In the whole wide world again
> Such a constant lover.
> Suckling, "The Constant Lover"

Apostrophe: the direct address of a person not present or living, of inanimate objects, or of abstract qualities.

> Roll on, thou deep and dark blue Ocean—roll!
> Byron, "Apostrophe to the Ocean"

Metonymy: the naming of one thing to suggest another associated with it.

> . . . For 'twas that hand that gave away my heart.
> Shakespeare, *Othello*

Synecdoche: the use of a part to suggest the whole or of the whole to suggest a part.

> I am a man of unclean lips.
> Old Testament: Isaiah

While figurative language usually includes any of the preceding figures of speech, it need not do so. If you say, for example, "It's raining cats and dogs," you're not speaking literally, yet it is hard to pinpoint the figure of speech being used. Nonetheless, it is metaphorical language, for something is being described in terms of something else. The possible subtleties of metaphorical language can be seen in the excerpt on the next page. What is Blake saying?

To see a world in a grain of sand
And a heaven in a wild flower
Hold infinity in the palm of your hand
And eternity in an hour . . .
Blake, "Auguries of Innocence"

THREE FLOORS

STANLEY KUNITZ

Mother was a crack of light
And a gray eye peeping;
I made believe by breathing hard
That I was sleeping.

Sister's doughboy[1] on last leave
Had robbed me of her hand;
Downstairs at intervals she played
Warum[2] on the baby grand.

Under the roof a wardrobe trunk
A boy had learned to pick
Contained a red Masonic hat
And a walking stick.

Bolt upright in my bed that night
I saw my father flying.
The wind was walking on my neck,
The window-panes were crying.

1. What are the "three floors" of the title and by what means are they portrayed?
2. In what ways does Kunitz use figurative language to portray the mother? the sister? the weather?
3. What might the Masonic hat and walking stick suggest? Explain in literal terms the situation stated in the first two lines of the poem. In what ways does your description differ from Kunitz's?

FIGURATIVE LANGUAGE: a writer's use of words apart from their ordinary, literal meanings in such a way as to restore freshness, conciseness, and vitality to them. (See APOSTROPHE, HYPERBOLE, METAPHOR, METONYMY, PERSONIFICATION, SIMILE, SYNECDOCHE.)

1. *doughboy,* an infantryman in the United States Army. 2. *Warum* (vä rŭm'), why. [*German*]

figures of speech See *figurative language.*

foot See *rhythm.*

free verse

DRINKING COLD WATER

PETER EVERWINE

Almost twenty years
Since you put on your one good dress
And lay down in the shale hills of Pennsylvania.
What you expected from life was nothing much,
And it came
And so it was.
In California I mourned and then forgot,
Though sometimes, in a mirror,
I saw someone walk from the weeds,
Stepping from a shine of water,
And it was you, shining.

Tonight I brought my bundle of years
To an empty house.
When I opened it, a boy walked out,
Drinking cold water, watching the
Moon rise slim and shining over your house.
Whatever it was I wanted
Must have come and gone.

Twenty years, grandmother.
Here I stand
In the poverty of my feet,
And I know what you'd do:
You'd enter your black shawl,
Step back into the shadows of your hair.
And that's no help tonight.
All I can think of is your house—
The pump at the sink
Spilling a trough of clear
Cold water from the well—
And you, old love,
Sleeping in your dark dress
Like a hard, white root.

1. How many stanzas does this poem contain? Are they equal in length?
2. Is there any pattern of line length? of rhythm?

The preceding poem is considered *free verse*: poetry which breaks from fixed stanzaic patterns and makes use of unpatterned or irregular rhythms rather than uniform metrical feet. In free verse the unit of rhythmic control is the rise and fall within the entire poem rather than the metric line or stanza. Although free verse has gained great popularity in the past century, it is not a new form, nor is it confined to English poetry.

The term *free verse* explains itself—it is free from the demands of rhyme (although rhyme may occur), free from the necessity of following regular metrical patterns. Free verse allows for a variety of rhythmical effects; such free-verse rhythms are less regular than those of conventional verse, and are achieved through a subtle handling of the cadences of words, phrases, and lines. Line length may vary. Often the rhythm is described as organic, varying with the emotion, flowing with the entire poem. ASSONANCE, CONSONANCE, ALLITERATION, IMAGERY and almost any other poetic device may be used to bind lines together and to help create mood or atmosphere.

Walt Whitman was the first recognized American writer to use free verse extensively. Read the poem on the following page.

FOR YOU O DEMOCRACY

WALT WHITMAN

Come, I will make the continent indissoluble,
I will make the most splendid race the sun ever shone upon,
I will make divine magnetic lands,
      With the love of comrades,
        With the life-long love of comrades.
I will plant companionship thick as trees along all the
      rivers of America, and along the shores of the
      great lakes, and all over the prairies,
I will make inseparable cities with their arms about
            each other's necks,
    By the love of comrades,
      By the manly love of comrades.
For you these from me, O Democracy, to serve you ma femme![1]
For you, for you I am trilling these songs.

1. Note the poet's use of repetition. What effect does it create?
2. What other poetic devices does Whitman use?

FREE VERSE: a type of poetry which differs from conventional verse
forms in being "free" from a fixed pattern of meter and rhyme, depending for its effects on more subtle patterns of rhythm and sound.

---

1. *ma femme*, French for my woman or my wife.

---

heroic couplet See *couplet.*

1. I am very sad.
2. Why, man, if the river were dry, I am able to fill it with
   my tears; . . .
                    Shakespeare, *Two Gentlemen of Verona*

Which of the preceding two statements might be taken literally? Which makes its point more emphatically? Explain.

Hyperbole is the use of exaggeration for effect. Depending on tone and subject matter, that effect may range from the satiric, to the sentimental, or the comic.

In each of the following, what effect do you think the poet was trying to create through the use of hyperbole?

> Tears too are useful; with tears you can melt iron.
>   Ovid, *Ars Amatoria*

THE KING'S EPITAPH

JOHN WILMOT, EARL OF ROCHESTER

> Here lies a great and mighty King,
>   Whose promise none relies on;
> He never said a foolish thing,
>   Nor ever did a wise one.

HYPERBOLE: exaggeration for effect. Shakespeare uses hyperbole in the words of Romeo to his beloved Juliet:

> . . . there lies more peril in thine eye
> Than twenty of their swords: . . .

FOUL SHOT

EDWIN A. HOEY

With two 60's stuck on the scoreboard
And two seconds hanging on the clock,
The solemn boy in the center of eyes,
Squeezed by silence,
Seeks out the line with his feet,
Soothes his hands along his uniform,
Gently drums the ball against the floor,
Then measures the waiting net,
Raises the ball on his right hand,
Balances it with his left,
Calms it with fingertips,
Breathes,
Crouches,
Waits,
And then through a stretching of stillness,
Nudges it upward.

The ball
Slides up and out,
Lands,
Leans,
Wobbles,
Wavers,
Hesitates,
Exasperates,
Plays it coy
Until every face begs with unsounding screams—

And then

        And then

                And then

Right before ROAR-UP,
Dives down and through.

"Foul Shot" by Edwin A. Hoey. Special permission granted by *Read* magazine, published by Xerox Educational Publications, © Xerox Corporation, 1962.

In the preceding poem, find words, phrases, and/or lines that appeal to
(1) the sense of sight; (2) the sense of hearing; (3) the sense of touch; and
(4) the sense of movement. Do any words, phrases, or lines appeal to
more than one sense at a time? To which sense does the poem make its
primary appeal?

Sensory appeals made through description are called *images*. An
image is inherent in any word or group of words which represents an
experience that can be known through the senses. An image may appeal
to any of the following senses: sight (visual image), hearing (auditory
image), taste (gustatory image), smell (olfactory image), touch (tactile
image), or the so-called motor sense which has to do with motion or
muscle activity. Think of any word or phrase that appeals to each of
these senses.

An image may be a simple, literal representation; that is, it may use a
word to call up the sight, sound, or feeling it usually evokes. The images
in "Foul Shot" are primarily literal ones (the ball "wavers").

An image may also be figurative, depending for its effect on unexpected associations or figures of speech. The image of a ball that "plays
it coy," relies on the kind of unexpected association that constitutes
figurative language.

Effective *imagery* (all the images taken collectively), whether literal
or figurative, seldom appeals to one sense only. You have already noted
the variety of senses to which the imagery in "Foul Shot" appeals. When
skillfully used, imagery not only presents sensory details but also helps
communicate mood, tone, atmosphere, and meaning.

Try to describe the atmosphere of "Foul Shot"—is it relaxed, tense,
climactic, expectant, or something else altogether? Can you pick out any
images that are especially good at communicating that atmosphere?

Read the following poem, noting how the poet uses a variety of images
to express both mood and meaning.

A LADY

AMY LOWELL

You are beautiful and faded
Like an old opera tune
Played upon a harpsichord;
Or like the sun-flooded silks
Of an eighteenth century boudoir.
In your eyes
Smolder the fallen roses of outlived minutes,
And the perfume of your soul

"A Lady" from THE COMPLETE POETICAL WORKS OF AMY LOWELL. Reprinted by permission of Houghton Mifflin Company.

Is vague and suffusing,
With the pungence of sealed spice-jars.
Your half-tones delight me,
And I grow mad with gazing
At your blent colors.

My vigor is a new-minted penny;
Which I cast at your feet.
Gather it up from the dust,
That its sparkle may amuse you.

1. To which of the senses do the images in the poem appeal? Cite lines.
2. What idea about the lady of the title does the cumulative effect of the images suggest?
3. What idea does the image of the last stanza express?

IMAGERY: the sensory details in a literary work. Whether literal or figurative, an image provides vividness and immediacy, evoking in the reader a complex of emotional suggestions.

irony

The poet Anna Wickham comments on the dubious advantage of being a woman.

> I have to thank God I'm a woman,
> For in these ordered days a woman only
> Is free to be very hungry, very lonely.
> Wickham, "The Affinity"

When the speaker here says that she is thankful, do you think she is literally saying what she really means?

MANY WORKMEN

STEPHEN CRANE

Many workmen
Built a huge ball of masonry
Upon a mountain-top,
Then they went to the valley below,

Excerpt from "The Affinity" by Anna Wickham. Reprinted from her volume, THE CONTEMPLA-
TIVE QUARRY, by permission of Harcourt Brace Jovanovich, Inc.

And turned to behold their work.
"It is grand," they said;
They loved the thing.

Of a sudden, it moved:
It came upon them swiftly;
It crushed them all to blood.
But some had opportunity to squeal.

Why do you suppose the workmen built the ball upon the mountain? Why do you think they "loved the thing"? What unexpected event occurs?

A statement that contradicts the real attitude of the speaker, or a situation that contrasts what is expected with what actually happens, is called *irony*. The quotation from Wickham illustrates *verbal irony*: here the surface meaning of what the writer or speaker says is opposite of the intended meaning. The Crane poem illustrates *irony of situation*: here the opposite of what is expected or intended occurs.

Read the following poem.

SURPRISE

DOROTHY PARKER

My heart went fluttering with fear
Lest you should go, and leave me here
To beat my breast and rock my head
And stretch me sleepless on my bed.
Ah, clear they see and true they say
That one shall weep, and one shall stray
For such is Love's unvarying law. . . .
I never thought, I never saw
That I should be the first to go;
How pleasant that it happened so!

Does this poem contain irony of situation, verbal irony, neither, or both? At what point in the poem does the speaker's tone appear to shift?

IRONY: use of words which imply the opposite of what they literally mean (verbal irony), or a state of affairs that is the opposite of what is expected (irony of situation).

PORTRAIT OF THE ARTIST AS A PREMATURELY OLD MAN

OGDEN NASH

It is common knowledge to every schoolboy and even every
    Bachelor of Arts,
That all sin is divided into two parts.
One kind of sin is called a sin of commission, and that is very
    important,
And it is what you are doing when you are doing something
    you ortant,
And the other kind of sin is just the opposite and is called a
    sin of omission and is equally bad in the eyes of all right-
    thinking people, from Billy Sunday to Buddha,
And it consists of not having done something you shudda.
I might as well give you my opinion of these two kinds of sin
    as long as, in a way, against each other we are pitting them,
And that is, don't bother your head about sins of commission
    because however sinful, they must at least be fun or else
    you wouldn't be committing them.
It is the sin of omission, the second kind of sin,
That lays eggs under your skin.
The way you get really painfully bitten
Is by the insurance you haven't taken out and the checks you
    haven't added up the stubs of and the appointments you
    haven't kept and the bills you haven't paid and the letters
    you haven't written.
Also, about sins of omission there is one particularly painful
    lack of beauty,
Namely, it isn't as though it had been a riotous red letter day
    or night every time you neglected to do your duty;
You didn't get a wicked forbidden thrill
Every time you let a policy lapse or forgot to pay a bill;
You didn't slap the lads in the tavern on the back and loudly
    cry Whee,
Let's all fail to write just one more letter before we go home,
    and this round of unwritten letters is on me.
No, you never get any fun
Out of the things you haven't done,

But they are the things that I do not like to be amid,
Because the suitable things you didn't do give you a lot more
      trouble than the unsuitable things you did.
The moral is that it is probably better not to sin at all, but if
      some kind of sin you must be pursuing,
Well, remember to do it by doing rather than by not doing.

1. Ogden Nash states his subject in the first two lines. What clues do you have that his is not a serious treatment of sin? How does the poem develop the idea that "all sin is divided into two parts"?
2. What do you make of the title? What does it add to the verse?
3. Where does Nash enhance humor by forcing the rhyme?
4. Describe the overall pace or tempo of the poem. (Is it slow, rapid, halting, sporadic, gentle—what?)

"Portrait of the Artist As a Prematurely Old Man" is an example of *light verse*: poetry that deals lightly with its subject, its first goal being laughter. Light verse usually includes elements that are unexpected or incongruous, often in the form of an abrupt punch line. It can range from highly sophisticated SATIRE to absolute nonsense. Often it deals, lightly of course, with human foibles. While light verse may take almost any form, rhyme and rhythm are usually a part of its structure; both elements can be manipulated by the poet for humorous effect.

INSOMNIA THE GEM OF THE OCEAN

JOHN UPDIKE

When I lay me down to sleep
My waterbed says, "Gurgle gleep,"
And when I readjustment crave
It answers with a tidal wave
And lifts me like a bark canoe
Adrift in breakers off Peru.

Neap to my spring, ebb to my flow,
It turns my pulse to undertow,
It turns my thoughts to bubbles, it
Still undulates when I would quit;
Two bags of water, it and I
In restless sympathy here lie.

LIGHT VERSE: poetry that deals lightly with its subject and is directed toward amusement or laughter. Light verse can range from nonsense to satire.

"Insomnia the Gem of the Ocean" by John Updike from *The New Yorker*, (September 16, 1972). Reprinted by permission; © 1972 The New Yorker Magazine, Inc.

literary ballad See *ballad.*

---

lyric

REMEMBERING YOU

MAXINE KUMIN

Skiing the mountain alone
on a day of difficult moods
with snowflakes of rottenstone
at the liverish altitudes

and the bones of the birches pale
as milk and the humpbacked spine
of an untouched downhill trail
turned suddenly serpentine,

a day comes into my head
when we rose by aerial tram,
bubbles strung on a thread
of a mobile diagram,

rose to the mountain's crest
on a day of electric blue
and how, my enthusiast,
I made the descent with you,

the beautiful greed of our run
taken on edge, tiptoe
with a generous spill of sun
on the toytown roofs below

as on powder side by side
running lightly and well
we lipped and took the untried,
easily parallel.

NIGHT FRIENDS

S. J. MARKS

Terror we expect, but we are always surprised by love.
                                    —Thomas Williams

What you taught me
        and how I remember it
        when I lie in the dark
I write on the cold trees.
I see what you see through the corner of my eyes

Walking slowly,
        we touch the empty silences
        that lie in wait, settling to slow
        decay.
We are here. These gray weathered branches
        are facts.

You meet me, your eyes, your lips, your yellow
        hair blown among long grasses.
There you are.
This is the way it seems to happen.

I am insane with words, with grief.
I am alone.
For two days now the one sound inside my head
        has been your name.

1. What is the basic emotion expressed by the speaker of each poem?
2. In each case, is the speaker concerned primarily with communicating an emotion or the circumstances that led to the emotion, of expressing a feeling or telling a story?
3. Would you characterize the speaker's tone in each case as personal or impersonal? Explain.

Both "Remembering You" and "Night Friends" belong to a broad classification of poetry called *lyric.* Usually short, the lyric is a personal reflection by a single speaker, either the poet or some voice adopted by the poet, which presents some basic emotion such as grief, love, or happiness. SONNETS are a kind of lyric; ELEGIES and ODES are lyrics that are generally longer and more complex.

"Night Friends" by S. J. Marks from *The New Yorker,* (December 4, 1971). Reprinted by permission; © 1971 The New Yorker Magazine, Inc.

Though the term *lyric* has come a long way from its original definition—poetry intended to be sung to the accompaniment of a lyre—it still retains the characteristic of music in its sounds and its structural pattern, which may be as formal as a sonnet or as irregular as free verse. Because of its emotional quality, lyric poetry relies heavily on sound to reinforce its ideas, using rhythms and repetition of sound patterns to intensify response.

LYRIC: a poem, often short, presented by a single speaker and expressing some basic emotion.

---

metaphor

APARTMENT HOUSE

GERALD RAFTERY

A filing-cabinet of human lives
Where people swarm like bees in tunneled hives,
Each to his own cell in the towered comb,
Identical and cramped—we call it home.

1. Raftery compares an apartment house to a "filing-cabinet of human lives." What does this comparison suggest about the apartment house?
2. To what else are the apartment house and its dwellers compared? What similarities exist between the items compared?
3. Raftery might have chosen to make a literal statement: "We live in identical and cramped quarters called apartments; yet we consider this home." Instead, he expressed his message in the form of nonliteral comparisons. Which is more effective—the poem or its literal equivalent?

It is the very nature of poetry to express one thing in terms of another in order to expand meanings through unexpected, yet valid, associations. When things that are essentially unlike are related through implied comparisons, they are called *metaphors*.

A metaphor resembles a SIMILE in that both compare two things that are literally unlike. The distinction between these two *figures of speech* is basically this: in a simile the items compared are both mentioned, with their similarity indicated by a connective, usually *like* or

---

"Apartment House" by Gerald Raftery. Reprinted by permission of the author.

as; in a metaphor, the comparison is merely implied, which can cause it to be more subtle, less easy to identify. In a metaphor, for example, only one item may be mentioned, while the other is unnamed or merely suggested. Whereas a simile might state, "Night came like a bird of prey," the same idea could be stated in a metaphor thus: "The wings of hungry night swooped down to earth." The following simile from a Shakespearean sonnet is relatively easy to identify.

> How like a winter hath my absence been
> From thee.

The objects compared in the following Shakespearean metaphor, however, may be less easily recognizable.

> That time of year thou mayst in me behold
> When yellow leaves, or none, or few, do hang
> Upon those boughs which shake against the cold, . . .

Some effort is required on the part of the reader to determine what the poet is comparing in the preceding metaphor. The poet is expressing his situation and feelings in terms of nature. What do you learn about the speaker's condition from this comparison?

What objects are being compared in the following metaphor? Do you think the comparison is effective?

> O, beware, my lord, of jealousy;
> It is the green-ey'd monster which doth mock
> The meat it feeds on: . . .
>
> Shakespeare, *Othello*

Sometimes an entire poem is used to develop a single metaphor. This is called an *extended* or *sustained metaphor*. Here is an example.

MOTHER TO SON

LANGSTON HUGHES

Well, son, I'll tell you:
Life for me ain't been no crystal stair.
It's had tacks in it,
And splinters,
And boards torn up,
And places with no carpet on the floor—
Bare.

But all the time
I'se been a climbin' on,
And reachin' landin's,
And turnin' corners,
And sometimes goin' in the dark
Where there ain't been no light.
So, boy, don't you turn back;
Don't you set down on the steps
'Cause you finds it's kinder hard.
Don't you fall now—
For I'se still goin', honey,
I'se still climbin',
And life for me ain't been no crystal stair.

1. Point out the first metaphor the woman uses. Restate the meaning conveyed by this comparison in literal terms.
2. What words or phrases in the poem refer to a stairway? What kind of stair do they describe—crystal or otherwise?
3. Which images emphasize the point the speaker makes about life?
4. In what way does the very movement of climbing a stairway serve to reinforce the message of the poem?

Every image in the poem helps to sustain or extend the basic metaphor of a stairway; thus, the term *extended* or *sustained metaphor*.

You may occasionally come upon the term *metaphorical language*; it is a general classification which includes any language used in a nonliteral way and is synonymous with *figurative language*.

METAPHOR: a figure of speech which involves an implied comparison between two relatively unlike things. Wordsworth begins his poem, "To a Skylark," with two metaphors, addressing the bird as:

Ethereal minstrel! pilgrim of the sky!

metaphorical language See *figurative language*.

meter See *rhythm*.

metonymy

Explain each of the following, making your explanation as literal as possible.

1. The pen is mightier than the sword.
2. If you use your head, you can figure out this problem.
3. My uncle sets a good table for Thanksgiving.

In each of the above, a word has been substituted for another term which it suggests. One instance contains two such substitutions. This change of name is a figure of speech called *metonymy*. Metonymy involves the substitution of one term for another that is closely associated with it, usually a part for the whole, or an item for another related one (*pen* for writing and *sword* for fighting in example 1). Common in daily speech, metonymy is also valuable in poetry because it allows for a combination of conciseness and concreteness. Shakespeare uses metonymy in *The Winter's Tale*, when he writes:

> The crown will find an heir.

What does he use the word *crown* to suggest? Try restating Shakespeare's line in literal terms.

METONYMY: a figure of speech in which one term is substituted for another closely associated with it, usually a part or a single attribute for the whole. Metonymy occurs in the following use of the word *sift* to represent sand.

> I am soft sift
> In an hourglass . . .
> Hopkins, "The Wreck of the
> Deutschland"

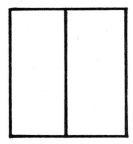

Excerpt from "The Wreck of the Deutschland" from POEMS OF GERARD MANLEY HOPKINS, 4th Edition. Published by Oxford University Press, London.

PRIZE-GIVING

GWEN HARWOOD

Professor Eisenbart, asked to attend
a girls' school speech night as an honoured guest
and give the prizes out, rudely declined;
but from indifference agreed, when pressed
with dry scholastic jokes, to change his mind,
to grace their humble platform, and to lend

distinction (of a kind not specified)
to the occasion. Academic dress
became him, as he knew. When he appeared
the girls whirred with an insect nervousness,
the Head in humbler black flapped round and steered
her guest, superb in silk and fur, with pride

to the best seat beneath half-hearted blooms
tortured to form the school's elaborate crest.
Eisenbart scowled with violent distaste,
then recomposed his features to their best
advantage: deep in thought, with one hand placed
like Rodin's Thinker. So he watched the room's

mosaic of young heads. Blonde, black, mouse-brown
they bent for their Headmistress' opening prayer.
But underneath a light (no accident
of seating, he felt sure), with titian hair
one girl sat grinning at him, her hand bent
under her chin in mockery of his own.

Speeches were made and prizes given. He shook
indifferently a host of virgin hands.
'Music!' The girl with titian hair stood up,
hitched at a stocking, winked at near-by friends,
and stood before him to receive a cup
of silver chased with curious harps. He took

"Prize-Giving" by Gwen Harwood from POEMS. Reprinted by permission of Angus & Robertson
(U.K.) Ltd.

her hand, and felt its voltage fling his hold
from his calm age and power; suffered her strange
eyes, against reason dark, to take his stare
with her to the piano, there to change
her casual schoolgirl's for a master's air.
He forged his rose-hot dream as Mozart told

the fullness of all passion or despair
summoned by arrogant hands. The music ended,
Eisenbart teased his gown while others clapped,
and peered into a trophy which suspended
his image upside down: a sage fool trapped
by music in a copper net of hair.

1. What story does the poem tell?
2. The events of this story reveal a great deal about both the professor
and the girl with titian hair. Characterize each, and cite details that help
reveal their characters.

"Prize-Giving" is a *narrative*—a poem that tells a story or relates a
series of events leading up to a climax. In effective poetry of this type,
condensation enables the events to move with speed; a high degree of
suggestivity provides a certain sense of suspense. Through the relating
of incidents in a narrative, vivid characterization can be achieved, as is
the case in this narrative.

There are three common types of poetry which fit the general description *narrative*. One of these, the BALLAD, is discussed on page 325. The
second is the *metrical tale* or romance in which the scenes, situations,
and characters are remote, exotic or fantastic. The third type of narrative
is the *epic*, which is characterized by extreme length, dignified tone, and
heroic characters and events. *Beowulf*, the Old English folk epic, and
Paradise Lost by John Milton are examples of this type of poetry.

NARRATIVE POEM: a poem that tells a story or relates a series of
events.

ode

The *ode* is a type of LYRIC that dates from ancient Greek poetry to the
present; it is formal in style, serious in tone, and complex in structure.
Originally, the ode had a rigid structure and adhered to certain strict
rules of composition. The most elaborate kind of ode, termed *Pindaric*
after the Greek poet Pindar (522?–443 B.C.), is divided into various

stanza structures called *strophes* (specifically, the *strophe,* the *anti-strophe,* and the *epode*). Another type of ode, called *Horatian* after the Roman poet Horace (65–8 B.C.), has a less rigid stanza form. A third type of ode, the *irregular* ode, is much more flexible in its stanza form, rhyme scheme, and meter than the other ode forms. Although these types of ode vary in their degree of formality, all of them share a dignified or enthusiastic tone, solemn diction, and serious theme.

In contemporary poetry, the ode in its traditional form has nearly disappeared. What remains is a shortened, less structured meditation that resembles the lyric. Occasionally, the ode form is altered in subject matter, TONE, and purpose to produce IRONY or SATIRE. Here is an example of a modern ode. How would you describe its tone?

YOUR COMPLIMENTARY RIVER ODE   J. D. REED

Trout mouths dimple this long pool
as if the Manistee had acne.
Songbirds are busy
with a Golden Guide
to Humans of the Northern Forests
trying to identify me.
(Odd—a half-ton Silver-Throated Hollarer.)

I am busy trying to untangle
this leader, which has
just survived a gang-rape of wind.
In these situations
it is impossible not to think.
The raccoons are thinking "prehensile."
The bears are thinking "lunch."
And I am thinking

"What am I doing in this sport coat?
Why this tin of Klassy Kar Wax?
How come I'm out here,
about this business
our fathers nearly fathomed?"

What, if anything, does Reed's ode have in common with the traditional ode? Consider, in answering, its tone, subject, and language.

ODE: a long lyric poem, formal in style, serious in tone, and complex in form. The modern ode, usually shorter and less complex in form, is often ironic or satiric.

"Your Complimentary River Ode" by J. D. Reed from *The New Yorker,* August 5, 1972. Reprinted by permission of *The New Yorker* and The Sumac Press.

onomatopoeia

All the lines that follow were written to describe the same thing. Can you determine what it is?

> I chatter, chatter as I flow
> I babble on the pebbles . . .
> Tennyson, "The Brook"

> The hell of waters! where they howl and hiss,
> And boil in endless torture . . .
> Byron, *Childe Harold*

> And liquid lapse of murmuring streams . . .
> Milton, *Paradise Lost*

The authors of the preceding quotations were trying to convey the sound of water in motion. In each case, what different picture of water do you get? How is the image of water that "chatters" different from the image of water that "murmurs"?

The poets quoted above have used words whose sounds suggest their sense (*chatter, babble, hiss, murmuring,* etc.). When the sound echoes the sense of a word, *onomatopoeia* is said to occur. Onomatopoeia, which is an extremely effective poetic device, occurs commonly in daily speech. Words such as *crash, plunk,* and *zoom* probably owe their existence to the effort of someone to make the sound of a word echo its meaning.

Following are some examples of the use of onomatopoeia. Read each aloud to determine what image, tone, mood, atmosphere, or meaning the poet is attempting to suggest.

> The moan of doves in immemorial elms
> And murmuring of innumerable bees.
> Tennyson, *The Princess*

> And wow he died as wow he lived,
> going whop to the office and blooie home to sleep and
> biff got married and bam had children and oof got fired,
> zowie did he live and zowie did he die . . .
> Fearing, "Dirge"

Excerpt from "Dirge" by Kenneth Fearing from NEW AND SELECTED POEMS. Copyright © 1956 by Kenneth Fearing. Reprinted by permission of Indiana University Press.

Tlot-tlot; tlot-tlot; Had they heard it? The horse hoofs
    ringing clear!
Tlot-tlot, tlot-tlot, in the distance! Were they deaf that they
    did not hear?

Noyes, "The Highwayman"

ONOMATOPOEIA: the use of words whose sounds suggest their sense.
Tennyson coined his own onomatopoetic words in this description of a
cantering horse:

Coom oop, proputty, proputty—that's what I 'ears 'im saäy—
Proputty, proputty, proputty—canter and canter awaäy.

---

paradox

Try to explain how the following statements could be true.

Victory is defeat.

She is a poor little rich girl.

Sanity is madness.

Though each of these examples seems a contradiction, all are nevertheless in some sense true. Such a statement is called a *paradox.*

A poet may use paradox for emphasis (the seemingly contradictory
statement makes us stop and give it special attention) or to create a sense
of irony.

The following paradox was stated by Tennyson. Under what condi-
tions might a "good" mother really be a "bad" mother?

Good mother is bad mother unto me!
A worse were better; . . .

The poem that follows is based on a paradox. What do *darkness* and *light* mean in this context?

TO SEE

CID CORMAN

To see that the
darkness is

darkness is
already light.

PARADOX: an apparent contradiction that is nevertheless true. The statement, "Failure is success," expresses a paradox.

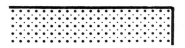

personification

What kind of wind does Stephens describe in the following poem?

THE WIND

JAMES STEPHENS

The wind stood up and gave a shout;
He whistled on his fingers, and

Kicked the withered leaves about,
And thumped the branches with his hand,

And said he'd kill, and kill, and kill;
And so he will! And so he will.

Stephens' wind acquires a special life of its own. What human characteristics does the poet attribute to the wind?

In portraying the wind as a wild man, Stephens makes use of a figure of speech called *personification*. Through personification, human characteristics are assigned to nonhuman things. When we speak of a tea-kettle "singing" or leaves "dancing," we are assigning human attributes to nonhuman things. In poetry, effective use of personification enables a reader to see abstractions, events, inanimate objects, or animals in terms of human qualities, thus expanding the literal into the metaphorical. Try describing the wind Stephens portrays without using personification.

Sometimes life, but not necessarily human life, is attributed to inanimate objects or abstractions. You might say, for example, that your stomach is "growling" or that your imagination "ran wild." Explain how Milton, in the following lines, seeks to impart life to an abstraction.

> How soon hath Time, the subtle thief of youth
> Stolen on his wing my three and twentieth year!
> Milton, "On His Having Arrived at the
> Age of Twenty-three"

PERSONIFICATION: a figure of speech in which human characteristics are assigned to nonhuman things.

> Blow winds, and crack your cheeks! rage! blow!
> Shakespeare, *King Lear*

---

prose poem

Smithers-Cromby provides all its employees with an annual chest X ray. On Tuesday, April 5, a mobile X-ray unit will be stationed in the company's west parking lot from 1 P.M. to 4 P.M. Blank X-ray forms will be available on that day at the front desk of the Personnel Office, Room 1130. Pick up a form, fill it out as directed, and take it to the X-ray mobile unit. Give the X-ray form to the X-ray operator as you enter the mobile unit. Results of your X ray will be mailed to you within two weeks. We encourage all of our employees to take advantage of this service.

Do you consider the preceding lines prose, or poetry? Why?

It is a tale of love and lovers that they tell in the low-
lit Causeway that slinks from West India Dock Road to the
dark waste of waters beyond. In Pennyfields, too, you
may hear it; and I do not doubt that it is told in faraway Tai-Ping, in Singapore, in Tokio, in Shanghai, and
those other gay-lamped haunts of wonder whither the
wandering people of Limehouse go and whence they return
so casually. It is a tale for tears, and should you hear
it in the lilied tongue of the yellow men, it would awaken
in you all your pity. In our bald speech it must, unhappily,
lose its essential fragrance, that quality that will lift
an affair of squalor into the loftier spheres of passion
and imagination, beauty and sorrow. It will sound
unconvincing, a little . . . you know . . . the kind of
thing that is best forgotten. Perhaps . . .

Burke, Limehouse Nights

Read the preceding passage aloud, noting how Burke uses parallel con-
struction to control rhythm and movement. Note also his use of AL-
LITERATION, FIGURATIVE LANGUAGE, and IMAGERY. Is this poetry?
Explain.

PROLETARIAN PORTRAIT

WILLIAM CARLOS WILLIAMS

A big young bareheaded woman
in an apron

Her hair slicked back standing
on the street

One stockinged foot toeing
the sidewalk

Her shoe in her hand. Looking
intently into it

She pulls out the paper insole
to find the nail

That has been hurting her.

Is this work by Williams a poem? Explain.

Suppose Burke had set up his lines something like this:

> It is a tale of love and lovers
> That they tell
> In the low-lit Causeway
> That slinks
> From West India Dock Road
> To the dark waste of waters
> Beyond.

Suppose Williams had set up his lines in a paragraph (you might try this arrangement to see how it looks and sounds). Given this rearrangement, could you know definitely if one work is poetry, the other prose? Explain.

No matter how Burke's lines appear on the printed page, their imagery and their structured rhythms are always in evidence. The lines by Williams, with their emphasis on the natural rhythms of speech and their use of antipoetic DICTION, might plausibly be mistaken for prose if set up in a proselike structure.

It is almost impossible to put into words the essential difference between poetry and prose; the dividing line is often shadowy because much prose has qualities considered poetic and much poetry is proselike. Here, for example, is Cervantes' prose description of the dawn:

> Now had Aurora displayed her mantle over the blushing skies, and dark night withdrawn her sable veil.
>
> Cervantes, *Don Quixote*

Carlyle casts his thought about dawn in a metrical structure:

> So here hath been dawning
> Another blue Day:
> Think, wilt thou let it
> Slip useless away?

Cervantes' lines are alive with the kind of metaphor usually associated with poetry; Carlyle's are little more than a bouncing, moralistic jingle. Still, Cervantes called his lines prose, and Carlyle called his lines poetry.

The author of the work that follows calls it a *prose poem*, a term used to describe a piece of tightly knit writing set down upon the page as prose but possessing the rhythms, conciseness, language, scope, and other characteristics usually associated more with poetry than with prose.

WHY AM I HAPPY WRITING THIS TEXTBOOK   KARL SHAPIRO

Why am I happy writing this textbook? What sublime idiocy!
What a waste of time! A textbook on prosody[1] at that.
Yet when I sit down to comb the business out, when I
address the easel of this task, I burn with an even
flame, I'm cooking with gas. There are some things
so dull they hypnotize like the pendulum of a clock;
so clockwork and quotidian they make the flesh de-
lirious like fresh water. X-ray the poem, give it a
thorough physical, a clean bill of health. We can see
everything but the flow of blood. What Latin and
Greek nomenclature! But this is order, order made to
order. This is system to plot and plan. This is definition, edges clean as razors. Simplification, boldface,
indented. I know there is no such thing as a textbook.
I know that all textbooks are sold the second the
course is over. I know that a book sold is a dead book.
And I dream, like others, of writing a textbook that
is not a textbook, a book that not even a student would
part with, a book that makes even prosody breathe.
So, when the sun shines with the nine o'clock bright-
ness and the coffee swims in my throat and the smoke
floats over the page like the smoke of a ship's funnel,
then I romanticize. I make a muse of prosody, old hag.
She's just a registered nurse, I know, I know, but I
have her sashay, grind and bump, register Alcaics,
Sapphics, choriambs[2] (my predilection). She's trained
all right. She's second nature herself. She knows her
job, I mine. We'll work it out: it may be poetry. Blue-
prints are blue. They have their dreams.

Do you think this is a poem? Consider: the natural rhythms of thought,
the connotations of the language, the use of parallelisms, the repetition of sounds, the use of imagery and figurative language.

PROSE POEM: a piece of writing set down as prose but having the
rhythms, language, scope, and imaginative quality usually associated
with poetry.

---

1. *prosody* (pros′ə dē), the science of poetic meters and versification. 2. *Alcaics* (al kā′iks), *Sapphics*
(saf′iks), *choriambs* (kōr′i ambs′). Alcaics is a Greek lyrical meter, so called from Alcaeus, a lyric
poet who is said to have invented it. Alcaic measure is little more than a curiosity in English verse.
Sapphics is a four-lined verse form of classical lyric poetry, named after the Greek poetess Sappho,
who employed it. A choriamb is a metrical foot of four syllables.

So runs my dream; but what am I?
An infant crying in the night;
An infant crying for the light,
And with no language but a cry.
Tennyson, *In Memoriam*

Lord Thomas said a word in jest,
Fair Annet took it ill:
"A, I will nevir wed a wife
Against my ain friends' will."
Anonymous, "Lord Thomas and Fair Annet"

For Mercy has a human heart,
Pity a human face,
And Love, the human form divine,
And Peace, the human dress.
Blake, "The Divine Image"

Examine the RHYME scheme of each of the preceding stanzas. In addition to the fact that each stanza consists of four lines, can you find any similarities in the structure?

Any stanza of four lines, regardless of line length, meter, or rhyme pattern is called a *quatrain*. Perhaps the most familiar quatrain form is the old English ballad meter, which is a stanza made up of alternating iambic tetrameter and iambic trimeter lines (see RHYTHM), rhyming *a b c b* (the second example).

QUATRAIN: any stanza of four lines, regardless of line length, meter, or rhyme pattern.

The curfew tolls the knell of parting day,
The lowing herd winds slowly o'er the lea,
The ploughman homeward plods his weary way,
And leaves the world to darkness and to me.
Gray, "Elegy Written in a Country Churchyard"

---
refrain

While you read the following poem, note the poet's use of repetition.

GRASS

CARL SANDBURG

Pile the bodies high at Austerlitz[1] and Waterloo.
Shovel them under and let me work—
　　　　　　I am the grass; I cover all.

And pile them high at Gettysburg
And pile them high at Ypres and Verdun.
Shovel them under and let me work.
Two years, ten years, and passengers ask the conductor:
　　　　　　What place is this?
　　　　　　Where are we now?

　　　　　　I am the grass.
　　　　　　Let me work.

1. What physical image does this poem communicate?
2. What phrases are repeated in the poem?
3. A connection exists here between image and repetition. What is this connection?

The repetition of phrases or lines in a poem is called a *refrain*. The refrain may be an exact repetition, or the poet may make some alterations in it. In English poetry, an early extensive use of refrain occurred in the folk ballads of the Middle Ages. While ballad refrains sometimes served to advance plot, they were more often used for their entertainment or musical value. (See BALLAD, page 325.) When it occurs in modern poetry, refrain often serves to intensify or vary meaning, as in the Sandburg poem above.

"Grass," from CORNHUSKERS by Carl Sandburg, copyright, 1918, by Holt, Rinehart and Winston, Inc.; renewed, 1946, by Carl Sandburg. Reprinted by permission of Harcourt Brace Jovanovich, Inc.
1. *Austerlitz*. Austerlitz, Waterloo, Ypres (ē′pr), and Verdun (vėr dun′) are sites of fierce European battles. Gettysburg is the scene of a bloody Civil War battle in Pennsylvania.

REFRAIN: the repetition of phrases or lines in a poem or song.

> The day is cold, and dark, and dreary;
> It rains, and the wind is never weary;
> The vine still clings to the mouldering wall,
> But at every gust the dead leaves fall,
>   And the day is dark and dreary.
>   Longfellow, "The Rainy Day"

---
rhyme

> He that first invented thee,
> May his joints tormented be,
>   Cramped forever;
> Still may syllables jar with time,
> Still may reason war with rhyme,
>   Resting never.
>   Jonson, "A Fit of Rhyme
>   Against Rhyme"

Although poets acknowledge certain limitations in rhyme, as does Jonson above, they likewise recognize its power to please the ear, provide unity to a work, and lend emphasis. Rhyme is to poetry as melody is to music; its recurring echo helps to set off a line as a rhythmic whole and to organize lines into a larger rhythmic pattern.

Like all sound, rhyme should complement and reinforce the sense of what is being said. Along with tone, mood, meaning, and all the other devices, rhyme contributes toward the total communicated effect.

See how rhyme is handled in the following stanza. The italicized letters on the right identify the rhymes. The first rhyme is labeled *a*, as are all the words rhyming with it; the second is labeled *b*, and all the words rhyming with it *b*; the third is *c*, and so on. This pattern of rhymes is called a *rhyme scheme.*

There is sweet music here that softer falls	*a*
Than petals from blown roses on the grass,	*b*
Or night-dews on still waters between walls	*a*
Of shadowy granite, in a gleaming pass;	*b*
Music that gentlier on the spirit lies,	*c*
Than tired eyelids upon tired eyes;	*c*
Music that brings sweet sleep down from the blissful skies.	*c*

Tennyson, "The Lotos-Eaters"

What atmosphere is established in this stanza? Suppose Tennyson had used unrhymed lines and written the following.

> There is sweet music here that softer falls
> Than petals from blown roses on the ground,
> Or night-dews on still waters between rows
> Of shadowy granite, in a gleaming path . . .

1. How would this change affect the poem?
2. By what various means does Tennyson keep the rhyme in this stanza from becoming monotonous? (Consider the rhythms and length of his lines as well as the variety of rhymes.)

A rhyme, like those in the Tennyson excerpt, in which the last syllable of a line is accented and rhyming is called *masculine rhyme.*

A rhyme scheme may involve words of more than one syllable. Consider the following.

> The cock is crowing,
> The stream is flowing,
> The small birds twitter,
> The lake doth glitter . . .
> > Wordsworth, "Written in March"

On which syllable does the accent occur in each of the rhymed word pairs? Rhymes such as *twitter/glitter* are called *feminine rhymes.* In this kind of rhyme, stressed rhyming syllables are followed by identical unstressed syllables (*nickel/pickle; fortify/mortify*).

A poet may rhyme a word within a line with the word that ends it, such as the following.

> The splendor falls on castle walls . . .
> > Tennyson, *The Princess*

This *internal rhyme,* as it is called, can be used to achieve variety or emphasis within a line.

Rhymes can be *slant rhymes (half rhymes)* in which the sounds of words are similar but not identical. The following lines fit this classification. (See CONSONANCE.)

> A Horse misused upon the Road
> Calls to Heaven for Human Blood.
> > Blake, "Auguries of Innocence"

When lines of a poem end in words that are pronounced differently but have a similar spelling, they offer a *sight rhyme* or *eye rhyme*.

> The tree was bent by winds so rough,
> It swept and dipped in every bough.

Rhyme is at its best when it contributes to the development of mood and meaning. It is at its worst when it is forced and destroys the natural rhythms of a word (*thing/evening*), when it is manipulated with little regard for meaning, or when it is hackneyed (*moon/June*). Along with all other language devices, rhyme contributes toward the total communicated effect—in tone, mood, or thought. Some critics classify any patterns in sound as rhyme. Under this very broad classification, techniques such as alliteration and assonance might be considered a form of rhyme.

RHYME: the repetition of similar or identical sounds.

rhythm

When we pronounce words of more than one syllable, we give more emphasis to certain syllables than to others. In each of the following words, which syllable is accented: *pro nounce; faith ful ly; quick ly; per verse?* Just as certain syllables in words are stressed, so also certain syllables or words are emphasized in a phrase or sentence. It is these accented syllables that determine the *meter* or *rhythm* in poetry. Read the following lines aloud; which syllables do you think should be stressed in each line?

> If thou dost love, pronounce it faithfully:
> Or if thou thinkest I am too quickly won,
> I'll frown and be perverse and say thee nay . . .
> Shakespeare, *Romeo and Juliet*

In determining the meter or rhythm of this passage, a reader might mark the stressed syllables with the symbol ⁄ , the unstressed syllables with the symbol ˘ . Further, each line can be divided into smaller units, each with an accented syllable and at least one unaccented syllable. Such units of measure, called *feet,* are divided by a slash. The result looks like this.

> If thou / dost love, / pronounce / it faith / fully:
> Or if / thou think est / I am / too quick / ly won,
> I'll frown / and be / perverse / and say / thee nay . . .

Determining the metrical pattern in poetry is called *scansion*. In a poem with fairly regular rhythm, smaller patterns of accent repeat themselves within a line. The number of these patterns or feet within a line may range from one to eight. The preceding passage has five feet per line. The following terms are used to represent the number of feet which occupy a line of poetry.

FEET

one foot:	*monometer*
two feet:	*dimeter*
three feet:	*trimeter*
four feet:	*tetrameter*
five feet:	*pentameter*
six feet:	*hexameter*
seven feet:	*heptameter*
eight feet:	*octameter*

Pentameter, tetrameter, and trimeter are probably the most common line lengths in regular English verse.

In analyzing rhythm, not only the number of feet per line, but also the pattern of stressed and unstressed syllables that comprise the foot, must be considered. The four basic kinds of feet are illustrated by the following words, according to their accent patterns: *defy, helmet, ascertain, happiness*.

STRESS PATTERNS

A foot which follows the pattern ⌣ ∕ (defy) is called an *iamb* or *iambus*.
A foot which follows the pattern ∕ ⌣ (helmet) is called a *trochee*.
A foot which follows the pattern ⌣ ⌣ ∕ (ascertain) is called an *anapest*.
A foot which follows the pattern ∕ ⌣ ⌣ (happiness) is called a *dactyl*.

To classify a poetic line in terms of its parts, we consider the elements labeled FEET and STRESS PATTERNS above. We determine first the kind of foot and then the number of feet in a line. Examine, for example, the following line.

In October the gold of the trees overwhelms.

First, mark the accents required by the multisyllabic words themselves —*October* and *overwhelms*. Would you emphasize any other words in reading the line? If so, mark them with an accent. Can you easily place stress on the words *in, the, of*? Mark these words appropriately. By now, all the syllables should be marked, with the result looking like the following.

In Oc to / ber the gold / of the trees / o ver whelms.

By referring to the STRESS category above, you can determine that the pattern is anapest. To find the number of feet in the line, count the number of anapests. Refer to the preceding classification of FEET to determine the technical name for a line of four feet. By this procedure, you can determine that the line is anapestic tetrameter.

Repeat the analytical process, determining the number and type of foot in the following.

Fortune is fickle and friendship ephemeral.

Reexamine the passage from *Romeo and Juliet*. Is the general accent pattern of each foot iambic, trochaic, anapestic, or dactylic? How many feet to a line? These lines, as most of Shakespeare's, are *iambic pentameter*.

Occasionally, a poetic foot may be made up of two stressed syllables, such as the phrase *blue notes* in the following line.

Blue notes / are all / she sang / to me.

A foot consisting of two stressed syllables is called a *spondee* (adjective, *spondaic*). Locate the spondee in the following line.

The sprightly lads enjoyed their childhood.

At times, a poetic foot may be made up of two unstressed syllables, such as the phrases *in the* and *of the* in the following line.

In the / forest / of the / witches . . .

A foot consisting of two unstressed syllables is called a *pyrrhic*. Where is the pyrrhic foot in the following line?

Of their lovers they will whisper.

The spondee and pyrrhic serve, not as the predominant foot in a poetic line, but as an occasional substitute foot to vary the basic meter.

Scan each of the following lines to determine the rhythm. First classify the line as to the type of foot, then as to the number of feet.

1. The city now doth like a garment wear . . .
2. Like a child from the womb, like a ghost from the tomb   . .
3. Care is heavy, therefore sleep you . . .
4. Higgledy, piggledy, Agatha Kennedy . . .
5. Away went hat and wig.

The preceding lines can be described as follows: (1) iambic pentameter; (2) anapestic tetrameter; (3) trochaic tetrameter; (4) dactylic tetrameter; (5) iambic trimeter.

The person who dances to music responds to the rhythm of the music almost unconsciously. Only the beginner counts beats and exaggerates rhythm. So it should be with the reader of poetry. The rhythm is there, almost inescapable, having its effect. It should contribute to, not obliterate, all other aspects of the poem.

The following poem has lines of iambic monometer, dimeter, trimeter, tetrameter and pentameter. See if you can identify them.

ODE TO BEN JONSON

ROBERT HERRICK

> Ah Ben!
> Say how or when
> Shall we, thy guests,
> Meet at those lyric feasts,
>   Made at the Sun,
> The Dog, the Triple Tun;
> Where we such clusters had
> As made us nobly wild, not mad;
>   And yet each verse of thine
> Outdid the meat, outdid the frolic wine.

RHYTHM: the measured movement or beat in the musical flow of poetry.

---

run-on line See *end-stopped line and run-on line.*

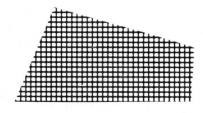

IN CHURCH

THOMAS HARDY

"And now to God the Father," he ends,
And his voice thrills up to the topmost tiles:
Each listener chokes as he bows and bends,
And emotion pervades the crowded aisles.
Then the preacher glides to the vestry-door,
And shuts it, and thinks he is seen no more.

The door swings softly ajar meanwhile,
And a pupil of his in the Bible class,
Who adores him as one without gloss or guile,
Sees her idol stand with a satisfied smile
And re-enact at the vestry-glass
Each pulpit gesture in deft dumb-show
That had moved the congregation so.

What do you think the purpose of this poem is?

"In Church" is a *satire*—a type of literature that views any aspect of life or human nature with a critical attitude. Although designed to instruct or inform, satire, with its sharp, incisive wit, also serves to entertain. Satire may range in its intensity from a gentle prodding to a savage attack; it may include exaggeration, humor, ridicule, or IRONY.

Explain the point the poet is making in the following. Why might this be considered satire?

PLAYS

WALTER SAVAGE LANDOR

Alas, how soon the hours are over
Counted us out to play the lover!
And how much narrower is the stage
Allotted us to play the sage!
But when we play the fool, how wide
The theater expands! beside,
How long the audience sits before us!
How many prompters! what a chorus!

"In Church" from COLLECTED POEMS OF THOMAS HARDY, reprinted by permission of Macmillan Publishing Co., Inc., the Trustees of the Hardy Estate, Macmillan London & Basingstoke, and The Macmillan Company of Canada Limited.

SATIRE: criticism of human nature or any aspect of life. Using techniques of exaggeration, ridicule, sarcasm, irony, humor, or absurdity, satire can range in degree from gentle needling to fierce attack. The following poem makes its satiric point succinctly.

ON A WAITER

DAVID MCCORD

By and by
God caught his eye.

---

scansion See *rhythm*.

---

simile

In each of the following examples, a comparison is being made. What things are being compared?

> . . . kisses balmier than half-opening buds of April . . .
> Tennyson, "Tithonus"

> Laws, like houses, lean on one another.
> Burke, *Tracts on the Popery Laws*

In what sense might kisses be compared to buds; laws to houses? What single word in each example indicates that there is a link between the two items compared?

A directly expressed comparison between two unlike things, indicated by *like* or *as,* and less commonly by words such as *seems, appears,* and *than,* is called a *simile.* A simile is a type of FIGURATIVE LANGUAGE; therefore, the things compared must be literally unlike. "Mary's mouth is like her mother's" is not a simile because the two things compared are essentially alike. "Mary's mouth gaped like an open clamshell" is a simile. Why? In a successful simile, the common attribute should be ap-

---

parent. Such a comparison should provide a new perspective, a novel insight. Often a simile introduces IMAGERY to reinforce the comparison.

An elaborate, long, and involved simile in which the object suggested for comparison is itself developed into a picture or image is called an *epic* or *Homeric simile.* Matthew Arnold makes use of such similes in the following passage from *Sohrab and Rustum.* Rustum, the old warrior, is watching the approach of the young Sohrab, a man he has heard about but never met.

> And Rustum came upon the sand, and cast
> His eyes toward the Tartar tents, and saw
> Sohrab come forth, and eyed him as he came.
> As some rich woman, on a winter's morn,
> Eyes through her silken curtains the poor drudge
> Who with numb blackened fingers makes her fire—
> At cock-crow, on a starlit winter's morn,
> When the frost flowers the whitened window-panes—
> And wonders how she lives, and what the thoughts
> Of that poor drudge may be; so Rustum eyed
> The unknown adventurous youth, who from afar
> Came seeking Rustum, and defying forth
> All the most valiant chiefs; long he perused
> His spirited air, and wondered who he was.
> For very young he seemed, tenderly reared;
> Like some young cypress, tall, and dark, and straight,
> Which in a queen's secluded garden throws
> Its slight dark shadow on the moonlit turf,
> By midnight, to a bubbling fountain's sound—
> So slender Sohrab seemed, so softly reared.

1. To what is the waiting Rustum compared? the approaching Sohrab?
2. Read the passage, omitting the epic similes. What is lost?

SIMILE: a figure of speech which involves a direct comparison between two unlike things, usually with the words *like* or *as.*

> . . . the dragon-fly
> Hangs like a blue thread loosened from the sky: . . .
> > Rossetti, "Silent Noon"

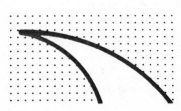

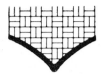

sonnet

A special poetic form is the *sonnet*—a fourteen-line LYRIC with any one of several, particular rhyme schemes. The following is a sonnet whose title means, literally, "I believe."

CREDO

EDWIN ARLINGTON ROBINSON

I cannot find my way: there is no star
In all the shrouded heavens anywhere;
And there is not a whisper in the air
Of any living voice but one so far
That I can hear it only as a bar
Of lost, imperial music, played when fair
And angel fingers wove, and unaware,
Dead leaves to garlands where no roses are.

No, there is not a glimmer, nor a call,
For one that welcomes, welcomes when he fears,
The black and awful chaos of the night;
For through it all—above, beyond it all—
I know the far-sent message of the years,
I feel the coming glory of the Light.

1. Chart the RHYME scheme of Robinson's sonnet. This sonnet appears to fall into two parts. Judging from the rhyme scheme and punctuation, where do you think this break occurs?
2. Where, in the last six lines, does the poet express the fact that, although he cannot *see*, he *believes*?
3. What is the RHYTHM of the sonnet?

A sonnet that can be divided into eight opening lines rhyming *abba abba* and six concluding lines rhyming *cde cde* is called an *Italian* or *Petrarchan sonnet*. The eight-line stanza or *octave* usually presents a proposition, dilemma, or question, while the six-line stanza or *sestet* provides a comment, application, or solution. The predominant meter is iambic pentameter, although in certain cases both meter and rhyme scheme may depart from the norm.

The following is a different type of sonnet. Can you determine in what ways it differs from the Italian sonnet?

PITY ME NOT

EDNA ST. VINCENT MILLAY

Pity me not because the light of day
At close of day no longer walks the sky;
Pity me not for beauties passed away
From field and thicket as the year goes by;
Pity me not the waning of the moon,
Nor that the ebbing tide goes out to sea,
Nor that a man's desire is hushed so soon,
And you no longer look with love on me.
This have I known always: Love is no more
Than the wide blossom which the wind assails,
Than the great tide that treads the shifting shore,
Strewing fresh wreckage gathered in the gales:
Pity me that the heart is slow to learn
What the swift mind beholds at every turn.

1. Chart the rhyme scheme of Millay's sonnet.
2. Millay's sonnet falls into a classification that characteristically embodies four divisions: three groups of four lines each, called *quatrains,* and two concluding rhymed lines called a *couplet.* The concluding couplet usually provides a comment or a mental twist to the preceding train of thought. Note the shift in thought in the last two lines of Millay's sonnet.
3. What is the predominant meter? Where do metrical variations occur? A sonnet such as Millay's that can be divided into three quatrains and a concluding couplet (rhyme scheme: *abab cdcd efef gg*) is called an *Elizabethan (English)* or *Shakespearean sonnet.*

Modern sonneteers may occasionally use this verse form with a great deal of poetic license, as does Sara Henderson Hay in the following sonnet. Examine the rhyme scheme, tone, and meter of Hay's poem to determine what similarities and differences it bears to the conventional Shakespearean and Petrarchan sonnet. Could it be considered a lyric?

ONE OF THE SEVEN HAS SOMEWHAT TO SAY

SARA HENDERSON HAY

Remember how it was before she came—?
The picks and shovels dropped beside the door,
The sink piled high, the meals any old time,
Our jackets where we'd flung them on the floor?
The mud tracked in, the clutter on the shelves,
None of us shaved, or more than halfway clean . . .
Just seven old bachelors, living by ourselves?
Those were the days, if you know what I mean.

She scrubs, she sweeps, she even dusts the ceilings;
She's made us build a tool shed for our stuff.
Dinner's at eight, the table setting's formal.
And if I weren't afraid I'd hurt her feelings
I'd move, until we get her married off,
And things can gradually slip back to normal.

SONNET: a lyric poem of fourteen lines, usually iambic pentameter, and having a fixed rhyme scheme. Depending upon the patterns of rhyme and organization of thought, the sonnet may be classified as *Shakespearean (English, Elizabethan)* or *Petrarchan (Italian).*

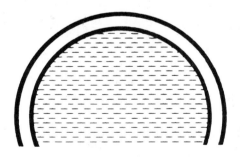

John Milton was a seventeenth-century English poet, as well as a writer of political pamphlets attacking the King. His poetry is marked by eloquence, dramatic power, intense moral preoccupation, and an effective use of sonorous, dignified BLANK VERSE. A staunch Puritan, he was appointed to a government post while Oliver Cromwell and the Puritans ruled England. He held this position until the Restoration of the Stuart kings, when he was arrested and fined, but not imprisoned. Fairly early in life he became blind and dictated his poetry to his daughters. In the following poem, Carl Sandburg writes about Milton.

TO THE GHOST OF JOHN MILTON

CARL SANDBURG

If I should pamphleteer twenty years against royalists,
With rewards offered for my capture dead or alive,
And jails and scaffolds always near,

And then my wife should die and three ignorant daughters
5 Should talk about their father as a joke, and steal the
Earnings of books, and the poorhouse always reaching for me,
If I then lost my eyes and the world was all dark and I
Sat with only memories and talk—

I would write "Paradise Lost," I would marry a second wife
10 And on her dying I would marry a third pair of eyes to
Serve my blind eyes, I would write "Paradise Regained," I
Would write wild, foggy, smoky, wordy books—

I would sit by the fire and dream of hell and heaven,
Idiots and kings, women my eyes could never look on again,
15 And God Himself and the rebels God threw into hell.

1. What do you learn about Milton in the Sandburg poem that is not stated in the short sketch given above?
2. Describe Sandburg's DICTION: is it formal, conversational, homely? To what sort of audience does the diction indicate the poet is speaking?
3. What is the subject of the first eight lines? What shift of idea begins with line 9? Does the cadence of the lines change to echo this change in idea? What is the effect of the piled-up adjectives in line 12?

4. The last line of the poem mentions God and the rebelling angels. What is the implied connection between these factions and Milton?

5. Does the poem contain any unnecessary words or details?

6. Comment on Sandburg's use of IMAGERY and FIGURATIVE LANGUAGE. Do you find it effective?

7. Sandburg's poem is written in FREE VERSE. Given his subject and his attitude toward this subject, why do you think Sandburg chose this form for his poem?

Following is a poem about Milton by Longfellow.

MILTON

HENRY WADSWORTH LONGFELLOW

I pace the sounding sea-beach and behold
    How the voluminous billows roll and run,
    Upheaving and subsiding, while the sun
    Shines through their sheeted emerald far unrolled,
5 And the ninth wave, slow gathering fold by fold
    All its loose-flowing garments into one,
    Plunges upon the shore, and floods the dun
    Pale reach of sands, and changes them to gold.
So in majestic cadence rise and fall
10   The mighty undulations of thy song,
    O sightless bard, England's Maeonides![1]
And ever and anon, high over all
    Uplifted, a ninth wave superb and strong,
    Floods all the soul with its melodious seas.

1. In this poem do you learn any details about Milton's life that are not given in the biographical sketch above?

2. Identify some of the images and figures of speech Longfellow uses and comment on their effectiveness.

3. Longfellow makes extensive use of ALLITERATION, ASSONANCE, and CONSONANCE. Find examples of these sound devices and comment on their effect.

4. Longfellow's poem about Milton is an Italian SONNET. What is the relationship between the octave and the sestet?

5. Longfellow uses classical ALLUSION by comparing Milton to the blind poet Homer. What does the fact that Longfellow refers to this Greek poet as "Maeonides" rather than as "Homer" tell you about Longfellow himself?

6. From the earliest times the number nine has been looked upon as a mystical number of peculiar significance. There were nine Muses, nine rivers of Hell, nine orders of angels. In his own work Milton makes

---

1. *Maeonides* (mē on′i dēz), a name applied to the blind Greek poet Homer.

several references to this number. What do you think might have been Longfellow's purpose in alluding to *nine* (lines 5 and 13) in his poem? What does the use of this allusion and the one mentioned in question 5 tell you about the audience Longfellow is writing for?

7. Which of the two poems—Longfellow's or Sandburg's—did you enjoy more? Why?

Sandburg's and Longfellow's poems are done in two very different *styles*. Style is the outward expression, through words, of the inner personality of a writer. It is the writer's way of looking at a subject, through a particular use of written language.

In the analysis of style, there are several important elements to consider.

1. There is first a study of the poet's diction or word choice. This choice reflects not only the poet's ideas, reading, and knowledge, but also indicates the kind of audience for whom the work is intended. In analyzing diction, try to determine whether it is conversational, formal, informal, vivid, pedantic, ornate, simple, quaint, or conventional.

2. The second element to consider is organization of ideas. Some poets write blunt, abrupt lines; some use graceful, smooth phrases; some write in an informal manner that sounds like conversation; some produce neat, mechanical patterns; some pit one idea against another through parallel structures or antithesis.

3. The third element is a consideration of the structure of a poem—its basic architecture. This includes both the form in which the poet casts the poem (sonnet, free verse, blank verse, heroic couplet, ode, etc.) and the way the various elements of the poem are treated in developing the idea. A poet may structure a poem by posing a series of questions, by presenting an argument, or by arranging words on a page for visual effect as in the concrete poem.

4. Fourth, consider imagery and figurative language. The poet may use these devices sparingly, or depend heavily on them to develop an idea. They may be merely ornamental, or essential in establishing meaning.

5. A fifth point to consider is the poet's fluency. Do thoughts move smoothly from one line to the next, guiding the reader with transitions, or are changes in thought abrupt?

6. Sixth, consider the tone. The poet's attitude toward a subject is made apparent through focus, word choice, and arrangement of details.

7. Last, look at the way the poet uses sound. Does it enhance or obscure meaning?

Choose any one poem printed in this Handbook, and analyze its style, using the seven preceding guidelines.

STYLE: the distinctive handling of language by a given poet, involving the specific choices made with regard to diction, syntax, imagery, figurative language, and tone.

WHY WEAVERS OBJECT

THEODORE SPENCER

The shuttle went weaving efficiently on and
"Ha!" said the thread as it entered the shuttle
"Now I'm alive and important!" the shuttle
Went weaving efficiently on and the thread
Was tossed in the shuttle tossed in the shuttle
Until it was firm in the cloth and the shuttle
Went weaving efficiently on and the next
Thread that came into the shuttle said "Ha!
Now I'm alive and important!" the shuttle
Went weaving efficiently on and the
Shuttle went weaving efficiently on and
"Ha!" said the thread as it entered the shuttle.

In this poem, the process of weaving individual threads into a single
fabric represents the process of life by which individuals are united in
various, collective efforts. There is also the suggestion of the daily routine, the workings of fate, perhaps even the loss of individuality. How do
the phrases, "Now I'm alive and important," and "Went weaving efficiently on," reinforce the meaning of this poem? In what way does the
singsong rhythm, along with repetition of phrases, contribute to the
meaning of the poem?

Although interpretations of this poem may vary, it is obvious that
Spencer has used a concrete process to represent an abstract concept.
The entire process of weaving functions as a *symbol* in this poem. In
its broad sense, *symbolism* is the use of something to suggest or represent something else. Originally, the word *symbol* meant a throwing
together or fusion. Such a fusion or association occurs in symbolism
when one element, usually concrete (a person, object, or event), is used
to represent an abstraction.

In analyzing a poem, you might ask questions such as the following to
determine whether it contains a symbolic meaning.

1. Does the author make a direct equation between something concrete
and something abstract?

2. Does emphasis upon certain words suggest a symbolic interpretation?

3. Do characterization or imagery suggest a symbolic interpretation?

4. Is a particular idea or image stressed, perhaps through repetition?

A symbol may form the framework of an entire poem. Some symbols are based on traditional associations—a dove for peace or a snake for evil. Others are less universal in the associations they evoke; a V sign, for example, may suggest the idea of victory for some, while it may have another significance, or none, for others.

SYMBOLISM: anything used to represent something else. In literature the term *symbol* usually refers to a concrete image used to designate an abstract quality or concept. The lovely, short-lived rose is often used to symbolize a young, beautiful, beloved girl.

---

synecdoche

> Toll for the brave!
>   The brave that are no more,
> All sunk beneath the wave . . .
>   Cowper, "On the Loss of the Royal George"

If the poet wanted to express his thought as literally as possible, what word might he have substituted for *wave*?

A figure of speech in which a whole is used for a part or a part for a whole is called *synecdoche;* it is a special kind of METONYMY, and sometimes this latter term is used to cover both. Generally, synecdoche is employed when a poet wishes to emphasize a particular characteristic. For example, in the quotation above, the word *wave* does more to suggest the force of moving water than the terms *sea* or *ocean*.

Find the synecdoche in the following quotations; in each case, try to determine what it is used to emphasize.

> . . . false, flattering tongue . . .
>   Lamb, "Letter to Southey"

> Arthur with a hundred spears
> Rode far; . . .
>   Tennyson, "The Last Tournament"

SYNECDOCHE: a figure of speech in which a whole is used for a part or a part for the whole. Synecdoche is generally used to emphasize a certain characteristic, as in the following example by Tennyson.

> About his feet
> A voice clung sobbing.

THE SLOTH

THEODORE ROETHKE

In moving slow he has no Peer.
You ask him something in his ear;
He thinks about it for a Year;

And then, before he says a Word
There, upside down (unlike a Bird)
He will assume that you have Heard—

A most Ex-as-per-at-ing Lug.
But should you call his manner Smug,
He'll sigh and give his Branch a Hug;

Then off again to Sleep he goes,
Still swaying gently by his Toes,
And you just know he knows he knows.

Plot the RHYME scheme of the above poem.
   The *tercet* (also called *triplet*) is a stanza form made up of three rhyming lines.
   Read the lines below.

O wild West Wind, thou breath of Autumn's being,
Thou, from whose unseen presence the leaves dead
Are driven, like ghosts from an enchanter fleeing,

Yellow, and black, and pale, and hectic red,
Pestilence-stricken multitudes: O thou,
Who chariotest to their dark wintry bed

The wingèd seeds, where they lie cold and low,
Each like a corpse within its grave, until
Thine azure sister of the Spring shall blow

Her clarion o'er the dreaming earth, and fill
(Driving sweet buds like flocks to feed in air)
With living hues and odors plain and hill: . . .
                    Shelley, "Ode to the West Wind"

1. Chart the rhyme scheme. How does it differ from that of "The Sloth"?
2. What is the meter?

When the rhymes in a tercet are linked from verse to verse as in Shelley's "Ode to the West Wind," the form is called *terza rima* (ter'-tsä rē' mä). The most commonly used meter is iambic pentameter. (See RHYTHM.)

TERCET: a stanza of three rhyming lines. A special type of tercet is called *terza rima,* a series of three-line stanzas, in which the first and third lines rhyme and the middle line forms the rhyme scheme of the following stanza; the rhyme scheme is *aba bcb cdc,* etc.

theme

THERE WAS A MAN WITH A TONGUE OF WOOD
STEPHEN CRANE

> There was a man with a tongue of wood
> Who essayed to sing,
> And in truth it was lamentable
> But there was one who heard
> The clip-clapper of this tongue of wood
> And knew what the man
> Wished to sing.
> And with that the singer was content.

1. Why was the singer content when someone recognized what he wished to sing?
2. Relate the singer's contentment to the main idea of the poem. What is the human need Crane is expressing?

In answering question 2, you are stating the poem's *theme*: the central idea or the essential meaning of a literary work. Seldom is a theme stated explicitly; instead it is implied through characterization, action, image, and tone. We come to grasp the theme of a work by determining the central idea that work embodies.

Try to determine the theme of the following poem.

BLUE GIRLS

JOHN CROWE RANSOM

Twirling your blue skirts, travelling the sward
Under the towers of your seminary,
Go listen to your teachers old and contrary
Without believing a word.

Tie the white fillets then about your lustrous hair
And think no more of what will come to pass
Than bluebirds that go walking on the grass
And chattering on the air.

Practice your beauty, blue girls, before it fail;
And I will cry with my loud lips and publish
Beauty which all our power shall never establish,
It is so frail.

For I could tell you a story which is true:
I know a lady with a terrible tongue,
Blear eyes fallen from blue,
All her perfections tarnished—yet it is not long
Since she was lovelier than any of you.

THEME: the central idea developed in a literary work.

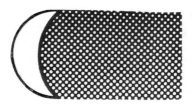

REFUGEE—1945 RUTH MOORE

She was an American civilian in Hong Kong
When the Japanese took the city;
She saw death,
Not decently, as we at home see death,
Embalmed in a coffin with carnations,
But splashed in shapeless masses on the stones of the street.

Now she is safe at home;
She lectures;
She has written a book.
She invariably ends her talk to the Women's Club
With "Why were we attacked? Why? Why?"

I have read her book.
In it she says, on page so-and-so,
"I had eight trunks,
Full of lovely things,
Picked up for a song from the dealers of the Far East . . .
Jade and jewelry,
Ivory,
Old scrolls,
A Buddha, carved a thousand years ago.
Matchless possessions that cost very little;
They were looted from me and I lost them."

On page such-and-such, again, she says,
(And listen, you ghosts of men who died at Hong Kong)
"Most of the roads are beautiful, fit for motor traffic,
But the steepest peak of the mountain, two thousand feet,
Is a matter for coolies and a sedan chair."

Why were we attacked? Why?

Lady, for Christ's sweet sake,
Who do we think we are?

1. Moore gives us a picture of the American civilian by describing her activities and by quoting certain passages from her book. What clues do these details provide about the American civilian?

2. The italicized statement at the end of the poem expresses, most strongly, the poet's attitude toward this lady. What is this attitude? How does this statement serve to qualify all the details that precede it?

The attitude a poet expresses in a given work is called *tone*. In establishing tone, we determine whether a poet views the subject with sympathy, disdain, humor, objectivity, ridicule, or affection. Sometimes, a poet's tone will involve a mixture of feelings, or it may change within a given work. (Try putting a label on the tone Moore projects.)

Since written language does not allow the actual, audible voice of the writer to be heard, the poet must rely instead on such things as word choice and arrangement to convey the desired impression. Any of the following techniques might provide a clue to the tone of a work: point of view, word choice, style, choice of images, treatment of characters and events—even sound and rhythm.

Determine the tone of the following poem. Note that different readers may vary in their interpretation of the tone in a particular work.

THE BLOODY SIRE   ROBINSON JEFFERS

It is not bad. Let them play.
Let the guns bark and the bombing-plane
Speak his prodigious blasphemies.
It is not bad, it is high time,
Stark violence is still the sire of all the world's values.

What but the wolf's tooth chiseled so fine
The fleet limbs of the antelope?
What but fear winged the birds and hunger
Gemmed with such eyes the great goshawk's head?
Violence has been the sire of all the world's values.

Who would remember Helen's face[1]
Lacking the terrible halo of spears?
Who formed Christ but Herod and Caesar,
The cruel and bloody victories of Caesar?
Violence has been the sire of all the world's values.

Never weep, let them play,
Old violence is not too old to beget new values.

TONE: the attitude and feelings of an author expressed in a given work, as determined by word choice, style, images, connotation, sound, and rhythm.

---

1. *Helen's face*, Helen of Troy, the immortal type of beautiful woman. In Greek legend she was the wife of Menelaus, king of Sparta. She eloped with Paris, thus bringing about the siege and destruction of Troy.

Pronunciation Key

The pronunciation of each word is shown just after the word, in this way: **ab bre vi ate** (ə brē′vē āt). The letters and signs used are pronounced as in the words below. The mark ′ is placed after a syllable with primary or heavy accent, as in the example above. The mark ′ after a syllable shows a secondary or lighter accent, as in **ab bre vi a tion** (ə brē′vē ā′shən).

Some words, taken from foreign languages, are spoken with sounds that do not otherwise occur in English. Symbols for these sounds are given in the key as "foreign sounds."

a	hat, cap	o	hot, rock	ə	represents:
ā	age, face	ō	open, go	a	in about
ä	father, far	ô	order, all	e	in taken
		oi	oil, voice	ı	in pencil
b	bad, rob	ou	house, out	o	in lemon
ch	child, much			u	in circus
d	did, red				
		p	paper, cup		**foreign sounds**
e	let, best	r	run, try		
ē	equal, be	s	say, yes	Y	as in French *du*. Pronounce (ē) with the lips rounded as for (ü).
ėr	term, learn	sh	she, rush		
		t	tell, it		
		th	thin, both	à	as in French *ami*. Pronounce (ä) with the lips spread and held tense.
f	fat, if	ŦH	then, smooth		
g	go, bag				
h	he, how				
		u	cup, butter	œ	as in French *peu*. Pronounce (ā) with the lips rounded as for (ō).
i	it, pin	ủ	full, put		
ī	ice, five	ü	rule, move		
				N	as in French *bon*. The N is not pronounced, but shows that the vowel before it is nasal.
j	jam, enjoy				
k	kind, seek	v	very, save		
l	land, coal	w	will, woman		
m	me, am	y	young, yet	H	as in German *ach*. Pronounce (k) without closing the breath passage.
n	no, in	z	zero, breeze		
ng	long, bring	zh	measure, seizure		

The pronunciation key is from the *Thorndike-Barnhart Advanced Dictionary*, copyright 1973 by Scott, Foresman and Company.

Index of Authors and Titles